UNCERTAINTY AND ECONOMIC EVOLUTION

Few economists can rival the impact which Armen A. Alchian has had in so many areas of economics. From economic law to industrial organization, macroeconomics to finance and basic economic theory, his dynamic style and far-reaching ideas have influenced generations of economists.

In this collection leading economists pay tribute to Armen A. Alchian's life and work. All aspects of his work are discussed, including topics little studied by economists, such as the influence social norms have on the success of government institutions and notions of cost for the definitions of coercion and freedom.

The essays continue Armen A. Alchian's work in a variety of areas and make clear that his ideas and writings have withstood the test of time. Economists in a number of disciplines will find this collection fascinating.

John R. Lott, Jr. is the John M. Olin Visiting Law and Economics Fellow at the University of Chicago Law School.

ROUTLEDGE STUDIES IN BUSINESS ORGANIZATION AND NETWORKS

UNCERTAINTY AND ECONOMIC EVOLUTION

Essays in honor of Armen A. Alchian

Edited by John R. Lott, Jr.

Routledge
Taylor & Francis Group

LONDON AND NEW YORK

First published 1997
by Routledge
2 Park Square, Milton Park, Abingdon, Oxon OX14 4RN

Simultaneously published in the USA and Canada
by Routledge
52 Vanderbilt Avenue, New York, NY 10017

First issued in paperback 2018

Routledge is an imprint of the Taylor & Francis Group, an informa
business

Typeset in Garamond by Florencetype Ltd, Stoodleigh, Devon

British Library Cataloguing in Publication Data
A catalogue record for this book is available from the British Library

Library of Congress Cataloguing in Publication Data
A catalogue record for this book has been requested

ISBN 13: 978-1-138-98637-4 (pbk)
ISBN 13: 978-0-415-15166-5 (hbk)

CONTENTS

CONTENTS

ILLUSTRATIONS

FIGURES

TABLES

LIST OF ILLUSTRATIONS

NOTES ON CONTRIBUTORS

Armen A. Alchian is a professor emeritus in the Department of Economics at the University of California at Los Angeles.

Terry L. Anderson is a professor in the Agricultural Economics and Economics Department at Montana State University.

Jim Buchanan is a professor in the Department of Economics at George Mason University.

Stephen Cornell is Professor of Sociology, University of California at San Diego.

Harold Demsetz is Professor Emeritus in the Department of Economics at the University of California at Los Angeles.

Arthur De Vany is a professor at the Department of Economics, University of California at Irvine.

Gertrud M. Fremling received her Ph.D. in economics from the University of California at Los Angeles.

William T. Gavin is Vice President and Research Coordinator at the Federal Reserve Bank of St Louis.

Peter J. Hill is a professor in the Department of Economics at Wheaton College.

Jerry L. Jordan is President and Chief Executive Officer at the Federal Reserve Bank of Cleveland.

Joseph P. Kalt is a professor at the John F. Kennedy School of Government, Harvard University.

Benjamin Klein is an assistant professor in the Department of Economics at the University of California at Los Angeles.

Daniel B. Klein is Associate Professor of Economics, Santa Clara University.

Bruce H. Kobayashi is an associative professor of law at George Mason University.

Axel Leijonhufvud is Professor Emeritus in the Department of Economics at the University of California at Los Angeles.

John R. Lott, Jr. is the John M. Olin Visiting Law and Economics Fellow, School of Law, University of Chicago.

Larry E. Ribstein is Professor of Law at George Mason University.

William F. Sharpe is the STANCO 25 Professor of Finance at the Graduate School of Business at Stanford University.

Robert H. Topel is a professor at the Graduate School of Business at the University of Chicago.

Benjamin Zycher is the Vice President for Research at the Milken Institute.

INTRODUCTION

Armen A. Alchian's influence on economics

John R. Lott, Jr.*

Armen Alchian's influence has been felt in many areas of economics from law and economics to industrial organization to macroeconomics to finance to basic economic theory. Few economists have the impact in even one area that Armen has had in so many fields. Articles like his 1950 piece "Uncertainty, Evolution, and Economic Theory" were seminal pieces that are still widely cited almost half a century after they were published. Yet, Armen's influence not only stems from his articles, but from the truly dominant force that he represented in UCLA's economics department. Few students made it through the program without being deeply affected by his penetrating style. All but one of the authors for this collection have had Armen as either a professor or colleague, and for each of us these pieces represent but a small repayment of our debt to him.

In testament to the importance of Armen's article "Uncertainty, Evolution, and Economic Theory," three of these ten papers deal extensively with it, though others are also influenced by it to varying degrees. The first piece by Harold Demsetz sets for itself the ambitious goal of showing that for over forty-five years economists have too easily accepted Armen's claim that many economic phenomena can be explained without reference to rationality. Demsetz rejects Alchian's claim that rationality and natural selection are substitute explanations of behavior by claiming that Alchian implicitly requires rationality elsewhere in the model (e.g. the reaction of creditors to losses they bear). Possibly, Armen would respond that natural selection and not rationality could be what determines which creditors exist; those that lend to the wrong clients or adopt the wrong rules go out of business. We leave to the reader to judge who is right.

Arthur De Vany's innovative chapter pushes the bounds of the evolutionary discussion by showing how evolution helps us learn and in turn helps us understand the different conditions different institutions face. As De Vany phrases it, "Every economic organization, contract, firm, or coalition, is the

* John M. Olin Visiting Law and Economics Fellow, School of Law, University of Chicago.

product of and contains information." His chapter provides a useful start into explaining why organizations take the forms that they do.

While Alchian's (1950) piece was limited to describing the actions of firms, the general notion that efficient rules or organizations will tend to survive and inefficient ones fail can also apply to political markets. Kobayashi and Ribstein take this tack and analyze whether there is a tendency towards efficiency in the evolution of uniform state laws. They claim that the most "efficient" statutes are the ones to be most widely and quickly adopted. A topical theoretical issue these days is the notion of herding behavior, whether it be in financial or political markets, and Kobayashi and Ribstein provide empirical evidence that state legislators are able to correctly discern why other states adopt the statutes that they do. Simply because one state adopts a statute is not sufficient to cause other states to mimic their behavior. The nature of the statute seems to be more important than whether others have already adopted it.

Another important strand of Alchian's work has been the organization of firms. Benjamin Klein's chapter fills a gap in his earlier work with Armen (Klein *et al.*, 1978) by introducing uncertainty into whether hold-up problems will occur. In Klein's new article, the returns to cheating vary with changes in demand and other variables; reputations help prevent hold-ups for some level of changes in the returns to cheating. The greater are the reputations, the larger the shocks that are necessary before it will pay for a firm to hold up the other party in a contract. Klein then applies his discussion to interesting real world cases involving Fisher Body–GM and Alcoa–Essex.

Alchian's impact on macroeconomics is generally not well understood, for his impact was not just through his published writing but also through conversations that he had with individuals like Karl Brunner and Allan Meltzer. As Jerry Jordan and William Gavin write, however, Alchian's published work made fundamental contributions to explaining money's role in economizing on information costs, the problems of measuring inflation, the credibility of policy makers, and the distinctions between anticipated and unanticipated inflation. Alchian and his coauthors might not always have gotten the credit that they deserved for their insights in these areas, but Jordan and Gavin's piece clearly shows that they anticipated many of the major issues that have arisen in macroeconomics during the last couple of decades.

The next three chapters deal with the relationship between property rights and the incentives in government institutions. Armen's important (if not always appreciated) work in this area can be best seen by his papers on "Competition, Monopoly, and the Pursuit of Money," with Reuben Kessel (1962); "Private Property and the Relative Cost of Tenure" (1958); and "The Economic and Social Impact of Free Tuition" (1968).

Terry Anderson and Peter Hill describe the motivations behind creating the federal park system's "crown jewel" – Yellowstone National Park. While the Northern Pacific Railroad would have preferred that it itself owned Yellowstone and thus solved any successive monopoly problems that might arise with it controlling access to the area, Anderson and Hill describe how public ownership of the park was preferable to the checkered ownership that was likely to result from federal homesteading laws. They also describe how, despite official government ownership, the in-principle ownership exercised by the Northern Pacific gave it the incentives to protect the tourist aspects of Yellowstone from damage by sightseers. Their piece provides an interesting alternative to the public interest view of the state.

Stephen Cornell and Joseph P. Kalt discuss a little-studied topic by economists: the role of social norms in deciding the success of governmental institutions and the economies that they regulate. They use a truly unique data set which allows them to analyze American Indian tribal governments and the success of their communities. Benjamin Zycher discusses what effect the absence of private property rights had on environmental degradation in Eastern Europe when it was communist.

The final two chapters demonstrate Alchian's influence in an area not normally influenced by economists. The chapter by Fremling and Lott illustrates the implications of Alchian's notions of costs for the definitions of both coercion and freedom. Dan Klein's far-ranging paper builds upon the work of Alchian, Coase, and Kirzner to discuss what he sees as three aspects of freedom. These include the freedom to respond flexibly to opportunities, the freedom to discover opportunities by "epiphany," and the freedom to discover opportunities by "serendipity." It is the last that he attributes to Alchian.

In sum, these chapters continue Armen's work in a wide variety of areas. If time is the ultimate test of the value of these ideas, Armen's work has met that test. His work continues attracting interest and providing new insights into how the world works many decades after his pieces were first published.

We wish to thank *Economic Inquiry* for allowing us to republish the essays by Anderson and Hill, Demsetz, Jordan and Gavin, Benjamin Klein, and Kobayashi and Ribstein.

REFERENCES

Alchian, Armen A. (1950) "Uncertainty, Evolution, and Economic Theory," *Journal of Political Economy* 58,3: 211–21.

—— (1958) "Private Property and the Relative Cost of Tenure," in *The Public Stake in Union Power*, ed. Philip D. Bradley. Charlottesville, VA: University Press of Virginia.

—— (1968) "The Economic Cost and Social Impact of Free Tuition," *The New Individualist Review* 5,1: 42–52.

Alchian, Armen A. and Reuben Kessel (1962) "Competition, Monopoly, and the Pursuit of Money," in *Aspects of Labor Economics*. Princeton, NJ: Princeton University Press.

Klein, Benjamin, Robert G. Crawford, and Armen A. Alchian (1978) "Vertical Integration, Appropriable Rents, and the Competitive Contracting Process," *Journal of Law and Economics* 21,2: 297–326.

1

RATIONALITY, EVOLUTION, AND ACQUISITIVENESS

Harold Demsetz

A classic article has "staying power" and impact. Alchian's 1950 article "Uncertainty, Evolution, and Economic Theory" has plenty of both, and there is no need to extol its obvious virtues. Yet, I am sure that Alchian would find things to modify in this article were he to rewrite it today, some forty-five years after its publication. One task I set for myself here is to supply some food for thought should Alchian be tempted to engage in a rewrite. I also discuss arguments and concepts put forth by other economists whose writings have influenced perceptions about rationality and evolution, thus moving the discussion beyond the limits of Alchian's article. The meaning of rational economic behavior is discussed next. Finally, I explore how rational behavior might be a product of evolution.

The notion of evolution as the shaper of economic institutions has been a minor theme in economics for two centuries. It is present in the works of Malthus and Smith, whose writings later influenced Darwin, Marx, and Schumpeter. The evolution theme even played a role in the late nineteenth century policy debates about the Sherman Antitrust Act. Many of the leading economists of that time, particularly those who helped to create the American Economics Association, opposed the Sherman Act. One of the more important economists, John Bates Clark, who was not among those most enamored with evolutionary concepts, wrote:

> Combinations have their roots in the nature of social industry and are normal in their origin, their development, and their practical working. They are neither to be depressed by scientists nor suppressed by legislators. They are the result of an evolution, and are the happy outcome of a competition so abnormal that the continuance of it would have meant widespread ruin. A successful attempt to suppress them by law would involve the reversion of industrial systems to a cast-off type, the renewal of abuses from which society has escaped by a step in development.[1]

Clark's negative view of the efficacy of an antitrust law, shared by many leading economists of the time, had little influence on legislative matters.

The Sherman Act became law.

These earlier references by economists to evolution are mainly casual and superficial, and in this respect they do not anticipate and are no substitute for Alchian's discussion. Alchian's unique contributions were to use evolution analytically in a model of economic behavior and to offer it as a substitute for rationality. Alchian's critique of the presumption that economic behavior is to be explained by rational action, which means profit maximization in the case of the firm of neoclassical theory, constitutes a fundamental challenge to one of orthodoxy's cherished principles. Part I of the present chapter discusses the difficulties in analyzing economic behavior without recourse to rationality, and it illustrates these by reference to Alchian's article.

PART I

Four major themes run through "Uncertainty, Evolution, and Economic Theory." The first is the difficulty that uncertainty creates for the neoclassical assumption that businesses maximize profit, or, to put this more broadly, the difficulty that uncertainty creates for the rational behavior assumption. The second is that there is a process at work – natural selection – that determines which business decisions lead to viable outcomes and which do not. The present chapter takes for granted and does not discuss the proposition that a natural selection process is at work. The third theme relates to the particular filter that is used by the evolutionary process when it comes to business decisions; the filter that Alchian puts in place is the test of whether decisions result in positive profit. The fourth theme is that decisions that survive this filter are disseminated through the economy by the imitative efforts of other firms.

The difficulty in behaving rationally (and irrationally also)

Knight (1921) was the first prominent economist to attack the notion that all or that most economic decisions are guided by rational calculation. Simon (1947, 1957, 1959) launched his attack at about the same time as Alchian. Although all three take roughly the same position in regard to the limits of rationality, they differ somewhat as to the source of these limits.

Knight rejects rational behavior if decisions must be made under conditions of uncertainty, which he distinguishes from conditions of risk. To a large extent, he denies the ability to calculate rationally if experience relevant to the decision problem is absent. With sufficient experience, probability distributions can be inferred, and these can be, and are, used to cope with risk through rational calculation (as in the provision of insurance). Failure of rationality, then, is a reflection of the paucity of experience. Alchian rejects rational behavior on the basis of similar reasoning, but his rejection seems to extend even into conditions that Knight would describe as risk rather than

5

as uncertainty. To Alchian, a major obstacle to rational maximizing is the lack of a one-to-one correspondence between decision and outcome; two different decisions can lead to the same outcome, although possibly with differing probabilities, so how can one decision, but not the other, be identified as rational maximizing? However, both Knight and Alchian stress inadequacies of available information. Simon's rejection is based on inadequacies of the human mind. The mind possesses only a limited capacity for understanding complex relationships and for handling large masses of data. Decisions cannot be made on the basis of rational calculation if they require mental capabilities beyond this limit. The differences between these views are fairly obvious, but the three are similar in that all cite the difficulty of making rational calculations in a world in which information is imperfect.

However, rejecting rational calculation leads to another problem. If we do not decide rationally, how do we decide? One might think the answer should be that we decide erratically or, perhaps, randomly, but this is not the answer given by these three economists. Simon substitutes "satisficing" – a decision criterion that accepts the desirability of settling for something less than the best and better than some lower bound – for maximizing. Since Simon is very much concerned about our mental limitations, he presumably believes, but does not demonstrate, that satisficing makes fewer mental demands than does maximizing. Knight does not comment much on substitute methods of making decisions, but he clearly sensed a problem here for he briefly describes his belief about the manner in which businesses, facing uncertainty, decide on their investments. He asserts the presence of a psychological tendency for overly optimistic estimates of the likely outcomes of their investments. Optimism leads to more investment than is needed, leading, on average, to negative returns and lower product prices.

Neoclassical theory uses maximization to guide its deductions because this seems a sensible or desirable decision criterion, but this criterion seems to spring willy-nilly from within the mind. The same is true for satisficing, optimism, pessimism, etc. It seems that Simon's satisficing criterion is chosen voluntarily by persons whose decisions are being frustrated by the limited capabilities of their minds. Knight's optimism is a starkly *ad hoc* psychological quirk. All these criteria suffer from the absence of a more basic explanation for their existence and survival in the psyche, and the same is true for maximization. Alchian looks not to the inner workings of the mind but to evolution for the criterion that determines the viability of business decisions, or at least so it seems. This criterion is whether businesses realize a positive profit from their decisions. Neoclassical theory, like Alchian's criterion, while it holds to maximization of profit by businesses also requires the realized maximum to be positive if business activities are to meet the market test. In this respect, Alchian's selection of criterion seems a quite easy extension from economic theory. But this is not so.

6

The positive profit criterion

Positive profit is an appealing evolutionary filter. Firms experiencing positive profit on a continuing basis usually survive; firms experiencing continuing losses usually fail, or they are reorganized. But these facts are also consistent with rational behavior. In fact, it is rational behavior that lies behind neoclassical theory's reliance on a non-negative profit to define equilibrium. Alchian cannot rely on neoclassical theory to buttress his choice of the positive profit criterion, for he is arguing against the use of a rational behavior postulate. He proposes positive profit as a survival filter that natural selection, not rational behavior, applies to business decisions. To distinguish positive profit from maximum profit in this way requires that its source should be different from rational pursuit of ends. Positive profit criterion, like ice ages, must be part of the environment in which business decisions are made. Alchian's objection to profit maximization, it must be remembered, is based on our inability to link business decisions to outcomes. Positive profit in Alchian's argument, therefore, cannot be predictively forward looking. If it were, he would be justified in presuming that business decisions can be linked to profit outcomes, or, at least, to the algebraic sign of these outcomes. To satisfy Alchian's needs, positive profit must be to business decisions as the ice age was to survival of species. The positive profit criterion must be external to our decisions; its application must not rely on human calculation if we are to avoid relying on rational behavior indirectly. From this perspective, positive profit is simply an *ex post* fact the occurrence of which leads to the survival of a firm, much as ice age temperature led to the survival of only some animals. Unfortunately, the demonstration of this independence is lacking, and, on consideration, it seems very difficult to supply.

Positive profit clearly is not independent of thought processes. Profit is itself a result of conscious calculation, and positive profit is a filtering criterion that we *choose* to impose on ourselves. If positive profit is to have meaning, there must be some reason to think our calculation methods are at least roughly accurate and that positive profit is not being confused with negative profit. That is, we must think that these methods taken in their entirety make *sense*, and if they do not make sense we no longer know what is accomplished by a natural selection filter that relies on calculations of positive profit.

That positive profit is not exogenous to the economic system, and that it is not a necessary criterion of success, is suggested by the soft budget constraints and subsidies that have characterized socialist economies and to a lesser extent our own also. Despite negative profit, socialist firms of all types continue to survive, and so does our own Continental Bank and Chrysler Corporation. Positive profit, therefore, is not necessary to survival, nor is its application independent of conscious thought, whether rational or irrational. Subsidies might be treated as just another source of revenue, one

7

that converts loss and prospective failure into profit and survival, but this would make the positive profit filter much too tautological since any method of survival can be interpreted as a source of revenue. Alchian's discussion makes it clear that he means business profit to depend on voluntary exchange across markets. The firm receives revenue from customers or financial market creditors. If this revenue is less than the firm's cost, loss results.

But why does loss imply business failure? Is it because consumers are unwilling to pay more for the same quantity of purchases? Is it because the legal system bars the firm from using violent means to obtain resources? Is it because suppliers of inputs refuse to take less for their inputs? Is it because lenders refuse to make capital available to a firm whose prospects are not promising? Is it because creditors can shut down the firm or reorganize it? All these are reasons for the firm to fail if profit is negative, but all of them suggest a dependency on rational calculations made by consumers and suppliers of inputs.

The failure of a firm is brought about by the reaction of creditors to losses they bear. This reaction makes sense only if the firm's history of losses can be used to predict its future. If a firm that suffers a series of losses is thought to be just as likely to enjoy great profit in the future as a firm that has a record of rising profits, creditors have no more reason to refuse to lend to the first firm than to the second. A reliable system of forecasting future profit on the basis of past profit is implied, and this suggests, of all things, the possibility that rational behavior is at work. If there were no reliable forecasting system, lenders would be as likely to recapture their capital and realize a profit from funds provided to firms with a record of negative profit as from funds provided to firms with a record of positive profit. The positive profit filter seems to require rejection of the very condition that made it appeal to Alchian, this condition being our asserted inability to map today's decisions into probabilistically reliable forecasts of tomorrow's outcomes.

If lenders pay no heed to the past profit of potential borrowers and if consumers are quite willing to purchase randomly from firms – one way to interpret irrational behavior – there is no compelling reason for firm survival to be associated with positive profit. Survival would be random. Suppose survival is not random but accords with the pattern that is described by Alchian's use of the positive profit filter. If we wish to use this fact to deny the relevance of rational behavior, we our obligated to explain the source of this filter in terms not easily tied to rational calculation. This, we have just seen, is difficult to do.

Even if such an explanation could be given, the positive profit criterion would not seem capable of explaining survival as well as another criterion that requires no more, or only a little more, information. A survey of business firm profits is necessary to determine which firms enjoy positive profit and which do not, but this reveals a profit ranking or, with slightly more information, a rate of return ranking. Why not assume that the filter natural selection applies to the economic system associates a higher probability of survival with a higher rate of return ranking? Just as thicker skin increased the probability of surviving the ice age, so higher profit rate increases the probability of surviving the competitive age. This criterion brings the natural selection filter closer to that of profit maximization, but without requiring, as pure maximization would seem to require, that there is a comparison of all possible opportunities. Moreover, it would be consistent with the factually greater willingness of lenders to favor higher rate of return firms. Of course, a criterion based on relative profit (rates) smacks much more of rational calculation.

Irrationality and budget constraints

The appeal of the positive profit criterion to Alchian undoubtedly is related to the notion of feasibility or of the need to satisfy budget constraints. A firm that has earned a positive profit finds its resources undiminished by its past activity and available for use in the next future period. A firm that has suffered a loss has diminished the resources available to it during the next period. Carried to an extreme with a string of negative profits, and coupled to requirements that lenders of capital lend only to positive profit firms, the negative profit firm cannot continue at the same level of activity because to do so requires more resources than it possesses.

A later analysis by Becker (1962) of the relationship between price and quantity is similar to this view of the problem, but it is based quite explicitly on the role of budget constraints. Becker demonstrates that budget constraints imply a negative relationship between price and quantity that is sold even if buying behavior is not rational. In his analysis, the budget constraint divides the choice set into the possible and the impossible. He shows that if product prices are allowed to vary, consumer purchases change in accordance with the law of negatively sloped demand. This happens because at least some consumers of the good whose price has risen relatively will find it impossible to purchase as many units as they could have if the price had not risen, even if their purchase intents are determined randomly rather than rationally. It is a well-drawn demonstration of the power of budget constraints. Yet, for reasons similar to those brought to bear above on the positive profit criterion, it is not fully convincing as a demonstration of the redundancy of rational behavior in our models. Whence the budget constraint? That there is a budget constraint seems to require rational decisions by others. Goods are not made available by others to those who cannot pay for them; funds to buy these goods are not made available by lenders. The people behind the budget constraint behave as if they husband their resources. Without this behavior, budget constraints lack meaning as long as wealth exists in the community.

These aspects of the budget constraint reflect social interactions. Becker's analysis would seem to be independent of rational behavior in an economy like that of Robinson Crusoe, in which the operability of the budget constraint derives not from the decisions of others but directly from the limits set by real resource availability. Alter the mix of resources and some previously exercisable opportunities are no longer possible. But this establishes only a *pseudo* law of negatively sloped demand. The statistical relationship between opportunities exercised and the relative supplies of inputs, although it conforms in appearance to what one would expect from the law of negatively sloped demand, is in fact only the appearance. It reflects only the impossibility of doing that which nature does not allow to be done. The law of negatively sloped demand is more than a demonstration of this. It is also a claim that *all* who purchase a good will purchase less of it if its price is raised, even though nothing bars them from purchasing more of the good by doing with less of other goods.[2] This proposition will be violated by Becker's example of random purchases, since some random (irrational) purchasers do buy more of the good whose price has risen. It is only the total of purchases that must fall because of operable budget constraints.[3]

Alchian's and Becker's arguments do suggest that patterns of observations that we explain in terms of rational behavior can also result from behavior that is not rational. However, as imaginative and informative as these arguments are, they cannot be sustained in full without appealing to rationality or without introducing a natural selection explanation that remedies the shortcomings of their present arguments. As they stand, rational behavior seems to be at work below the surface of their analyses. Consider, for example, Alchian's reliance on imitation to propagate success.

Propagation through imitation

The firm is not a biological organism. It does not mate with another firm and sexually breed biological offspring. A firm that experiences positive profit might grow; it might even spin off parts that follow the very practices that made the "parent" firm a positive profit firm (Nelson and Winter, 1982). To some extent, through processes such as these, we might predict a slowly increasing sphere of influence for business practices that happen to have worked well. But there are limits to the rate at which a firm can grow efficiently (Penrose, 1959; Marris, 1974). More important, we know factually that the sphere of influence for successful practices is extended more rapidly than it could be through internal growth only, and that this is accomplished primarily through imitation by rivals. The growth in fast food retailing was achieved not just by McDonald's growth, as rapid as this was, but by the imitation of McDonald's methods and organization by rival chains.

Alchian recognizes the importance of imitation and relies upon it to spread successful business practices. However, imitation, like positive profit, is difficult to disassociate from behavior that at least appears rational. Conscious and generally correct forecasting is involved. Past success must be separated

10

from past failure, projections from these past histories must be made and must be correct on average, and successful histories must be imitated more often than unsuccessful histories. If imitation were guided by randomly exercised choice, both unsuccessful and successful business practices would be adopted. The rush of resources into profitable markets and out of unprofitable markets, which we know to happen, cannot be explained by random choice. If imitation is to lead to adoption of successful and to rejection of unsuccessful variants, there must be some predictive value to the projections made from past records. Imitation, in extending the sphere of influence of successful variants, depends on rationality-supporting conditions.

PART II

To this point, I have argued that it is difficult to give meaning to natural selection for economic actions without placing some reliance on rationality. Far from being an alternative to natural selection, rationality may be a product of natural selection, but let us begin this section simply by assuming as fact that we behave rationally. To understand the economic consequences of this fact, it is necessary to have some agreement as to what we mean by rational behavior and about the goals this behavior is expected to pursue. The meaning of rational behavior is discussed here. Goals are discussed in the last part of this chapter.

Defining rational behavior

There is a clear difference between the rationality implicit in positive economic theory and that gleaned from the axioms of choice that are used to buttress utility theory (e.g. completeness of ordering, continuity of choice alternatives, independence from irrelevant alternatives, and transitivity). Positive economic theory links decisions to the service of our goals, and it uses rational behavior to instruct us about the nature of the linkage. The monopolist's output rate is set so that marginal revenue equals marginal cost because the monopolist *seeks* maximum profit. The axioms of choice, in contrast, do not depend at all on goal fulfillment. Consider that these axioms can be satisfied by a Roman general whose battle decisions are made on the basis of the pattern taken by a slaughtered chicken's entrails. Pattern one is judged to forecast a better chance of winning, pattern two a somewhat slimmer chance, and pattern three not much chance at all. His choice psychology is transitive if his preference of one over two and two over three leads him to prefer one over three, yet he may be defeated as many times as he wins by following signals he deciphers from these entrails. The problem here may be a belief in "superstition" or it may be in a failure to measure correctly the correlation between the shape of entrails and the winning of battles, but either deficiency is consistent with the notion that the rationality of decision rules cannot be determined only by their consistency with the axioms of choice. Let there be two rules of decision making. The first satisfactorily achieves results but sometimes violates transitivity. The second seldom achieves desired results but never violates transitivity. Which rule should, or does, a rational person prefer?

The ability of a rule to deliver results depends in part on its internal logic, but only in part. Good results depend also on whether a rule is well suited to the conditions under which it must be applied. A rule for making decisions that yield desired outcomes in a world populated by persons of goodwill may not work well in a world populated by persons deeply suspicious of each other. Moreover, if we are to rely on rationality to understand economic outcomes, we must have some notion about the goals that guide its application. Many more people would be living the life of a monk if perfection of the ascetic side of our lives was of utmost importance to us.

Precondition for behaving rationally

Goal-oriented decision rules rely on the existence of many stable correlations between events. If these correlations change through time, they should change slowly. Without steadiness over time in at least some of the relationships between natural events it becomes impossible to devise useful rules of decision making. Because rain tends repeatedly to come in the spring, and because dampness repeatedly results in the sprouting of seeds, patterns in the occurrence of these events can be observed and learned and useful rules of farming can be devised. What I mean by rationality is *the ability to recognize patterns in worldly phenomena, to project the conditions that govern these patterns into the future, and to select patterns and extrapolations from these that help to achieve desired goals.* Assertedly, business decisions conform with this notion of rationality.

To the extent that reasoning ability of this sort is influenced by genetic endowment, it is plausible to think of our current state of intelligence as a product of natural selection. Intelligence experts believe that the variability in intelligence that is explained by genetic differences is between 40 and 80 percent, with the remainder of variation being explained by such things as family and cultural environment. Thus, natural selection is indirectly at work in filtering business decisions, and the criterion it has evolved might depend very much on rationality as described above. Projections of expected profit and risk of profit are made on the basis of past experience with correlation patterns. From the limited choice sample these provide, the best profit–risk combination is chosen, and persons who supply additional resources to the firm will be influenced in making their supply decisions by their projections of the results they expect to realize. This is not simply profit maximization because risk matters and because not all possible profit–risk combinations are contained in our experiences. It is the best of what is available on the basis of a profit–risk tradeoff. Expectations seldom are confirmed exactly.

Different decisions may yield the same results. These realities do not undermine a claim that business men and women rely heavily on rational thought processes. However, even if such behavior were both plausible and reflective of natural selection, it would not carry us very far in understanding economic outcomes. Two types of issues arise. First, why is reasoning power devoted to the extent that it is to improving our material well-being? Our rationality could be, and is to some extent, directed to serve purposes other than improvement in our material well-being. If we are to understand rational behavior, we must be able to draw conclusions about the directions in which our preferences will guide our choices and actions. Second, why do we not observe much, if any, improvement through time in the reasoning power of other species? Most other species have existed over an evolutionary time span much greater than humans, yet no other species seems to have developed reason power equal to that which is characteristic of humans. From the ameba to the chimpanzee, survival seems to depend largely on characteristics very different from reasoning power (as defined here). Progress in answering these questions requires that we delve into the nature of our preferences or goals.[4,5]

PART III

Economic theory avoids the task of describing or explaining the goals we pursue, and, instead, to a large extent, it takes goals as unspecified givens. Theory allows us to discuss the tradeoff between apples and oranges or between income and leisure because it presumes these are utility-conferring goods and activities, but it gives no justification for the presumption. Even so, economic theory allows us to understand economic behavior without explicit justification of the goals it assumes. This is because economists think rationally (as defined above). We implicitly use recurring patterns of behavior to infer plausible goals. Apples are a good because we take the *fact* of repeated past purchases of apples as evidence of this. In its practical application to the details of economic behavior this implicitly empirical procedure works quite well, so that an explicit analysis of human wants is not needed. There is good reason to avoid saying more about our wants than can be inferred from our past behavior, for theory offers no economics-based explanation for why we want some things and not others.[6] The explanation is to be found in a combination of medical facts (apple consumption provides needed nutrients) and natural selection theory (taste patterns influence survival probabilities and reflect natural selection).

The acquisitive species

The same technique for inferring our preferences can be applied to a more general description of our proclivities. What it reveals is that we are an acquisitive species. We prefer more (generalized) wealth to less. This is similar

13

to the notion of insatiability of wants that we employ in theory, but it is not exactly the same. Not much, if any, evidence is given, or even could be given, to support the notion that our wants are insatiable. In fact, people often behave as if their wants are, or have been, satiated (e.g. "I cannot eat even one more slice of pizza"). This fact is obscured by our tendency to use insatiability tautologically. Thus, altruistic behavior is not interpreted as a violation of insatiability but, rather, as evidence that helping others confers positive utility on us. People retire early and earn less than they could, but this is not a problem for insatiability because we allow leisure to enter positively into our utility functions. But if we are to interpret behavior in this way, honesty would seem to require us to substitute the notion that we behave with "purpose" for the notion that our wants are "insatiable." Rather than being a description of our wants, our use of insatiability makes it a description of the choice situations we seek to analyze. These are situations in which resources are too meager to meet the demands for them that would be brought forth with a zero price. The fact that some goods or resources are superabundant (i.e. free) is not used to refute the insatiability of our wants. It is used to delineate the situations we wish to study, those for which the price system is the allocator of resources.

Here, I wish to use acquisitiveness in a less tautological way than we use insatiability. Acquisitiveness means not only a preference for *more* wealth (for self, family, and friends) over less. It also means the *realization* that more wealth can be had. Generalized wealth, of course, means command over goods. Which items enter our utility functions positively (goods) and which negatively (bads) depends partly on available supplies and partly on exogenous considerations, including natural selection among the latter. Acquisitiveness can be cast into a specific proposition such as "the typical person in each generation seeks wealth greater than that enjoyed by the typical person in the prior generation" and even that this person seeks this increment to wealth "if securing it requires somewhat harder work than that done by the typical person in the prior generation." Acquisitiveness is thus described by wealth comparisons through time as "wanting more and realizing that more can be had." My claim is that the typical person believes that an increase in wealth is desirable (our preference) and possible (our understanding of "nature"). Not everyone's wants, at all times, are acquisitive in this sense, or, if they are, not everyone is capable, at all times, of acquiring more wealth, but acquisitiveness in this sense is a valid description of our perceptions for a large fraction of the world's population. It is not tautological, however. There can be ascetics. More importantly, acquisitiveness may not be an equally strong characteristic of people who live in different cultures, and it is difficult to say if a society's culture reflects the particular perceptions of its people or if these preferences are shaped by the society's culture. As I shall argue below, acquisitiveness does not seem to be a characteristic that is as strong in other animals as it is in the human.

Although acquisitiveness is not tautological, analyzing economic activity in ways that reveal its presence is not always easy. As an example of this difficulty consider the behavior of parents and children in Becker's (1976) discussion of altruistic behavior toward parents by a "rotten kid." A selfish child finds it in his or her interest to behave "altruistically" toward his or her parents, taking some of his or her own wealth and giving it to the parents. The parents reciprocate by leaving their estate to the child. This transpires despite the essential selfishness of the child because of an empirical assumption that the parents are able to make much better use of funds than is the child. A sacrifice today by the child results in an increase in the parents' wealth that is larger than the sacrifice, so that when the child receives his or her inheritance a very good return on the investment has been made. The child's parents reciprocate this "altruistic" donation of wealth by designating the child as their heir, and it is in their interest to do so in order to secure the donation that they can convert into a sum much greater. The seemingly altruistic actions of child and parents simply reflect an implicit contract from which both parties gain, such gain coming from the investment skills of the parents. The egocentric ends of all parties are served, and the same "deal" could have been struck just as well between strangers. Yet, what is essentially acquisitive behavior is hidden behind a cloak of seeming altruism.[7]

No carefully devised empirical test of our acquisitive propensity is offered here, but there is evidence consistent with its existence as a prevailing force. This is found in the long term trend in living standards experienced by Western industrialized nations over the last two or three centuries, and there has been an accompanying broadening of this phenomenon through much of the world's population.

Evidence of acquisitiveness is not equally strong for any other species, even though much of what individuals in these species do is purposeful. Taking in nourishment, mating, and protecting territory, for example, seem purposeful, and they serve the self-interests of individual members of these species insofar as we or natural selection have defined self-interest. Nonetheless, this behavior is not acquisitiveness or, at best, it is very weak acquisitiveness. No persistent trend of improvement in wealth has been exhibited by other species. Natural conditions good enough to stave off starvation, to mate, and to defend against attack do not seem to whet appetites for still higher living standards but simply seem to satisfy each generation. Squirrels do not behave as if they want much more than a supply of nuts ample to attract and support a mate and to feed offspring. We do not observe wealth accumulation beyond these amounts even when external conditions are good enough to permit such accumulation. The absence of confirming behavior for other species may be due to a true lack of concern about accumulating more than very limited amounts of wealth (a question of goals), or it may be due to an inability to understand past correlations and to execute forward-looking plans or devise solution institutions based on these correlations (questions of intelligence and rationality).[8]

One may argue that animals in other species do want more, but populations always rise to Malthusian limits and undermine growth in living standards. But this happens either because there is no willingness to accept fewer offspring or because there is insufficient reasoning power to develop rules of behavior suited to the goal of material improvement. Dogs simply refuse to inventory more than a few bones no matter how many you throw at them, and they see no value in staying behind their owners' fences when the season attracts them to the opposite sex. The human species, or a large percentage thereof, is unique in its penchant for birth control. Birth rates are deliberately held below biologically feasible limits *even when resources are ample to support these limits biologically.* No doubt there are many life-style motivations for this, but important among these is a desire to maintain or increase personal and family wealth.[9]

The very possession of wealth, as distinct from the act of acquiring wealth, has a net beneficial effect on the probability of surviving. Wealth, health, and longevity are positively correlated. Although good health and long life do facilitate the accumulation of wealth, the primary direction of causation surely is the reverse. Whether or not acquisitiveness is genetic, a significant part of reasoning power does seem to be inherited. This allows acquisitiveness to influence the outcome of natural selection. Assume two persons that possess different powers to reason. Both are acquisitive, but the person with superior reasoning power is more successful in acquiring wealth. This greater wealth confers a higher probability of surviving on the person possessed of genetically superior reasoning power, implying that acquisitiveness facilitates a more rapid breeding of intelligence into the human species. The strength of this effect is open to debate.

Other links between intelligence and probability of survival surely exist, but these must be preferential to humans if we are to use them to explain a seemingly rapid (by comparison to other species) increase in our reasoning power. A link between intelligence and survival like that which obviously exists when it comes to defending one's self and fending off dangers does not easily satisfy this requirement, since it is a link that should be present in all species. Acquisitiveness seems both to promote the selection of intelligence (through its health and defense implications) and to be especially strong in humans.

I do not argue that acquisitiveness is itself inherited, although it may be; only that it is and has been a characteristic of the preference pattern of a large part of human populations. Under property right conditions similar to those devised in Western civilizations, persons have been able to accumulate wealth through generations. The social or cultural ability to do so, when linked to positive correlations between intelligence and wealth accumulation, on the one hand, and between survivability and wealth accumulation on the other hand, should have encouraged a more rapid selection of reasoning power, and the force of this should have been at its strongest during periods when wealth was insufficient to pull large fractions of population through the child-bearing years. Societies that have not devised similar institutions for encouraging or tolerating wealth accumulation in large fractions of their populations will not have benefited from this source of accelerated evolution in intelligence. Other sources for such improvement may exist, but unless they correlate negatively with Western property right institutions, the absence of these institutions places a special burden on rapid improvement in reasoning power.[10]

NOTES

1 Quotation taken from "The Limits of Competition" by J. B. Clark, as reprinted in Giddings, *The Modern Distributive Process* (1988).

2 This of course assumes that preference systems remain unchanged and that we are not dealing with Giffen paradox goods. Becker's analysis is consistent with these assumptions.

3 For a different type of objection to Becker's analysis, see Kirzner (1963). Also note Becker's rejoinder (1963).

4 The current vogue among students of animal behavior is to call attention to the cognitive abilities of "lower" animals. This provides evidence of continuity of development of these abilities from lower to higher life forms. However, the discovery of a chimpanzee's use of a tree branch as a tool by which to secure food, while demonstrating that humans are not unique in the use of tools, also demonstrates, by virtue of the length of time it has taken to make this discovery and the apparent absence of (many) other examples in the totality of chimpanzee behavior, that there is a considerable difference between the degree of reliance placed on rational thought processes by humans and by chimps.

5 If we were to probe the relationship between rational behavior and natural selection, it would be necessary to give a large role to imperfect information. That inheritable aspects of superior reasoning have a greater probability of surviving, other things equal, is due to imperfect information. Limited knowledge cannot be used effectively by those possessing poor reasoning power. So, over time, in a variety of interactions between persons possessed of different reasoning competence and, much more important, in a variety of interactions betweeen persons and nature, persons with superior reasoning ability will fare better. The natural selection of superior rationality is made possible *because* of, not in spite of, imperfect knowledge. Ironically, the very condition that Knight, Simon, and Alchian use in different ways to limit the role of rational behavior, imperfect knowledge, is one source of evolution-related improvement in reasoning power.

6 This is not quite true. Once apples are empirically determined to enter our utility functions positively, we can show that some conditions, such as those that pertain to age and income, may increase or decrease the utility value we place on apples (Stigler and Becker, 1977).

7 Other examples of seemingly altruistic behavior may be given. Tit-for-tat negotiating strategies overcome problems facing persons locked into a prisoner's dilemma, but they work because they yield a mutual net gain to the interacting parties, given the underlying assumptions of tit-for-tat models. The voluntary acceptance of an increased probability of death in order to reduce the probability

of death of one's blood relatives is another example. Since 50 percent of a child's genes are identical to those carried by one of his or her parents, the probability that this strain of genes will be perpetuated by this seemingly altruistic behavior is increased if the probability of death of the parent who puts herself or himself in harm's way is increased by less than half the reduction in the probability of death that results for the child. From the perspective of this chapter, the proper classification of these actions is egocentric, not altruistic.

8 The skeptic who is well informed in biological matters will point to examples of investments made by animals, such as the beaver's construction of a dam. The small number of such examples and their insignificance when compared to the accumulative urge in humans makes of these examples the exceptions that prove the rule.

9 Smaller family size results in an increase in the per capita wealth in the family unless, as is possibly true of farming with old technology, there are increasing returns to family size. Since per capita wealth correlates positively (and causally) with probability of survival, acquisitiveness confers a survival advantage to the typical family member through its negative impact on family size. But smaller family size, aside from this wealth effect and simply by virtue of there being fewer children, also reduces the probability that the family gene pool is passed to succeeding generations. Just what the optimal family size is from the perspective of propagating a family's gene pool is unclear, but the positive effect of per capital wealth on the survival of the individual implies a smaller family size is optimal than if there were no such wealth effect. If acquisitiveness leads to properly proportioned reductions in the size of families, it will raise the probability of survival of the human gene pool. To put the matter more briefly, in an affluent setting the biological maximum birth rate may be too large to maximize the probability that a family's gene pool survives. Something like acquisitiveness may be required if survival of the gene pool is to be maximized.

10 To such propositions, one would need to add caveats about different methods of accumulating wealth, since some of these (crime, rent seeking of certain sorts, war, etc.) may have a deleterious effect on the aggregate wealth of a society. Having said this, thereby prompting readers to recognize that a society benefits more or less from acquisitiveness depending on the guidance it gives to behavior, it nonetheless remains an assertion of this chapter that acquisitiveness has been a powerful agent for the more rapid progress in intelligence enhancement that seems to have taken place in the human species.

REFERENCES

Alchian, A. A. (1950) "Uncertainty, Evolution, and Economic Theory," *Journal of Political Economy* 58: 211–21.

Becker, G. S. (1962) "Irrational Behavior and Economic Theory," *Journal of Political Economy* 70: 1–13.

—— (1963) "A Reply to Kirzner," *Journal of Political Economy* 71: 82–3.

—— (1976) "Altruism, Egoism, and Genetic Fitness: Economics and Sociobiology," *Journal of Economic Literature* 16: 817–26.

Clark, John B. (1988) "The Limits of Completion," in *The Modern Distributive Process: Studies of Competition and its Limits.* Boston: Ginn and Co.; originally published in *Political Science Quarterly.*

Demsetz, H. (1995) *Seven Critical Commentaries on the Economics of the Firm.* Cambridge: Cambridge University Press. See especially Commentary Four for a discussion of rational behavior and the "overshooting" phenomenon.

Kirzner, I. (1963) "Rejoinder," *Journal of Political Economy* 71: 84–5.
—— (1964) "Rational Action and Economic Theory," *Journal of Political Economy* 70: 380–5.
Knight, F. H. (1965) *Risk, Uncertainty, and Profit.* New York: Harper and Row; first published in 1921.
Marris, R. (1974) *The Economic Theory of Managerial Capitalism.* London: Macmillan.
Nelson, R. R. and S. G. Winter (1982) *An Evolutionary Theory of Economic Change.* Cambridge, MA: Harvard University Press.
Penrose, E. (1959) *The Theory of the Growth of the Firm.* Oxford: Basil Blackwell.
Schumpeter, J. A. (1934) *The Theory of Economic Development.* Cambridge, MA: Harvard University Press.
—— (1950) *Capitalism, Socialism, and Democracy.* New York: Harper.
Simon, H. A. (1947) *Administrative Behavior.* New York: Macmillan.
—— (1957) *Models of Man.* New York: John Wiley.
—— (1959) "Theories of Decision Making in Economics," *American Economic Review* 48: 253–84.
Stigler, G. and G. Becker (1977) "De Gustibus Non Est Disputandum," *American Economic Review* 67: 76–90.

2

INFORMATION, CHANCE, AND EVOLUTION

Alchian and the economics of self-organization

*Arthur De Vany**

The strong invisible hand theorem says there is emergent order in human affairs. Smith and Hayek described it; Alchian gave the evolutionary proof. He showed that profit maximization is an emergent property of evolution when survival depends on positive profits. I extend Alchian's argument to consider how evolution discovers and adopts successful organizational forms. "Lock-in" on inefficient equilibria occurs, but noise and imitation, the evolutionary operators Alchian stressed, promote learning and adaptation which move the organizing dynamic off inefficient paths. Evolution is orders of magnitude faster than optimization; the relative time scales make the processes observationally distinguishable.

INTRODUCTION

Alchian (1950) invoked the idea that selection could replace or supplement rationality or conscious design in economic theory. Evolution in Alchian's theory is a force which is complementary to and may even substitute for rationality. He showed that selection could lead firms to act in a way consistent with maximizing as an evolutionary adaptation in an environment where positive profits are necessary for survival. In such an instance, no one individual within the organization would know all that the organization knows because its intelligence is distributed and its goal-seeking behavior is an emergent behavior. Hence, no individual could know or say if or how his or her actions lead to any goal or outcome. The collective product of their interactions must earn positive profits so the organization can compete

* Department of Economics, Institute for Mathematical Behavioral Sciences, University of California, Irvine, and Associate, Center for Computable Economics, UCLA. The Private Enterprise Research Center of Texas A & M partly supported this research. Comments by John Lott and several anonymous referees improved the article. I alone am responsible for errors.

20

with others for scarce resources. Only to the observer–economist will the macroscopic patterns in their behavior appear to be goal oriented.

By applying the evolutionary metaphor to the firm, Alchian emphasized self-organization over deliberate design as a source of order in economic affairs. In tackling this problem, he reinvigorated the research program that Adam Smith (1776) and Hayek (1944) extolled. They called for the study of an invisible hand far more powerful than the modern version, which is little more than a proposition about the computation of a price vector. Their *strong invisible hand theorem* is a statement about the inherent order in human affairs, an order that is "the result of human action but not human design."[1]

Like Alchian, Smith (1776) and Hayek (1944) stressed decentralized and self-directed action over centralized and planned deliberation. And they stressed adaptation in far-from-equilibrium processes over optimizing in equilibrium. Their arguments have a strikingly modern tone to economists versed in evolution and chaos, and they have a contemporary proponent in Alchian.

My own understanding of economics is strongly influenced by Alchian's teaching. I have distilled his teaching to the phrase "Everything in economics is information-theoretic." This is evident from the role chance plays in his work, for what is chance but a series of coin flips giving yes/no answers to questions? A property right is a list of binary decision rules assigning authority to agents, so it, too, is information theoretic. Institutions are information theoretic as well, for they give yes/no answers to questions posed by agents seeking guidance from the social knowledge encoded in institutions. So is evolution information theoretic for it gives yes/no answers to questions about the survival of carriers of information.

In addition to Alchian, Williamson (1988), Jensen and Meckling (1979), and Friedman (1953) argue that evolutionary competition selects efficient forms of organization. The counterargument has been made by Penrose (1952) and Winter (1964, 1975), both of whom point out that the proponents of the evolutionary model fail to exhibit a mechanism through which heritable determinants of fitness are transmitted.[2]

In trying to uncover a mechanism through which selection can operate Nelson and Winter (1974, 1977, 1982) argue that internal culture and structure are transmitted as heritable characteristics. Winter (1982) argues that knowledge must reside in human beings, but its use and meaning derive from the interaction of individuals within the structure of an organization. The idea that information is distributed among members of an organization and becomes useful to the organization only through structure is closely linked to the idea of emergent behavior. I extend Alchian's evolutionary argument to show that goal seeking is an emergent property of the dynamic by which an organization comes into being and evolves. This dynamic is closely tied to Winter's theory of structure and to the enhanced performance that lies behind the idea of emergent behavior. For concreteness, I consider a network coordination game with a structure of local interaction.

ARTHUR DE VANY

THE DEBATE: EVOLUTION, LOCK-IN, OPTIMIZATION

In trying to answer the central issue raised by Winter and Penrose on how heritable characteristics correlated with fitness may be transmitted, I find that the ability to learn and to make productive use of noise to improve inherited structure is correlated with evolutionary fitness. Peter Allen (1993) makes the same point in a model of population growth. He shows that evolution selects populations with the ability to learn. Learning in his context, as in mine, is an appropriate error rate that fosters discovery of fitter alternatives. Even if there is no direct mechanism whereby evolution leads economic organizations to inherit traits that produce high fitness, a high learning rate (noise) may indirectly produce such a connection. Structure is a heritable characteristic of the evolutionary process and hierarchical organizations tend to have good evolutionary dynamics (Williamson, 1988). I study the morphogenesis of organizations where agents are hierarchically coupled, where structure is inherited, and agents act according to versions of a best-reply dynamic. Efficient organization is an attractor for certain versions of this dynamic in the space of organizations.

Another point of debate over evolution and economic efficiency concerns path dependence and lock-in. Evolving organizations do not always attain optimality and may lock onto inefficient equilibria. Langlois (1988) and North (1990) accept that path dependence is a property of evolutionary systems. Binger and Hoffman (1989) show that evolutionary change is not a sequence of steps to ever more efficient institutions. Brian Arthur (1989), Paul David (1985), and Katz and Shapiro (1985) have shown that evolution may freeze on a particular structure, or move along a path that can become trapped on an inefficient outcome. I show here that certain dynamics can freeze on inefficient outcomes. On the other hand, Liebowitz and Margolis (1990) show that institutions, like patents, free training, rentals, or discounts can overcome inertia by promoting early moves. I show that these symmetry-breaking institutions promote good evolutionary dynamics.

These evolutionary dynamics embody four forms of broken symmetry: asymmetric information, asymmetric orders of moves, asymmetric agent weights, and agent bias. Simulations are used to show how often lock-in occurs, how inefficient the frozen equilibria are, and what properties of the evolutionary dynamic overcome lock-in. Lock-in tends to occur more often in simultaneous move games, when agents rapidly adjust their choices, when the agents are highly interconnected, and when there is too little noise. An asymmetric and noisy best-reply dynamic among sparsely and hierarchically connected agents converges on efficient organizations.

INFORMATION, CHANCE, OPTIMIZING, AND EVOLUTION

Contracts as information

An organization is a complex, multi-lateral contract among agents. Consider, for exposition, that the organization is a contract between two agents that assigns authority to one of the agents in each state of the environment which it distinguishes. Let the binary string representing this contract contain 96 bits; the first 32 bits name the two parties, and of these 16 bits are used for each name, which is enough to identify the agents in a population composed of $2^{16} = 65,536$ agents. The remaining 64 bits are used for the state conditional clauses of the contract. These bits are the contract's decision rules. Let the contract take as its input a state description k bits long. This is sufficient to identify 2^k states of the environment. The space of decision rules from which the "optimal" rules are to be chosen contains 2^{2^k} possibilities. An optimal contract is the set of decision rules in this space that yields the highest outcome by some criteria over the possible states of the world. This criterion needn't concern us here.

Since we have 64 bits to work with, the contract can deal with $2^k = 64$ states of the world, which implies that $k = 6$. Hence, the contract requires as input a message 6 bits long, which is sufficient to identify which state obtains among the 64 possible ones. The contract then assigns a 0 or a 1 to reflect an allocation of authority to the first or second party to the contract in that state of the world. If we number the states from 0 to 63, then the 64 binary digits in the contract correspond to an allocation of authority in each state; for instance, a signal 111101 would indicate state number 61 and we would look at the sixty-first position in the contract to find a 0 or 1 indicating that the first or second party has authority in this state to choose the next action. This example shows that the contract can be coded as a binary string that names the parties and allocates residual authority. This model of a contract can be extended greatly to include more agents or more complicated actions, but this simple form is enough for our purposes.

Complexity

Note that the contract is both a description and a program. If we list the authority assignments in states, this listing is a description of its terms. On the other hand, if we take the state signal as input, we can use the contract to compute the action; in this respect the contract is a program for converting the input signal about the state into an authority ranking. The binary string coding of the contract tells us the parties and their relations in any state for which the contract specifies an action.[3]

So, the contract represents two kinds of information, depending on our point of view. It represents structure – authority assignments in states – and

23

it represents process – the conversion of state information into action. Information theory is the tool for analyzing these points of view of the information contained in the contract. Shannon information theory deals with structure; process information is the provence of algorithmic information theory.

The information theoretic complexity of the contract is given by Shannon's theory as $H(C) = \log(2^{2^k}) = 2^k$. The complexity of the contract turns out to be the number of state-contingent clauses it contains. This is the descriptive complexity of the contract, information that could be obtained by looking at it and noting its clauses and conditions. But, this is not its algorithmic complexity, which is information about what the contract does, not what it says.

We find the algorithmic information by another route, one geared to actions. Suppose we don't have the contract in front of us. How can we discover the information it contains? If we could observe the actions of the parties in various states, could we discover a model of the contract from the data? The data would be a time series of states and actions taken by the party granted authority by the contract in the state. This action sequence would, like the contract, be a binary string. After a long period of observation we may be able to identify many of the clauses and their corresponding states through these observations. The algorithmic complexity, K, is the length of the shortest program or model that will produce the observed actions from an input of the observed states; it is the model we would find if we used Occam's razor.

Chance and optimization

With this information theoretic representation of economic organization as a binary string coding a contract we can pose our questions about optimizing, chance, and evolution. Drop consideration of who the parties are and concentrate on the bits of the contract that determine authority in the states.

One meaning of optimizing is that an agent designs or finds a unique contract that dominates every other contract in the space. Such a determination would require a pairwise comparison among all the contracts in the space. If the space is large and complex, the notion of optimizing may have no operational meaning. We will consider the complexity of optimizing two agent contracts and an N-agent coalition; both are generic representations of organization, and show that the relevant spaces are so large that optimizing has little meaning.

The complexity of multi-agent contracts comes from the fact that the contracts must be mutually consistent; there are many internal constraints to be satisfied in each coalition, and all the coalitions must be stable with respect to one another.

Table 2.1 Dimensions and complexity of the space of coalition structures when there are N agents or of the space of contracts when there are N states

N	Structures	H	Contracts	H
3	5	2.32	8	3
6	203	12.35	6.4×10	6
12	4.3×10^6	22	4.09×10^3	12
24	4.46×10^{17}	58.63	1.67×10^7	24
44	8.70×10^{39}	132.67	1.75×10^{13}	44
64	1.72×10^{65}	216.71	1.84×10^{19}	64
104	3.83×10^{21}	403.89	2.02×10^{31}	104

The difficulties of forming an optimal organization are directly related to the size of the space of coalition structures and decision rules. In Table 2.1 the cardinality of the space of coalition structures for N agents is shown in the second column, labelled "Structures." This is given by Bell's number.[4] The fourth column contains the cardinality of the two-party, state-contingent rules space. This is given by 2^k. The first column is the number of agents when you are looking at the second column or the size, in bits, of the input identifying the state when you are looking at the fourth column. The third and fifth columns contain the information theoretic complexities of these objects.

The Table reveals, in the third and fifth columns, that it does not take a lot of information to *describe* a member of either of these large spaces. The amount of information one needs to describe the organizations only grows as the log of the size of the space. But, describing an object is no more complex than looking it up if you have its address, which can be done in a number of steps equal to the information theoretic complexity.

It is a far different matter to search the space to *find an optimal organization* when you don't know what it is or where it is located. The size of this task is directly related to the size of the space and, here, the numbers are huge. The size of the spaces explode as the size of the input (number of agents or number of states) increases. With only six agents there are 203 possible coalition structures and there are 6.4×10 state contracts that take 6 bit inputs. When there are just twelve agents, there are 4.21×10^6 structures and 4.096×10^3 contracts that take 12 bit inputs. From there on, the numbers explode. The implication is that an optimal contract lies in a space so large that neither chance nor rational design could find it.

Combining both these problems by bringing together agents and states in contracts that cover many states and are consistent and optimal would take computational resources on the scale of the product of the appropriate entries in Table 2.1. Resources of such magnitude are beyond imagining.[5]

25

Given the size of these spaces, the probability of finding an optimal organization by chance is nil. Moreover, you cannot know that it is optimal, even if it is.

Bounded rationality

The burden of enforcing consistency among the contracts is what makes forming the coalition structures so intractable. To meet all the constraints of an optimal organization, as we have shown, requires unbounded information. Let us define an unboundedly rational organization as one that meets all of a large set of optimal simultaneous constraints, but requires unbounded computational resources to do it. A boundedly rational organization then would violate some constraints and use only bounded computational resources. These constraint inconsistencies might never come to the surface in a complex organization. If they do, then some form of due process must be used to resolve the conflict. Hence, a boundedly rational organization with a dispute resolution mechanism would be a far simpler one to form than one that rigorously met all the internal constraints.

Evolution as an organizer

Evolution is a walk in the space of possible contracts. Each contract has many neighbors just 1 bit change away. Chance enters the process through mutation and imperfect imitation (recall that I am using reproduction as self-imitation, so that both reproduction and imitation of other contracts are subsumed in the one term) and it serves to expand the number of paths from each contract to new possibilities.

A random mutation can take the search into a distant region of the space; it represents leaps in the space of contracts. Imitation, which is imperfect, explores neighborhoods located near successful contracts. Together, these operations bring breadth (through chance) and depth (through imitation) to the search. The speed-up from deep search in promising neighborhoods can be large, depending on the properties of the space. If we know the content of a "successful" contract, this would be equivalent to knowing its binary address in the whole space of contracts. Then we could find it in just $\log(2^{64})$ = 64 binary searches. So, even partial knowledge of the terms that good contracts are likely to contain can vastly speed up the search, because other good contracts are likely to be located nearby. Imitation speeds the evolutionary process because it concentrates search in promising regions. The danger in imitation is that the contracts that are imitated are in the neighborhood of a local maximum. Mutation has value when the search relies on imitation because mutations can take the search into new regions.

Evolution opportunistically exploits depth and breadth of search by shifting emphasis to imitation or mutation as the search uncovers opportunities.

26

Imitation is inheritable learning, a characteristic which human systems exhibit and biological systems do not. Imitation floods the area with many additional searchers, shifting the emphasis from breadth to depth. This continues, moving the organization to higher fitness, until mutation uncovers a superior contract at another location in the space. Then imitation floods the new region with depth searchers. Imitation is a conservative strategy, innovation is a venturesome one. Evolution mixes these strategies by using chance to innovate new organizations and imitation to conserve successful ones. Inheritable learning through imitation may speed evolution. This is because fitness in the organization and the ability to learn are correlated.

Parallelism

Another way evolution speeds search is by exploiting parallelism. Evolution evolves many contracts simultaneously. Again, consider search as a walk in the space of contracts. If just one agent directs the walk of agents, we have a model of informationally centralized, sequential search. All the information goes through one processor which uses it to direct search. Even if the central director uses many searchers, the flow of information is choked by a bottleneck at the central processor. In evolutionary search, each searcher is self-directed and many contracts are explored simultaneously. They exploit the local information they acquire from their own searches and what they learn of other nearby trials. Searchers located in poor regions fail or migrate to new territories by imitating others. Diversity and noise locate searchers over the space and these contract variations are tested simultaneously against one another. Parallelism speeds search, but only if there is enough diversity. Otherwise search is flooded into a small region where many parallel agents are not much more effective than one agent. Noise is essential to the success and speed of evolutionary search because it broadens search and sustains the diversity needed to maintain parallelism.

A cost of parallelism is the loss of specialization. Maintaining many trials over a landscape requires resources to be spread over less fit points. If learning is rapid, these points quickly will be deserted in favor of those which are better. We will show later that noisy parallel processes overcome lock-in on low fitness points and are more likely to reach high fitness. The cost of parallelism is lower average fitness along the path.

The drawback to imitation can be overcome by failure. Organizations that are locked onto contracts that are not effective must compete for resources with organizations that use more effective contracts. Unless the less effective organizations are allowed to fail, they will not release resources to other organizations located in more effective regions of the contract space. There will be too few resources for search in regions that are promising, parallelism will break down, and evolutionary search will hit a resource bottleneck. Failure is essential to the success and speed of evolutionary search.

ARTHUR DE VANY

EVOLUTION AND EMERGENT ORDER

In De Vany (1995), I develop a model of emergent organization to explore the role of noise and evolution in producing order. Some of the results of that inquiry illustrate the points made in the discussion above.

Emergent order

Emergent order must come from the process without being its intention. An emergent process has these properties:

1 A collection of agents who follow instruction.
2 Interactions among the agents which form macroscopic patterns.
3 An economist–observer who interprets the patterns as structure or process.

An advantage of an emergent process is its use of low level agents that are directly connected to the problem domain. By studying economic order at the emergent level, we bypass the problem of representing how the macroscopic patterns are formed and we bypass the problem of how the agents learn and represent these patterns as part of their knowledge – their memory is in the world, and the intelligence they reveal is borne of their interactions at the emergent level; it is nowhere programmed in any agent. Even though this is computer science, it is precisely the message of Smith, Hayek, and Alchian.

As we have already seen, the difficulties which rational or emergent design must overcome are many.

1 The search space is large. There are 2^n possible contracts when a two-party contract must cover n states. And there are a Bell number of coalition structures when contracts must be consistent and optimal for n agents.
2 Information processing demands are large. When they are connected to k other agents and must coordinate with them, there are 2^k possible combinations of signals among the agents and there are 2^{2^k} possible decision rules.
3 The search space is complex. Because the returns to any one agent depend on the choices of some or all of the other agents, the landscape of coalitional values is rugged and complex and contains many local optima.
4 The search process is path dependent. Because coalitions evolve, they are constructed recursively and each structure must build on the structure it inherits. Earlier choices deform the value landscape and they condition and constrain later choices; thus, the value landscape, and what is fit or optimal, co-evolves with the coalitions.

Coordination on a network

Building on our binary representation of contracts and organizations, let us consider a model that is capable of representing local interactions among the

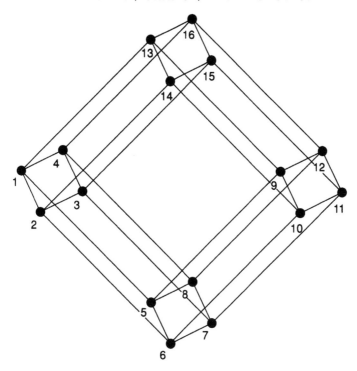

Figure 2.1 A hypercube of locally interacting agents

agents. Let us consider an organization to be a web of relationships among agents scattered in a space in which they interact with their local neighbors. This organization is a contract with local hierarchy. We represent this contract as a hypercube of suitable dimension with agents who make 0–1 choices located at the vertices. Such a four-dimensional hypercube is shown in Figure 2.1. The connections between agents are shown as links between the nodes of the graph. Each node represents an agent and the agents with whom it interacts are indicated by the links. We want to evolve organizations on this structure.

We will pose the objective to be a coordination of the agents in the network with a strong form of network externality. We will regard agents as being compatible with a linked neighbor whenever they both select either 0 or 1. For example, 0 might denote driving on the left side of the road and 1 driving on the right. Assume that either choice is equally effective, so that it only matters that the agents coordinate with their neighbors on that choice. Efficient coordination is reached when every agent selects the same action. Mixed choices are not efficient for they represent incompatible choices some-where in the network. The efficient coalitions are those consisting of all 0s or all 1s; no other combination of 0s and 1s will be equally well coordinated. Agents do not coordinate beyond their own neighborhoods, but compatibility throughout the system requires that if i is linked to k and k is linked to j that k uses the same choice for both neighbors. But, i and j are linked to other neighbors who may have made other choices and they will wish to be compatible with their other neighbors' choices. This holds over all the points in the network and presents a coordination problem considered by many economists to be very serious. The problem is, therefore, a good test of emergent order.

In order to be faithful to the idea of emergence, the solutions must be reached without deliberation. The agents must be autonomous and choose their actions independently. They must be informed only by the actions they observe and not through the acquisition of an understanding of the global situation. Their information must come only from local neighborhoods. No coordination through central processing or global signals is to be permitted. The search is done in parallel with each agent separately making choices without consultation with other agents. Each agent is a local hill climber interested only in improving its present situation with each new action. The solution must evolve, which means that each choice must build recursively on the choices laid down before it.

To study this process, I used a neural network to evolve coalitions of agents under a variety of parameter settings. Following an initial randomization, the choices evolve recursively until they reach their limit point, where they settle and show no further changes.

Deterministic choice

First, consider a base case that represents how the coordination game is solved by agents who take discrete actions in random sequence. Agents make choices that lie in the [0,1] interval. The moves begin with a randomly selected agent who makes a choice, and then another agent is randomly selected. This agent may be in the same neighborhood, or far away. The second agent is informed of the previous choice only if it is in the neighborhood of the first agent to move; otherwise, it receives no information about the previous move. Then the third agent is randomly chosen to act, again subject to the same information constraint that it is informed only of the previous moves of its neighbors. The process continues until all the agents have acted and this is termed one iteration of the network. The process is then iterated in the next round, starting from the configuration reached in the previous iteration. In the second round, the agents know all their neighbors' prior choices from the prior iteration and their information is updated as they go through the next round in random sequence.

Ten experiments were performed in which coalitions were evolved under these assumptions and parameter settings. The efficiency or fitness of the coalition represents the portion of the gains to coordination which it achieves. Fitness along the evolutionary paths is shown along the vertical axis in Figure

30

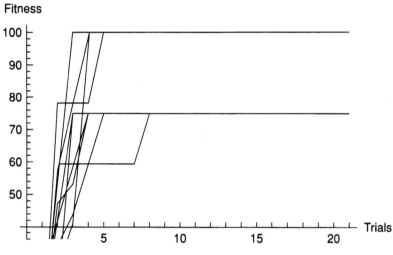

Figure 2.2 Fitness dynamics for the base case

2.2; the number of iterations is on the horizontal axis. Evidently, there is emergent order in the process for it locates two optima in short order. One optima is the highest available global optimum, where full coordination is reached. The other is a local optima that captures about 70 percent of the available gains from coordination. It is evident that the coalitions on the lower path found the lower optima and couldn't escape.

Noisy evolution of coalitions

Noisy evolution is implemented by a Boltzmann network in which information-weighted probabilistic choices are made by each agent. The agent's choice of 0 or 1 is random and the probability of either choice is influenced by signals about its neighbors. The probability of a choice of 0 or 1 depends on the agent's gain; when there is a large gain, that choice is made with high probability; if the gain is small, the choice becomes more uncertain.

Noisy choice can move the organization off local hills to global optima. Noise exponentially increases the paths over which the system may evolve from one state to another. As Figure 2.3 shows, there are many distinct fitness paths that rise and fall as the process searches different neighborhoods of the fitness landscape. Significantly, *all* these paths terminate on the globally optimal coalition. But, the cost of getting to the global optimum is lower fitness and reversals of fortune on the path leading there. Noisy search seems to be turbulent and error prone, but it is strongly error correcting. Because a larger space of organizations is sampled, noisy search is more apt to find the global optimum.

31

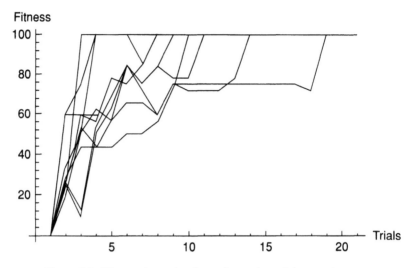

Figure 2.3 Fitness dynamics for noisy and partial commitment

Fitness on the path and at the rest point

A few more conclusions are suggested by the fitness statistics shown in Table 2.2. Here the sample size, mean, standard deviation, maximum and minimum fitness of coalitions are given for each history. In each evolution there are twenty generations of coalitions. The mean sample fitness includes the fitness of every coalition attempted. In addition, the final fitness realized in each evolution is averaged to obtain average final fitness. Note that the attainable fitness differs for the deterministic and noisy search, so we must rescale them to compare their efficiencies; this is done in the next table. What we learn from the present table has more to do with the fitness distributions produced by these search processes. What is evident is the long tails that are produced by noisy search. The fitness covariance of noisy search is nearly three times its mean, while the covariance is only about one-half of the mean fitness with deterministic search. On the other hand, the covariances of final fitness are reversed; here noisy choice produces less variation than deterministic choice. Selection trims the tails of fitness distributions. Imitation, or in these models recursive generation of coalitions from their predecessors (a form of inheritance and imitation), then searches the space surrounding extreme performance organizations. The result is a leveraging of fitness – fitness breeds fitness – into extremal points in the upper tail of the fitness distribution. Noise produces a log normal fitness distribution, and then selection takes over to drive organizations to the extreme tail of the fitness distribution, where fitness follows a power law, or Pareto, distribution.

Table 2.2   Fitness statistics

Case	N	Mean	SD	Max	Min	Covar.
			Sample			
Deterministic	210	5.11	1.83	6.40	0.00	3.35
Noisy	210	25.73	9.29	32.00	0.00	86.02
			Final			
Deterministic	10	5.92	0.77	6.40	4.80	0.54
Noisy	10	32.00	0.00	32.00	32.00	0.00

Table 2.3   Mean and final fitness relative to maximum fitness

Case	Mean	Final
Deterministic	79.84	92.50
Noisy	80.37	100.00

The equilibrium coalitions have higher fitness and less variance of fitness than do the coalitions formed on the path to the equilibrium. Relative to the maximum attainable fitness, the noisy process does best in terms of final fitness, but about as well in achieving average fitness. In Table 2.3 the normalized fitness is reported. Here, the fitness is scaled relative to the maximum attainable fitness. Once again, the noisy process achieves higher final and mean fitness.

Why does noise produce higher fitness? By sending search over a wide area of the fitness landscape, noise produces extreme tails in the fitness distribution. This is evident in the high standard deviation and covariances in the table for the noisy process. Selection trims the lower tail through failure and moves coalitions to high fitness through reproduction and imitation. Unless the unfit coalitions can be broken, the system freezes on a local optimum. The unfit coalitions that are inherited by subsequent generations must be broken or more fit coalitions cannot emerge. Failure is crucial to evolutionary success and an adaptable process that evolves to high fitness will have a high failure rate.

CONCLUSIONS, APPLICATIONS, AND CONJECTURES

Conclusions

Economic organization is information theoretic. Every economic organization, contract, firm, or coalition is the product of and contains information.

This information is of two kinds: descriptive and algorithmic. The former describes structure, the latter determines function. The complexity of the organization is related to its descriptive and algorithmic information. There are economies of scale in organizations, but they come from our knowledge of how to model the way they act, not from knowledge of their structure. An optimal organization is unboundedly rational because it contains unbounded information. Such an organization is too complex to be produced by chance or by design. But, a boundedly rational organization can be readily produced by evolutionary selection.

Evolution is a powerful and adaptive information processor. It opportunistically exploits breadth, depth, and parallelism to search the fitness landscape. The experiments reveal an emergent order in simple processes that do not rely on foresight and use only local interactions. Organizations of high, and even optimal, fitness were evolved in much less time than an optimum could be computed. Consider the simulations where we evolved organizations involving sixteen agents. This is a space containing $2^{16} = 65,536$ organizations. If one were to search this space directly there would be 2^{16} coalition values to be calculated and then these would be sorted according to value; this latter step can usually be done in $\log(2^{16}) = 16$ steps. So, the exhaustive search would take $2^{16} + \log(2^{16})$ steps. Simulations of this search by the noisy evolutionary method of the Boltzmann machine found optimal coalitions within twenty and usually within $\log(2^{16})$ steps. At each of these steps there were sixteen purely local calculations, so in all there were $16 + \log(2^{16})$ steps. Hence, evolution scales the search down from $2^{16} + \log(2^{16})$ steps to $16 + \log(2^{16})$ steps. How can evolution reduce the number of steps by an order of magnitude of 2^{16}? By using a search process that is innovative, conservative, and massively parallel. We use chance to find new contracts, but we preserve features of successful contracts and use them to direct search into promising regions.

One of the keys to achieving high fitness was the presence of noise. Noise promotes discovery and learning. Noisy, error-prone processes produce extreme outcomes. Noisy evolution produces a log normal fitness distribution and selection drives organizations into the extreme upper tail, where power laws hold. Selection trims the low outcomes and preserves the high outcomes. The result is that the diversity produced by noisy evolution leads through selection to the most fit organizations. Processes that yield less diversity produce less fit organizations in the end. There is a cost of evolutionary search. Because evolution generates fitness distributions with long tails, it reduces average fitness along the early part of the evolutionary path. In order to find superior outcomes, some resources must be used to try new solutions that turn out to be inferior. The payoff is the high and uniform fitness of the survivors.

34

Applications

Consider first some applications of the results to networks. By making partial commitments rather than all-or-nothing choices, the agents retain their adaptability and they can respond to the evolution of the system more gracefully by changing only part of their system. Leasing and renting equipment supports flexible commitment and it seems reasonable that leasing would be used in markets where there are network externalities and a high rate of technical change. Leasing preserves adaptation on the part of the lessee and, when there are network externalities, the larger firms who retain ownership and ultimate control of the leased equipment can coordinate better among themselves than can many smaller users of their equipment. The widespread use of leasing in the computer industry during its formative period is consistent with this view.

Another network industry where short term, partial commitments have been important is in natural gas. De Vany and Walls (1995) show that the natural gas pipeline network evolved a highly connected structure following deregulation. Instrumental to this transformation was the widespread use of short term transmission leases. These permitted traders to do hit and run entry in gas markets over the entire pipeline network and this brought about a convergence of prices.

The importance of partial commitments is that mixed systems can coevolve as one eventually replaces the other. Coordination is preserved in mixed systems if the agents mix their systems and choose the appropriate one to use for connecting to specific agents. As new systems are acquired, the network evolves toward a fully compatible set of systems. It just doesn't have to happen all at once. If there is sequential choice, the lock-in from simultaneous choice is avoided and the mixed solutions gradually give way. Hughes (1983) notes that mixed AC and DC power systems coexisted until DC eventually was replaced. The transition was smooth and not an all-or-nothing choice because there were means to permit both systems to interconnect. The use of mixed and multiphase systems let the power grid evolve into a coordinated system, illustrating again the importance of the adaptability that lies behind sequential choice, noise, partial commitments, and mixed strategies.

In addition to stressing the value of noise and adaptation, the model downplays the need for foresight. Liebowitz and Margolis (1995) argue that strong lock-in does not occur in markets where there is foresight. The agents can overcome network coordination failure by devising new, inclusive ownership structures. Inclusion internalizes and centralizes control. On the other hand, foresight is not required for the evolutionary dynamic to escape inefficient lock-in; what is needed is sufficient diversity of agent behaviors and a structure of interaction among the agents that is not too global. Diverse, locally coupled agents, acting in their own interests and with a sufficiently high error rate, seem to do quite well if the simulations can be taken seriously. They need

35

no foresight and, given the successes they can achieve with a decentralized ownership structure, an inclusive ownership structure may be no more effective than a decentralized one.

The point is not to deny that a more centralized, inclusive ownership structure might be better than a decentralized one in some situations. But, coordination is quite possible without centralization and may even be more readily achieved under a decentralized system of ownership. For example, strongly connected networks of agents tend to exhibit dynamics that more readily are trapped on local optima than sparsely connected networks (De Vany, 1995). In such a case, it would be better for the network to be locally connected than globally connected.

In the broader context of organization, many of these statements about the network problem also apply. Organizations that are decentralized, with modest hierarchies among locally coupled agents, and that tolerate noise and diversity are highly adaptive; they do not tend to lock in on inefficient solutions. They are, however, boundedly rational and even while this supports their adaptability, it requires some mechanism to resolve the disputes that must arise within an organization in which some constraints among agents must eventually come into conflict. Management in this context is more like due process and negotiation between clusters over conflicts that must arise when an organization uses noisy and adaptive methods to evolve efficient forms.

Evolution and optimizing operate on different time scales. It usually is thought that evolution takes far more time than optimizing, but that is not the case when optimizing is treated as an explicit process that also takes time. We have seen that evolution of a boundedly optimal organization operates on a time scale of about $\log(2^N)$, whereas optimization operates on a time scale of about 2^N. Evolution is much faster. This matters a lot for empirical economics for events on the time scale of optimization are unlikely to be observable, whereas events on the time scale of adaptive, evolutionary processes can, in principle, be observed. Applying this perspective to, say, the problem of modeling the behavior of cost suggests that the survivor technique is a more accurate method than estimating cost functions, which is based on optimization.[6] A diversity of organizational arrangements and production techniques permits the industry to be poised to adapt to changes; convergence to a common "optimal" arrangement and technique can take place only within a stationary environment and such arrangements are fragile, like single crop agriculture. The advantages of the poised adaptability of a heterogeneous industry over a homogeneous one that is in a statically efficient, but dynamically maladaptive and brittle, equilibrium seems underappreciated in equilibrium economics.

How can an organization exploit evolution as an adaptive mechanism? It is not natural selection, but the ability to take advantage of natural selection that is an advantage to organizations. A self-organized firm or industry almost certainly would evolve the ability to evolve as one of its primary character-

36

istics; it would evolve the capability to exploit evolution as an adaptive mechanism. The contrast of self-organized with centrally directed or regulated industries reveals the distinction between evolution and optimizing as organizing methods. De Vany and Walls (1995) show that a failing of regulation based on theories of static optimization is that it prevents the regulated firm and industry from exploiting evolution. The regulatory equilibrium is brittle and non-adaptive; on an evolutionary time scale, it is always out of equilibrium, does not achieve static efficiency, and adapts catastrophically to changes in the environment.

Some of our results have implications for information and game theory. While much of the recent literature has pointed to information asymmetries as a source of inefficiency, the evolutionary model of self-organized and decentralized coordination points to asymmetries as a source of good dynamics and efficient outcomes. In fully symmetric games, the agents freeze on inefficient outcomes to the network coordination game. The same point could be made about noise. While noise can be a source of inefficiency, it also is a source of learning and good evolutionary dynamics. In fact, we found that *only* the noisy, asymmetric, and constraint-violating dynamics converged on fully efficient coordination outcomes. Shifting our perspective from statics to dynamics in order to understand where structure comes from will cause us to reappraise many results of static analyses and to gain new appreciation for structure, noise, diversity, and dynamics as sources of order and to downplay the role of hyper-rationality and foresight.

Conjectures

The following conjectures expand (or go far beyond!) the conclusions.

In standard theories, contracts and authority relationships are the product of rational optimization. But, in a theory of economic organization based on Alchian's theory of chance and evolution, the firm would be self-organized. In a self-organized system, the order evident in economic activity is emergent. Emergent order comes from the interactions between agents and their environment that produces something that was not evident in our understanding of how the agents operate; it comes from the constraints under which the agents act, from their exploratory and adaptive actions, and from an evolutionary competition among adaptive behaviors.

Economic institutions are important to the task of creating complex organizations. If institutions create generic structures that can be used as templates for new organizations, this will produce an economy of scale in the institution. The templates solve the internal consistency problem by construction and ease the task of putting organizations together. Universal institutions promote evolvable organizations. Effective institutions preserve the integrity of the selection process. They establish a zone of autonomy, thus creating individuals over whom selection operates. They tolerate failure,

37

noise, and variation while stabilizing the learning environment. They promote local interaction. These sound like the institutions of capitalism.

Cultural transmission through learning and imitation favors intelligence, and the ability to learn and imitate may be selected in the evolutionary process. Cultural evolution is a means of arriving at viable solutions to recurrent situations without each generation paying the costs of trial and error learning. High decision costs – obtaining the information, computing the decision, evaluating the outcomes – can lead to reliance on cultural transmission of decision. Yet, too much imitation can lead to herding and uniformity which produce too little diversity in the population and produce an equilibrium that is brittle and maladaptive to shocks.

Only free, autonomous agents can produce emergent order. Personal freedom and freedom of contract are not small institutional matters that hinge only on transactions costs; they are fundamental (and universal) institutions on which everything else depends. One can contract around a problem if there are defective institutions, but if freedom and flexibility of action and contract are not available, then many problems must go unsolved.

NOTES

1 Dan Klein pointed out to me that Adam Smith's associate, Francis Hutcheson, put it this way.
2 Hodgson (1993) is a good discussion of this controversy and part of the following discussion draws upon his work.
3 There is more to it than this; see De Vany (1993) for the details. We need to specify the length of the string in its prefix, how many parties, and we need to give the most compact description of the decision rules, among other things.
4 There is no closed form for Bell's number, but it can be computed by a recurrence relation. The recurrence relation is $b(n) = S_k = \Sigma^{n-1} C(n-1, k) p(n - k - 1)$, where $C()$ is the binomial coefficient. The initial condition is $k = 0$ $b(0) = 1$, and higher numbers are calculated recursively.
5 A rough measure of the difficulty of either of these tasks can be gotten from a thought experiment by Stockmeyer and Meyer that is reported in Poundstone (1990). They estimate that the fastest computer using every particle in the universe running from the beginning of time could execute at most 10^{168} operations. This computer could compare at most all those coalition structures that could be formed with just 134 agents or all those two-party contracts that cover just 550 states.
6 I thank Rod Smith for suggesting this application of the evolutionary model.

REFERENCES

Alchian, Armen (1950) "Uncertainty, Evolution, and Economic Theory," *Journal of Political Economy* 58: 211–21.
Allen, Peter (1993) "Evolution: Persistent Ignorance from Continual Learning," in *Nonlinear Dynamics and Evolutionary Economics*, ed. Richard H. Day and Ping Chen. New York: Oxford University Press, pp. 1–38.
Arthur, Brian (1989) "The Economy and Complexity," in *Lectures in the Sciences of Complexity*, ed. D. L. Stein. Redwood City, CA: Addison-Wesley, pp. 713–40.

Binger, Brian and Elizabeth Hoffman (1989) "Institutional Persistence and Change: The Question of Efficiency," *Journal of Institutional and Theoretical Economics* 145: 67–84.

David, Paul (1985) "Clio and the Economics of qwerty," *American Economic Review, Papers and Proceedings* 75: 332–7.

De Vany, Arthur (1993) "Information, Bounded Rationality, and the Complexity of Economic Organization," Institute for Mathematical Behavioral Sciences Working Paper 93–08, University of California.

—— (1995) "The Emergence and Evolution of Self-Organized Coalitions," in *Computational Methods in Economics and Finance*, ed. M. Gilli. Würzburg, Vienna: Kluwer Scientific, pp. 235–58.

De Vany, Arthur and David Walls (1995) *The Emerging New Order in Natural Gas: Markets versus Regulation*. Westport, CT: Quorum Books.

Friedman, M. (1953) "The Methodology of Positive Economics," in *Essays in Positive Economics*. Chicago: University of Chicago Press, pp. 3–43.

Hayek, F. (1944, 1977) *The Road to Serfdom*. Chicago: University of Chicago Press.

Hodgson, Geoffrey (1993) *Economics and Evolution: Bringing Life Back into Economics*. Oxford: Polity Press.

Hughes, Thomas (1983) *Networks of Power: Electrification in Western Society, 1880–1930*. Baltimore, MD: Johns Hopkins University Press.

Jensen, M. and W. Meckling (1979) "Rights and Production Functions: An Application to Labor-Managed Firms," *Journal of Business* 52: 469–506.

Katz, M. and C. Shapiro (1985) "Network Externalities, Competition, and Compatibility," *American Economic Review* 75: 424–40.

Langlois, R. (1988) "Economic Change and the Boundaries of the Firm," *Journal of Institutional and Theoretical Economics* 144, September: 635–57.

Liebowitz, S. and S. Margolis (1990) "The Fable of the Keys," *Journal of Law and Economics* 33: 1–25.

—— (1995) "Path Dependence, Lock-in, and History," *Journal of Law, Economics, and Organization* 6: 463–81.

Nelson, R. and S. Winter (1974) "In Search of a Useful Theory of Innovation", *Research Policy* 11: 36–76.

—— (1977) "Neoclassical vs. Evolutionary Theories of Economic Growth: Critique and Prospectus," *Economic Journal* 114: 886–905.

—— (1982) *An Evolutionary Theory of Economic Change*. Cambridge, MA: Harvard University Press.

North, D. (1990) *Institutions, Institutional Change and Economic Performance*. Cambridge: Cambridge University Press.

Penrose, E. (1952) "Biological Analogies in the Theory of the Firm," *American Economic Review* 42: 804–19.

Poundstone, W. (1990) *Labyrinths of Reason*. New York: Anchor Books.

Smith, A. (1776, 1956) *An Inquiry into the Nature and Causes of the Wealth of Nations*, Oxford: Clarendon Press.

Williamson, O. (1988) "The Economics and Sociology of Organization," in *Industries, Firms, and Jobs: Sociological and Economic Approaches*, ed. G. Farkas and B. England. New York: Plenum Press, pp. 159–85.

Winter, S. (1964) "Economic Natural Selection and the Theory of the Firm," *Yale Economic Essays* 14: 225–72.

—— (1975) "Optimization and Evolution in the Theory of the Firm," in *Adaptive Economic Models*, ed. R. Day and T. Groves. New York: Academic Press, pp. 73–118.

—— (1982) "An Essay on the Theory of Production," in *Adaptive Economic Models*, ed. S. Hymans. Ann Arbor, MI: University of Michigan Press, pp. 55–91.

3

EVOLUTION AND SPONTANEOUS UNIFORMITY

Evidence from the evolution of the limited liability company

Bruce H. Kobayashi and Larry E. Ribstein

This chapter examines whether the process of unguided state by state evolution of limited liability company (LLC) statutes has led to efficient interstate uniformity. Our evidence suggests significant uniformity has been produced in cases where the net benefits of uniformity are positive, and that such uniformity has not been produced by herd behavior. Our results are consistent with Alchian's intuition about the role of market processes, and suggests that the survival of efficient rules, fostered by the rational behavior of decentralized economic actors, is produced by forces beyond the control or foresight of individual lawmakers or legislatures.

INTRODUCTION

Among Armen Alchian's many major contributions to economic analysis is his pioneering application of the principles of biological evolution and natural selection to economics. In his 1950 article, "Uncertainty, Evolution, and Economic Theory," Alchian used evolutionary principles to demonstrate that the standard tools of economics can be directly applied to situations where strong assumptions about individual behavior cannot be made. As Alchian noted:

> The essential point is that individual motivation and foresight, while sufficient, are not necessary. All that is needed by economists is their own awareness of the survival conditions and criteria of the economic system and a group of participants who submit various combinations and organizations for the system's selection and adoption. ... As a consequence, only the method of use, rather than the usefulness, of economic tools and concepts is affected by the approach suggested here; in fact, they are made more powerful if they are not pretentiously assumed to be necessarily associated with, and dependent upon, individual foresight and adjustment.

40

Alchian's approach emphasizing the "decisions and criteria dictated by the economic *system* as more important than those made by individuals in it" is especially relevant to the use of economics to study the creation of law. This approach does not require that one question the importance of rational calculation by actors within the system.[1] Rather, it suggests a more powerful approach to studying the creation of law – one that deemphasizes the motivation or foresight of judges or legislators in favor of a broad consideration of the numerous forces affecting the legal system. Such an evolutionary approach has been used to illustrate how the incentives of litigants can cause judge-made law to evolve toward efficiency without the active participation of judges.[2] Similar "evolutionary" forces can act upon individual legislators and legislatures to produce efficient statutory outcomes. Both competition between interest groups,[3] and competition between jurisdictions can cause statutes to evolve toward efficiency.[4]

Such evolutionary processes are particularly relevant to the creation of uniform laws. A large body of centrally produced federal and uniform state laws have been promulgated as a uniform solution to problems created by diverse state statutes. But there are defects inherent in centralized lawmaking by the federal government and uniform lawmaking bodies.[5] Such uniformity inhibits exit from perverse laws, and thus eliminates an important mechanism through which the evolutionary forces can operate.[6] Thus, it is important to consider whether decentralized processes, such as state jurisdictional competition, can better overcome both incentive and public choice problems and produce efficient uniformity. Yet little is known about the legal evolution of statutory law or the extent to which such decentralized evolution can produce efficient uniformity.[7]

This chapter extends the current literature on the decentralized evolution of law by examining whether the process of unguided state provision of statutes for closely held firms leads to interstate uniformity in areas where such uniformity can be expected to promote economic efficiency. Our focus is the recent evolution of the limited liability company (LLC) statutes, a form of closely held business which combines the benefits of limited liability with the tax advantages of partnership (Ribstein, 1992, 1995a), and Ribstein and Keatinge (1992). We adopt Alchian's suggestion by deemphasizing the often ambiguous predictions of theories based on the behavior of individual market or political actors in favor of an empirical examination of the ultimate evolution of LLC statutes. The evidence presented in this chapter is consistent with the hypothesis that unguided evolution can achieve uniformity, and that such uniformity occurs when the benefits of uniformity outweigh the costs of reduced variation and experimentation.

Our chapter suggests an expanded role for unguided jurisdictional competition and less reliance on centralized uniform lawmaking. Our results also suggest the applicability of Alchian's approach to other areas involving the centralized versus decentralized production of uniformity, including the

41

evolution of technological standards (Liebowitz and Margolis, 1990, 1994), and the choice between legal rules and standards.

The organization of the chapter is as follows: the next section reviews theories of evolution of the closely held firm through jurisdictional competition. The third section provides a theory of the costs and benefits of uniform laws. The theory is used to test whether the recent evolution of LLC statutes is consistent with appropriate spontaneous uniformity. The fourth section concludes.

EVOLUTION OF CLOSELY HELD FIRMS

Evolution of closely held firms confirms Alchian's insight that a study of the "adaptive mechanism" of the market may be more fruitful than that of "individual motivation and foresight." As noted in the introduction, jurisdictional competition can play a potentially large role in evolution of state statutory law. However, the existing literature on jurisdictional competition has focused primarily on state legislators' motives to maximize state revenues from chartering public corporations.[8] Commentators have noted that the law can achieve uniformity by firms moving to favored states, particularly Delaware, and by other states imitating these states to prevent further losses.[9] They disagree mainly about whether this process is a "race to the bottom" in which the states attract incorporation business by exploiting principal–agent problems resulting from the separation of ownership and control,[10] or a "race to the top" that is disciplined by efficient capital markets.[11]

With respect to closely held firms, by contrast, legislators seem to lack a motive to compete for chartering revenues. Because foreign incorporation is marginally costlier for close corporations than for public corporations, so that few close corporations will choose to incorporate outside the state in which they do business, states with inefficient statutes do not face the threat of loss of incorporation business. Thus, it has been suggested by Ayres (1992) that state legislators will not compete to supply close corporation statutes. It may be that, whatever legislators' motives, lawyers can drive jurisdictional competition.[12] Even so, lawyers in individual states probably lack the knowledge or foresight to know when to adopt *uniform* rules. Indeed, the rule must first be widely adopted before it becomes uniform.

The previous discussion suggests little reason to expect promulgation of close corporation statutes, much less the evolution of *efficient* close corporation statutes. Applying Alchian, however, regardless of the incentives, motivation, or foresight of individual legislators or other lawmakers, efficient rules can evolve if the *system* fosters survival of such rules. As noted in the introduction, adoption of the evolutionary approach does not imply the rejection of rational calculation by individuals within the legal system – indeed Demsetz (1996) rejects the notion that rational behavior and evolution are alternative or sub-stitute explanations of behavior. Rather, it suggests that the survival of efficient rules is fostered by rational behavior of economic actors where the end result is shaped by forces beyond the control or foresight of individual lawmakers or legislatures.[13]

One way in which the system can encourage the survival of efficient rules is if participants in the system – in this case, parties to closely held firms – rationally pursue alternative methods of earning profits. According to the contractual theory of the firm pioneered by Coase (1937, 1960) and by Alchian and Demsetz (1972), firms' choice of contractual arrangements, including their selection of particular business forms and legal default rules, reflects choices influenced by positive transactions and information costs.[14] Contractual terms can be defined by standard statutory forms provided by state or federal law, or in custom agreements. The transaction cost literature predicts that closely held firms will demand standard statutory forms when the benefits of using customized agreements are small relative to the additional transactions costs that would be incurred in using such agreements.[15] Statutory forms such as the close corporation compete with non-statutory business forms, which, in turn, compete across jurisdictions through the use of contractual choice of law clauses.[16] *Transaction cost considerations also determine when firms will demand uniform statutory provisions and when provisions will vary from state to state.* Following Alchian's theory, efficient rules will be selected as a result of this process of "jurisdictional" natural selection if the system widely adopts rules that are appropriate for a large number of firms. Ultimately, the extent to which such forces do or do not operate in this or any area remains largely an empirical question.

EVIDENCE FROM THE EVOLUTION OF LLC STATUTES

In this section, we describe a positive theory of desirable and undesirable uniformity. This theory is based on the tradeoff between, on the one hand, uniformity's benefits of reducing information costs, facilitating exchange, and improving the allocation of resources, and, on the other, diversity's benefits of increasing flexibility and promoting experimentation and innovation. We then attempt to explain the observed pattern of uniformity found in existing LLC statutes using this theory.

After identifying circumstances in which uniformity of statutory provisions relating to business associations would, and would not, be desirable, we review data on LLC statutes which show that, even without an NCCUSL proposal, the states have generated greater uniformity in exactly the circumstances transactions cost economics predicts uniform LLC provisions would be most desirable. Our examination suggests the pattern of evolution is consistent with appropriate uniformity, and inconsistent with non-efficiency rationales for uniformity, such as herd behavior.

The benefits of uniformity

Economic analyses examining the benefits of uniformity have stressed the information and other costs created by diversity. In particular, information costs are generated when parties face a large number of statutory variations among jurisdictions. But these information costs vary among different types of provisions. This forms the basic insight for our test for appropriate uniformity. Uniformity is relatively important for provisions affecting third-party creditors who engage in small, non-recurring transactions with many firms, where the creditors' marginal cost of learning an applicable provision likely exceeds their marginal benefit. Under these circumstances, parties will choose not to obtain the information and will instead apply a discount to reflect uncertainty. Firms have an incentive to avoid this penalty by adopting uniform provisions that reduce transaction costs and uncertainty.[17] By contrast, uniformity is less important regarding provisions that affect the members themselves. The members of closely held firms typically make relatively large investments in few firms and therefore have relatively large marginal benefit and small marginal cost in being informed about each provision. As a result, firms have less of an incentive to adopt uniform provisions of this type.[18]

Owners also may have a tax incentive to adopt uniform provisions. The tax rules for characterizing firms as partnerships require that the firm lack at least two of the "corporate" characteristics of limited liability – centralized management, continuity of life, and free transferability of interest.[19] In order to ensure against adverse tax consequences of surprise characterization of a firm as a corporation, the parties may insist that the firms adhere to a standard form that has been explicitly sanctioned by the Internal Revenue Service. Since almost all LLCs have limited liability, tax considerations suggest that LLC statutes will tend to ensure that LLCs lack at least two of the other corporate characteristics. For example, the vast majority of the statutes provide for a default rule of decentralized management.[20]

The benefits of diversity

A second consideration in determining whether uniformity is desirable with respect to a type of statutory provision is whether there are significant benefits from diversity. For some types of provisions it is important only that there is a clear rule, and not precisely what the rule is. For others, there may be a significant question as to what rule is appropriate for particular firms or for firms generally. Indeed, Romano (1992) suggests that close corporation arrangements generally are more idiosyncratic than public corporations, and therefore less amenable to standard statutory forms. Firms may want to be able to select the latter type of provision from a menu of alternatives. Perhaps more important in the context of closely held firms, there may be a need

44

for experimentation among jurisdictions to arrive at the appropriate default rule.

Many of the provisions listed above as involving high benefits of uniformity also involve relatively low benefits of diversity. These rules are designed to provide minimal protection from trade creditors above those provided by bankruptcy or state insolvency law. While there may be some debate about whether such provisions are necessary, there is little room for variation in the substance of the provisions themselves, and consequently relatively little benefit from state by state evolution. For example, the rules provide small trade creditors with a simple fallback rule that prevents the most egregious cases of debtor misconduct. Because this is only baseline protection, the precise contours of the rule are unimportant. By contrast, many of the provisions listed as involving low benefits of uniformity also involve relatively high benefits of diversity. These include provisions regarding such matters as management form and allocation of voting and financial rights. In fact, these provisions have undergone substantial evolution in the short history of LLC statutes.

In contrast to most provisions, tax-motivated provisions involve a conflict between the benefits of diversity and the benefits of uniformity criteria. There is significant room for evolution and variation in the rules regarding management, transferability, and dissolution. Indeed, the tax rules do not provide a strong reason for uniform statutes. Because, as noted above, firms must possess *three* of four "*corporate*" features to *fail to* qualify for partnership tax treatment, many firms may not want to adopt particular tax-compliant features. Moreover, the tax rules themselves provide enough guidance that there may be little need for business associations' statutes to mimic these rules. On the other hand, *lawyers* may prefer uniform rules that ensure tax compliance because they risk potential malpractice liability without incurring the benefits of diversity.[21] Lawyers are a highly coordinated interest group who can further their interests in state legislatures. Accordingly, tax-induced uniformity is less likely to be explained by efficiency considerations than by lawyer–client agency costs.[22]

The evidence on LLC evolution

This section shows evidence that spontaneous beneficial uniformity through the evolution of LLC statutes actually occurs, as predicted by Alchian's theory. Figure 3.1 shows the total number of states adopting LLC statutes and the total number of LLC statutes passed over time. In the fifteen-year period between 1977 and the end of 1991, only eight states had passed LLC statutes. Since a tax ruling opened the floodgates on LLCs, forty-seven states and the District of Columbia had passed LLC statutes by the end of 1994. These adoptions are listed chronologically in Table 3.1.[23]

Table 3.2 lists sixty-nine provisions found in the forty-eight LLC statutes, and whether each provision primarily affects the members, primarily affects

Table 3.1 Adoption of LLC statutes

Year	Order	State	Enactment date
1977	1.	Wyoming	June 30, 1977
1978		None	
1979		None	
1980		None	
1981		None	
1982	2.	Florida	April 21, 1982
1983		None	
1984		None	
1985		None	
1986		None	
1987		None	
1988		None	
1989		None	
1990	3.	Colorado	April 18, 1990
	4.	Kansas	May 11, 1990
1991	5.	Nevada	January 1, 1991
	6.	Virginia	March 21, 1991
	7.	Texas	June 16, 1991
	8.	Utah	July 1, 1991
1992	9.	West Virginia	March 27, 1992
	10.	Iowa	April 27, 1992
	11.	Minnesota	April 29, 1992
	12.	Oklahoma	May 1, 1992
	13.	Maryland	May 26, 1992
	14.	Arizona	June 2, 1992
	15.	Louisiana	July 7, 1992
	16.	Rhode Island	July 21, 1992
	17.	Delaware	July 22, 1992
	18.	Illinois	September 11, 1992
1993	1R.	Wyoming (revised)	March 5, 1993
	19.	South Dakota	March 13, 1993
	20.	Montana	March 18, 1993
	3R.	Colorado (revised)	March 22, 1993
	21.	Idaho	March 26, 1993
	4R.	Kansas (revised)	April 5, 1993
	22.	New Mexico	April 7, 1993
	23.	Arkansas	April 12, 1993
	24.	North Dakota	April 12, 1993
	25.	Michigan	April 14, 1993
	26.	North Carolina	April 23, 1993
	10R.	Iowa (revised)	April 26, 1993
	27.	Indiana	May 13, 1993
	11R.	Minnesota (revised)	May 13, 1993
	7R.	Texas (revised)	May 19, 1993
	28.	Alabama	May 20, 1993
	13R.	Maryland (revised)	May 27, 1993
	29.	Nebraska	June 2, 1993
	15R	Louisiana (revised)	June 9, 1993
	12R.	Oklahoma (revised)	June 11, 1993

Table 3.1 continued

Year	Order	State	Enactment date
	2R.	Florida (revised)	June 14, 1993
	30.	Connecticut	June 23, 1993
	31.	New Hampshire	June 23, 1993
	32.	Oregon	June 24, 1993
	33.	Georgia	July 1, 1993
	34.	Missouri	July 2, 1993
	5R.	Nevada (revised)	July 9, 1993
	16R.	Rhode Island (revised)	July 22, 1993
	35.	New Jersey	July 30, 1993
	36.	Wisconsin	December 13, 1993
1994	37.	Mississippi	March 15, 1994
	38.	Kentucky	March 19, 1994
	39.	Ohio	April 1, 1994
	40.	Washington	April 1, 1994
	6R.	Virginia (revised)	April 5, 1994
	41.	Tennessee	April 14, 1994
	3R.	Colorado (revised)	April 19, 1994
	14R.	Arizona (revised)	April 19, 1994
	42.	Maine	April 20, 1994
	43.	District of Columbia	May 18, 1994
	31R.	Connecticut (revised)	June 7, 1994
	44.	Alaska	June 8, 1994
	45.	South Carolina	June 16, 1994
	46.	New York	July 4, 1994
	47.	California	September 6, 1994
	48.	Pennsylvania	December 7, 1994
1995*	22R.	New Mexico (revised)	April 5, 1995
	32R.	Oregon (revised)	May 5, 1995

Note: * Through May 5, 1995

third parties, or primarily affects the firm's tax liability. The table also lists the number of adoptions of the form contained in the original Wyoming statute, and the number of adoptions of the leading form.[24] Examining Table 3.2, we see that large numbers of states have adopted similar forms of many types of provisions.[25] This evidence strongly refutes theories that suggest close corporation statutes will not be produced by state legislatures, and is consistent with the hypothesis that the states, without the help of a uniform lawmaking body,[26] have recognized and attempted to reduce the costs of diversity by adopting uniform default rules that reduce the transactions and information costs of operating close corporations. However, uniformity also could be consistent with inefficient behavior, a possibility discussed later in this section. Further, many provisions do not have a widely adopted form.[27]

In order to examine whether spontaneous uniformity has led to appropriate uniformity, we test to see if the amount of uniformity that has developed

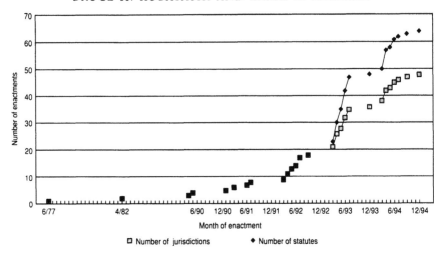

Figure 3.1 The number of LLC statutes enacted

for the types of provisions identified above correlates with the desirability of uniformity. As noted above, we divide LLC provisions into three mutually exclusive categories: those which affect primarily the members; those which affect third parties; and those which are primarily tax motivated. We identify the "uniform" provision for each category of provisions as the one that has the most adoptions.[28] Our theory predicts that if spontaneous uniformity promotes uniformity in situations where it is most desirable, provisions affecting members will be less uniform than provisions in the third-party or tax categories.

Table 3.3 lists the average number of adoptions and the share of the leading form, by category. We hypothesize that the average number of adoptions of the leading form will be smaller for provisions affecting members than for provisions affecting either third parties or the LLC's tax status. The data on existing LLC statutes are consistent with our hypothesis. The leading form in provisions affecting members are adopted, on average by 23.1 of the forty-eight jurisdictions that have adopted LLC statutes as of the end of 1994. That is, the leading form in provisions that affect members on average has a "market share" of less than one-half. By contrast, the leading form in provisions affecting third parties or affecting the LLC's tax liability are adopted, on average, by thirty of the forty-eight jurisdictions (a share of 62.5 percent).

Table 3.4 lists the difference between the average number of adoptions of the leading form along with a *t*-statistic testing the null hypothesis that the difference of the means is zero. The null hypothesis that there is no difference between the average number of adoptions of the leading form of the third-

Table 3.2 Provisions included in existing LLC statutes

Provision Adopted	Type of provision	Number of jurisdictions adopting original form	Number of jurisdictions adopting most form
1. Number required to form	Third party	16	32
2. How LLC is formed	Third party	36	36*
3. Number of owners	Tax	13	21
4. Contents of articles	Third party	1	6
5. Execution of articles	Third party	8	40
6. Consequences of false execution	Third party	29	29*
7. Purpose limitations	Third party	16	27
8. Powers	Third party	31	31*
9. Firm name (must include)	Third party	1	25
10. Firm name (must exclude)	Third party	8	11
11. Reservation of name	Third party	3	45
12. Maintenance of agent	Third party	48	48*
13. Service of process	Third party	7**	31
14. Erroneous statement of duty	Third party	21	27
15 Conseq. of non-compl. with formalities	Third party	17	17*,***
16. Operating agreements in writing	Member	23	23*
17. Operating agreement method of adoption	Member	8**	33
18. Firm property ownership	Third party	22	22*
19. Profit sharing and distributions	Member	3**	26
20. Required form of capital contribution	Third party	0	45
21. Oral agreement to contribute	Member	36	36*
22. Compromise	Third party	34	34*
23. Rights and obligations re non-cash dist.	Third party	7	38
24. Interim distribution rights	Member	43	43*
25. Wrongful distribution liability	Third party	5	14
26. Wrongful distribution definition	Third party	11	18
27. Definition of members' interest	Member	32	32*
28. Transfer of financial interest to assignee	Member	7**	23
29. Effect of assignment on membership stat.	Member	11**	18
30. Transfer of financial interest to assignor	Third party	6**	42
31. Transfer of management rights	Tax	18	23
32. Certification of interests	Member	24**	21***
33. Rights of member's creditors	Third party	7**	34
34. Disp. of mbr int. – divorce or inheritance	Member	16**	18
35. Default management	Tax	36	36*
36. Provision of management form	Member	25	25*
37. Allocation of member voting rights	Member	25	25*

Table 3.2 continued

Provision Adopted	Type of provision	Number of jurisdictions adopting original form	Number of jurisdictions adopting most form
38. Power to vote	Member	9**	9
39. Member agency power	Third party	8	30
40. Member agency power	Third party	7	30
41. Member agency power – non-member mgr	Third party	28	28*
42. Duty to disclose records to members	Member	3	19
43. Manager duty of care	Member	13**	13
44. Consent to conflict of interest transactions	Member	19**	11***
45. Waiver of fiduciary duties	Member	16**	10
46. Member duties	Member	19**	10***
47. Derivative suits authorized	Member	11**	18
48. Indemnification	Member	8	17
49. Suits against firm	Member	34	34*
50 Member dissociation right	Member	20	20*
51. Member dissociation events	Member	22	23
52. Rights of member who wrongful dis.	Member	19	21*
53. Causes of dissolution	Member	1	30
54. Agreement to continue	Member	8	31
55. Ability to contract around agmt to cont.	Tax	3	40
56. Articles of dissolution	Third party	16	18
57. Winding up	Member	17	17*
58. Distribution of assets	Member	5	32
59. Creditor's post-dissolution rights	Third party	15**	22
60. Merger authorization	Member	4**	15
61. Merger-conv. filing formalities	Member	4**	31
62. Personal liability of LLC owners	Third party	48	48*
63. Provision for bus. outside formation state	Member	33	33*
64. Foreign LLC (FLLC) definition	Third party	0**	18
65. FLLC registration	Third party	0**	48
66. FLLC internal affairs	Third party	1**	37
67. FLLC rights	Third party	21**	27
68. FLLC formalities failure	Third party	2**	31
69. Def. of transacting business	Third party	16**	32

Notes:
* The uniform form is the initial form adopted in the 1977 Wyoming Statute
** The initial statute did not include such a provision
*** If the leading form is the non-adoption of such a provision, the share of the second most adopted form is listed

Table 3.3   Average number of adoptions of the leading form (most adopted form as of May 5, 1995)

Category	Number of provisions	Average number of adoptions of the leading form	Standard deviation	Average share of the leading form
Third party	34	29.9	11.0	62.3 %
Member	31	23.1	8.8	48.2 %
Tax	4	30.0	10.9	62.5 %

Table 3.4   Tests of the difference of the means

H_0	H_1	Difference $(\mu_i - \mu_j)$	t-statistic	Degrees of freedom
$\mu_{3rd\ party} = \mu_{member}$	$\mu_{3rd\ party} > \mu_{member}$	6.8	2.68**	63
$\mu_{tax} = \mu_{member}$	$\mu_{tax} > \mu_{member}$	6.9	1.38*	33
$\mu_{3rd\ party} = \mu_{tax}$	$\mu_{3rd\ party} \neq \mu_{tax}$	−0.1	−0.01	36

Notes:
* Statistically different from zero at the 0.10 level (one-tailed test)
** Statistically different from zero at the 0.01 level (one-tailed test)

party and member categories is rejected at standard significance levels. The difference between the average number of adoptions of the leading form of tax and member provisions is also positive and statistically significant at the 0.10 level. Finally, the difference between the average number of adoptions of the leading form for third-party and tax provisions is negative, but not statistically different from zero at standard significance levels. [29]

We also examined the development of uniformity over time as new statutes were passed. If spontaneous uniformity has moved the states toward appropriate uniformity, then the theory discussed earlier predicts that uniformity (measured by the average share of the leading form) will rise for provisions in the third-party category, but that there will be no such movement toward uniformity for provisions in the member category.

The clearest test of evolution of statutory law concerns tax provisions. Lawyers' pressure for tax-compliant provisions is likely to cause at least initial uniformity. Without evolution, this uniformity is likely to persist. By contrast, our theory suggests that profit-seeking firms will seek alternatives to tax-motivated provisions, thereby eroding the market shares of initially popular provisions. However, because uniformity regarding this type of provision is more efficient than for other types of member provisions, our theory suggests that tax provisions ultimately may be more uniform than other member provisions.

The recent adoption history of LLC provisions is consistent with these predictions. Figure 3.2 shows the average share of the leading provision by

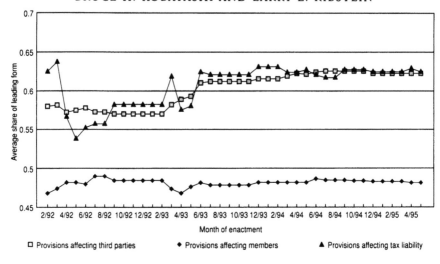

Figure 3.2 The average share of the leading form: by type of provision

category over the last three years when most LLC statutes have been passed. During this time, the difference between the average share of the leading form for the *third-party* and *member* categories has increased.[30] The average share of the leading form for provisions in the member category remained relatively constant, rising from 46.8 percent to 48.2 percent during the period February 1992 to May 1995, while the average share of the leading form for provisions in the third-party category has increased from approximately 58 to 62.3 percent during the same time period. The leading form share of the tax provisions fluctuated during this time period, showing initial uniformity, a period of diversity when the initial uniform law is being replaced, and finally, a return to the initial level of uniformity of 62.5 percent.

Non-efficiency explanation for spontaneous uniformity

This part has shown that the states have tended to move toward uniformity in situations in which our theory suggests uniformity may be desirable. This leaves the question whether the uniform provisions that have emerged are efficient.[31] As already suggested concerning tax-compliant provisions, uniformity may result from political pressure by a dominant interest group – that is, lawyers. Thus, it is possible that uniformity may reflect wealth-decreasing rather than wealth-increasing forces.[32]

Spontaneous uniformity may be undesirable for the additional reason that state legislators are engaging in "herd behavior" by ignoring their private information and simply adopting prior statutes.[33] If so, the states probably are not evolving toward a more efficient rule because legislators are disregarding the information generated by the experience of other states. The policy implication of either explanation would be that NCCUSL-promoted uniformity, despite its defects, may be superior to spontaneous uniformity that is generated by inefficient early statutes and a simple game of follow-the-leader.

Once again, our data support Alchian's intuition that overall market processes can produce desirable evolution even when individuals' motivations or foresight is suspect. Our evidence that the states are achieving uniformity in situations where our theory predicts it is efficient to do so suggests that legislators are sorting provisions according to the desirability of uniformity measured by independent criteria, and therefore are using private information rather than blindly following the leader.

Other data can be used to *test* more directly the herding hypothesis. One implication of the herding hypothesis is that early statutory forms would have disproportionate influence.[34] That is, the herding hypothesis predicts that initially adopted provisions are likely to be the uniform provisions. Table 3.5 suggests this is not the case. Overall, the form initially adopted in the Wyoming statute is the uniform statute in only twenty-four of the sixty-nine provisions. Even more striking, for provisions affecting third parties, the initially adopted form is the uniform form in only 26.5 percent (9/34) of the cases. The percentage is much higher for provisions affecting members (just over 45 percent).

Figure 3.3 illustrates the declining importance of the initial form over time by graphing the average share of the initial and leading (or uniform) form for each type of provision.[35] The path of the average share of initial provisions falls over time for all three types of provisions, while the average share of the uniform provisions consistently rises over time. As our theory predicts, this rise is less pronounced for the provisions that primarily affect members. In the third-party situation, spontaneous uniformity is not evidence of inefficient herding because in this situation the substance of the rule, and therefore legislators' private information about the "right" rule, matters least.

Table 3.5 Relationship between the leading and initial form

Category	Number of provisions where the leading form equals the initial form	Total number of provisions	Cases where leading form equals the initial form (%)
All	24	69	34.8
Third party	9	34	26.5
Member	14	31	45.2
Tax	1	4	25.0

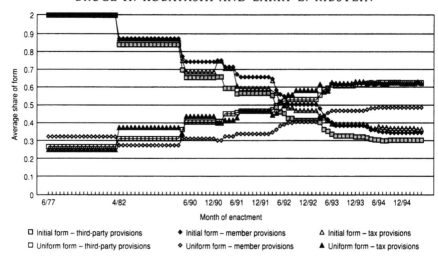

Figure 3.3 A comparison of the average share of the initial and leading form

CONCLUSION

The evidence from the recent evolution of the LLC shows that passage of state statutes has achieved significant uniformity in those situations predicted as appropriate by the transaction cost model of the firm. Further, the evidence suggests that early statutes do not have a disproportionate effect on subsequent statutes, suggesting that observed uniformity is not the result of inefficient herd behavior. These effects occur despite commentators' doubts about motives of individual legislators to produce efficient statutes, consistent with Alchian's intuition about the role of market processes. This strongly suggests that states can achieve desirable spontaneous uniformity without the "help" of uniform lawmaking bodies such as NCCUSL or the federal legislature.[36]

NOTES

1 For a critique of Alchian's attack on the importance of rational calculation, see Demsetz (1996). Although Alchian questioned the importance of rational calculation, he noted that adoption of the evolutionary approach "does not imply that individual foresight and action do not affect the nature of the existing state of affairs."

2 Much of the economic literature on the evolution of the common law was a direct response to the difficulties involved in defining non-arbitrary preferences of judges. See Rubin (1977), Priest (1977), Landes and Posner (1979), Cooter and Kornhauser (1980). For models of judicial behavior, see Posner (1993a, 1993b), Miceli and Cosgel (1994), Kobayashi and Lott (1993). The evolutionary approach was also suggested by Oliver Wendell Holmes as a way to examine the

progress of the common law. See Elliot (1984). For analyses of the choice between judge-made and statutory law, see Rubin (1982).

3 For example, Becker (1976, 1983) suggests that competition in political markets will cause political institutions that lower the cost of producing wealth transfers to survive over time, and that political policies that raise efficiency will be more likely to be adopted than policies that lower efficiency. Lott (1996) suggests, however, that political institutions that have the lowest cost of producing any given level of wealth transfers may not increase wealth, as such institutions can increase total amount and total costs of generating wealth transfers. See also Peltzman (1976).

4 See Hirshleifer (1976) for a discussion of within and between regime political competition as complements. The issue of jurisdictional competition is discussed in more detail below. For analyses of spontaneous evolution of laws, see Benson (1989) and Bernstein (1992).

5 Ribstein and Kobayashi (1995; 1996), Ribstein (1993b), Baysinger and Butler (1984), and Schwartz and Scott (1995) provide recent analyses of uniform lawmaking bodies. Ribstein and Kobayashi (1996) produce evidence that states have been adept at sorting proposals by the uniform lawmaking body, the National Conference of Commissioners of Uniform State Laws (NCCUSL) and determining when uniformity is likely to increase economic efficiency. Nevertheless, NCCUSL's promotional efforts still might cause some uniform provisions to be adopted when uniformity does not promote economic efficiency. Moreover, as Ribstein and Kobayashi (1995) and Schwartz and Scott found, *whether or not* uniformity increases economic efficiency, the uniform lawmaking process may tend to produce *poorly written laws*. For discussions of the problems with federal law, see Macey (1990), Easterbrook and Fischel (1983), and Carlton and Fischel (1983).

6 The classic paper on the benefits of diversity is Tiebout (1956). See also Easterbrook (1983) and Levmore (1987).

7 For discussions of the incentives of individual legislators see for example, Lott (1987), Lott and Reed (1989), Lott and Davis (1992), Kalt and Zupan (1984), Niskanen (1975), Maloney *et al.* (1984), and Stigler (1971).

8 For a review of non-corporate jurisdictional competition, see Ribstein (1993a). Easterbrook (1983) applies the jurisdictional competition model to the state action doctrine in antitrust. For broad-based discussions of the economics of federalism, see Kitch (1981), Rose-Ackerman (1980, 1981), Cover (1981), and Shapiro (1972).

9 See Romano (1985), noting the literature's emphasis on "survivorship," and that as "a corollary of the process's efficient (optimal) outcome, uniform statutes are predicted." Proponents of this view include Easterbrook and Fischel (1983) and Manne (1967). Some commentators, including Posner and Scott (1980), Easterbrook (1983), and Baysinger and Butler (1985), suggest that diverse public corporation statutes exist to allow different types of firms to select the set of legal rules most appropriate for their particular circumstances. Romano (1985) argues that empirical evidence is inconsistent with these corporate diversity theories, and suggests that partial diversity exists because firms shop for particular types of statutory provisions when they are planning to engage in certain types of transactions. Uniformity clearly has emerged in Canadian corporate law. See Daniels (1991) (arguing that the uniformity resulted from jurisdictional competition) and Macintosh (1993) (arguing that the uniformity resulted from the provinces' lack of incentive to compete to supply corporate law).

10 The original "race to the bottom" hypothesis was stated in Cary (1974). See also Nader *et al.* (1976). For a *more* recent treatment, see Bebchuk (1992). These

articles stress the agency costs created by the separation of ownership and control suggested by Berle and Means (1932). For general discussions of agency theory and the theory of the firm, see Fama and Jensen (1983a, 1983b), and Jensen and Meckling (1976).

11 For discussion of the race to the top, see Winter (1977). For empirical evidence favoring the race to the top hypothesis, see Carney (1993), Romano (1985), and Dodd and Leftwich (1980). For studies of the role of jurisdictional competition in the transition from special chartering to general incorporation, see Shughart and Tollison (1985) and Butler (1985).

12 Romano (1985) and Macey and Miller (1987) note the importance of the demand by lawyer and other professional interest groups in supplementing revenue maximization by the legislature as an incentive for legal change. Further, Ribstein (1993a, 1994) notes the role of contractual choice of law clauses and the incentives of lawyer interest groups in supplying Delaware corporate law. In any event, legislators face such weak incentives to innovate, and taxpayers are such a poorly coordinated group, that maximization of franchise tax revenues is unlikely to be a strong motive for corporate statutes. For a general theoretical discussion of the weak incentives faced by legislators, see Rose-Ackerman (1980, 1981). For an application to promulgation of public corporation statutes, see Ribstein (1995b).

13 Indeed, our research on the uniform lawmaking process under NCCUSL suggests that attempts by centralized decision makers to shape the ultimate result (i.e. deciding which rules should become uniform) often result in perverse outcomes. See Ribstein and Kobayashi (1996). Our results suggest that this centralized process results in a large number of uniform law proposals where uniformity is not efficient. Further, these attempts at achieving uniformity are largely unsuccessful, as we find that inefficient uniform proposals are not widely adopted. That is, our results suggest that the decentralized decisions by state legislatures to not adopt these uniform law proposals defeats the inefficient planned actions of the centralized body. For a critique of NCCUSL's Uniform Limited Liability Company Act, see Ribstein and Kobayashi (1995).

14 For a clear statement of this proposition, see Easterbrook and Fischel (1992). While a large literature has examined a firm's contractual choice of control structure using the transactions cost framework, little attention has been paid to the firm's choice of organizational form. It is often assumed that the choice of form merely reflects tax considerations. We take a broader view in this chapter by treating the choice of form as reflecting transactions and information costs in addition to tax considerations. See Ribstein (1988, 1992, 1995b).

15 See Ribstein (1994).

16 See Butler (1985), Ribstein (1995b, 1995c) for an analysis of competition between statutory and non-statutory forms. See Ribstein (1993a, 1994) for a discussion of jusridictional competition and choice of law clauses.

17 Provisions where uniformity is likely to be important include, for example, simple default terms that minimize the debtor–creditor agency costs inherent in limited liability. Specific examples of provisions in this category include: (1) requirements regarding the contents and execution of the filed document (certificate or articles); (2) limitations on purposes for which the firm may be formed; (3) place and form of filing the basic disclosure document; (4) mechanisms for enforcing obligations (e.g. rules on registered agents and service of process); (5) form of members' capital contributions (i.e. investments that are subordinated to creditor claims); (6) enforcement of capital contribution obligations; (7) definition of and penalties for wrongful distributions to owners by financially distressed firms; (8) members' personal liability for debts of the firm; (9) rules governing "foreign" firms (i.e.

those organized under the law of another jurisdiction); (10) rules ensuring accuracy of the disclosure document; (11) regulation of misleading names (i.e. names that might confuse creditors concerning the nature or identity of the firm); (12) limitation on members' or manager's powers to bind the firm; (13) rules for determining what property is owned by the firm; and (14) transfer or firm property. See Table 3.2 for a comprehensive list.

18 Examples of these provisions include: (1) formalities and other rules governing the "operating agreement" or similar document that spells out the agreement between the parties but is not intended as notice to third parties; (2) whether the statutory default provides for centralized or decentralized management; (3) the method of allocating profits and distributions; (4) the method of allocating voting rights; (5) matters on which members have a right to vote; (6) rules for meetings of members and managers; (7) rules regarding assignment of interests; (8) fiduciary duties of managers and remedies for breach; (9) dissolution and liquidation of the firm; (10) maintenance and inspection of records.

19 See Treas. Reg. Sec. 301.7701–2(a).

20 See Table 3.2, and Ribstein (1995b). For discussions of how state legislators tend to design their LLC and partnership statutes around federal tax regulations see Ribstein (1992, 1994).

21 For a discussion of lawyers' role in resisting flexibility that might trigger malpractice liability, see Ribstein (1994).

22 See Macey and Miller (1987) and Ribstein (1995b). Tax-based provisions represent a special case for lawyers' collective preference for clear, uniform rules. More generally, successful lawyer interest groups may not prefer simple rules. Increased complexity may increase the demand for lawyers' services in the absence of external sources of guidance (White, 1992). *On the other hand, lawyers also have incentives to produce efficient statutes in order to help their states compete for a larger share of the market for state law.* See Ribstein (1995a, 1995b).

23 Ten states passed new LLC statutes in 1992, eighteen states passed new statutes in 1993, and 12 states passed new LLC statutes in 1994. Only Hawaii, Massachusetts, and Vermont had not passed LLC statutes by the end of 1994. Further, seventeen states have revised existing statutes since March 1993. For a discussion of the effect of partnership tax classification rules on the terms governing LLCs, see Ribstein (1995b).

24 A comprehensive cataloging of the various forms for each of the sixty-nine provisions found in existing LLC statutes and listed in Table 3.2 was compiled. For a detailed description of LLC provisions and forms, see Ribstein and Keatinge (1992). For example, provision 5, which controls whether or not execution of articles is required, serves to provide simple default rules that minimize debtor–creditor agency costs inherent in limited liability, and is classified as one that primarily affects the LLC's interactions with third parties. For each state statute, we recorded whether the statute: (1) requires acknowledgment or verification; or (2) does not require acknowledgment or verification. The Wyoming statute adopted form (2), which is used in eight of the forty-eight jurisdictions. Form (1) is the most adopted or uniform form, adopted by forty jurisdictions.

25 For example, thirteen of the sixty-nine provisions have leading forms that have been adopted by at least thirty-six of the forty-eight jurisdictions, and thirty-nine have leading forms adopted by over half of the states. Note that classification of two statutes as adopting the same form means that the statute falls within the definition of the category, and is judged to have the same legal effect. It does not mean that the language in the statutes is identical. While this approach may arguably overstate the extent to which states have adopted "uniform" statutes (e.g. due to unforeseen differences in effect or due to differences in statutory

57

interpretation across the states) there is no reason to believe that any existing classification errors are systematically related to whether a provision falls into the third party, member, or tax categories. *Instead, a tendency to adhere closely to uniform language may depend on the characteristics of the adopting state.* In our examination of the uniform state lawmaking process, we found that states with full time legislatures were less likely, *ceteris paribus*, to adopt uniform law proposals. See Ribstein and Kobayashi (1996). An examination of the same factors found no significant correlations between characteristics of a state (e.g. size of legislature, volume of bills, population, general state expenditures) and the rate at which a state adopts the leading form of third-party or member provisions.

26 The states' *spontaneous* movement toward uniformity is similar to a social convention, where similarity can arise because people recognize the benefits of conforming to a single standard, such as driving on the same side of the road. See Schelling (1960) and Sugden (1986).

27 For example, eight provisions have leading forms with fewer than fifteen adoptions.

28 This is equivalent to the "one-firm" concentration (CR1) used in many studies in industrial organization. We also report the Herfindahl index, which takes into account the distribution of the provisions. Which index is used does not affect the substantive results of the chapter.

29 In comparing the average number of adoptions of the leading form of the member versus the average number of adoptions of either the third-party or tax categories, the alternative hypothesis is that the average number of adoptions of the member category is less than the average number of adoptions of the third-party or tax categories, suggesting a one-tailed test is appropriate. Our theory does not predict a clear relationship between the degree of uniformity of the third-party and tax categories, suggesting that a two-tailed test is appropriate in this situation. Similar results are obtained if a broader measure of uniformity is used. For example, results using the Herfindahl index (HHI) are consistent with those obtained by looking only at the leading form. The HHI for provisions primarily affecting members equals 0.333. By contrast, the HHI for provisions primarily affecting third parties or the LLC's tax liability equals 0.485 and 0.490 respectively.

30 This difference, however, is not statistically significant at standard levels (the *t*-statistic with sixty-three degrees of freedom equals 0.459): 58.8 percent of the third-party provisions (20/34) remained equally uniform or became more uniform (as measured by the share of the leading form) over this time period, compared to 54.8 percent (17/31) of member and 50 percent (2/4) of the tax provisions.

31 Although there is evidence of spontaneous uniformity in the corporate area, it is not clear why this uniformity has developed and, in particular, whether it is efficient. For example, Carney (1993) identified some circumstances which may account for the trend toward diffusion of corporate law provisions, including the role of lawyer and manager interest groups and of the Model Business Corporation Act. The interest group factor may explain why certain types of provisions have been adopted, but it does not explain why there is a move toward uniformity regarding these provisions. The role of the Model Act suggests that uniformity is not necessarily "spontaneous" in these situations.

32 More generally, uniformity may, in some cases, reduce the costs of rent seeking. See Ribstein and Kobayashi (1996). The predictions for efficiency in these cases are ambiguous – lowering the costs of transfers decreases the costs of achieving a given level of transfers, suggesting an increase in efficiency. However, decreasing the costs of transfers may increase the total amount and costs of such transfers, and can result in a decrease in efficiency. For a general discussion of these issues, see Lott (1996). Such problems may be minimized in the LLC context by the fact that uniform third-party provisions generally define simple default rules where

the content of the rule matters least, and where the wealth-transferring potential present with other mandatory rules is minimized. See Miller (1992) for a similar discussion of the efficiency of close corporation statutes. See Ribstein (1995b) for a more detailed discussion of the efficiency of the content of LLC provisions.

33 For theoretical treatments of herd behavior, see Banerjee (1992), Bikhchandani *et al.* (1992), and Scharfstein and Stein (1990). For an application of this theory to judicial lawmaking, see Johnston (1993).

34 The theoretical economic literature on technological standards has used examples of the persistence of early inefficient standards to suggest that inefficiency of markets is generating standards in the presence of network effects. The most common example used in the economics literature is the continued dominance of the QWERTY keyboard over the supposedly superior Dovrak keyboard. Theoretical papers suggest that the continued use of QWERTY represents the perpetuation of an inefficient standard, resulting from its early adoption and the inability of market forces to overcome the inertia created by QWERTY-specific human capital. However, Liebowitz and Margolis (1990) present empirical evidence suggesting that the assumptions of the theoretical literature about the relative efficiency of QWERTY are incorrect. See also Liebowitz and Margolis (1994). For an application of the network effects literature to explain the evolution of state corporate law, see Klausner (1995). Although our evidence of the evolution of state statutory standards suggests that there was no "lock-in" of an inefficient early LLC standard, the rules provided by the first LLC statutes probably were not sufficiently well established to produce network effects. Network effects in the LLC context are better indicated by LLC statutes' application of partnership rules in order to capitalize on the existing network of partnership *customs and precedents.* See Ribstein (1995c).

35 The graph uses the form adopted by the Wyoming statute as the initial form. Similar results are obtained if one compares a set of early statutes (e.g. those adopted prior to 1992). Using the leading form from either the first four or first eight statutes as the initial form results in a similar decline, suggesting the absence of a disproportionate influence from this group of early statutes.

36 This question is of some topical interest, as NCCUSL *recently produced* the Uniform Limited Liability Company Act. For *analyses* of this uniform act, see Ribstein and Kobayashi (1995) and Ribstein (1995a).

REFERENCES

Alchian, Armen A. (1950) "Uncertainty, Evolution, and Economic Theory," *Journal of Political Economy* 58: 211–21.

Alchian, Armen A. and Harold Demsetz (1972) "Production, Information Costs, and Economic Organization," *American Economic Review* 62: 777–95.

Ayres, Ian (1992) "Judging Close Corporations in the Age of Statutes," *Washington University Law Quarterly* 70: 365–98.

Banerjee, Abhijit (1992) "A Simple Model of Herd Behavior," *Quarterly Journal of Economics* 107: 797–817.

Baysinger, Barry D. and Henry N. Butler (1984) "Revolution versus Evolution in Corporate Law: The ALI's Project and the Independent Director," *George Washington Law Review* 28: 557–81.

—— (1985) "The Role of Corporate Law in the Theory of the Firm," *Journal of Law and Economics* 52: 179–91.

Bebchuk, Lucian A. (1992) "Federalism and the Corporation: The Desirable Limits on State Competition in Corporate Law," *Harvard Law Review* 105: 1435–510.

BRUCE H. KOBAYASHI AND LARRY E. RIBSTEIN

Becker, Gary S. (1976) "Comment," *Journal of Law and Economics* 19: 245–8.
—— (1983) "A Theory of Competition Among Pressure Groups for Political Influence," *Quarterly Journal of Economics* 98: 371–400.
Benson, Bruce L. (1989) "The Spontaneous Evolution of Commercial Law," *Southern Economic Journal* 55: 644–61.
Berle, Adolph A. and Gardner C. Means (1932) *The Modern Corporation and Private Property*. New York: Macmillan.
Bernstein, Lisa (1992) "Opting Out of the Legal System: Extralegal Contractual Relations in the Diamond Industry," *Journal of Legal Studies* 21: 115–57.
Bikhchandani, Sushil, David Hirshleifer and Ivo Welch (1992) "A Theory of Fads, Fashion, Custom, and Cultural Change as Informational Cascades," *Journal of Political Economy* 100: 992–1026.
Butler, Henry N. (1985) "Nineteenth-Century Jurisdictional Competition in the Granting of Corporate Privileges," *Journal of Legal Studies* 14: 129–66.
Carlton, Dennis W. and Daniel R. Fischel (1983) "The Regulation of Insider Trading," *Stanford Law Review* 35: 857–95.
Carney, William J. (1993) "Federalism and Corporate Law: Conditions for Optimal Development," mimeo, Emory University.
Cary, William (1974) "Federalism and Corporate Law: Reflections upon Delaware," *Yale Law Journal* 83: 663–705.
Coase, Ronald H. (1937) "The Nature of the Firm," *Economica* 4,2: 386–405.
—— (1960) "The Problem of Social Cost," *Journal of Law and Economics* 3: 1–44.
Cooter, Robert D. and Lewis A. Kornhauser (1980) "Can Litigation Improve the Law with the Help of Judges?" *Journal of Legal Studies* 9: 139–64.
Cover, Robert M. (1981) "The Uses of Jurisdictional Redundancy: Interest Ideology and Innovation," *William and Mary Law Review* 22: 639–82.
Daniels, Ronald J. (1991) "Should Provinces Compete: The Case for a Competitive Corporate Law Market," *McGill Law Journal* 36: 130–90.
Demsetz, Harold (1996) "Rationality, Evolution, and Acquisitiveness," *Economic Inquiry* 34: 484–95.
Demsetz, Harold and Kenneth Lehn (1985) "The Structure of Corporate Ownership: Causes and Consequences," *Journal of Political Economy* 93: 1155–77.
Dodd, Peter and Richard Leftwich (1980) "The Market for Corporate Charters: Unhealthy Competition versus Federal Regulation," *Journal of Business* 53: 259–83.
Easterbrook, Frank H. (1983) "Antitrust and the Economics of Federalism," *Journal of Law and Economics* 26: 23–50.
Easterbrook, Frank H. and Daniel R. Fischel (1983) "Voting in Corporate Law," *Journal of Law and Economics* 26: 395–428.
—— (1992) *The Economic Structure of Corporate Law*. Cambridge, MA: Harvard University Press.
Elliot, E. Donald (1984) "Holmes and Evolution: Legal Process as Artificial Intelligence," *Journal of Legal Studies* 13: 113–46.
Fama, Eugene F. and Michael Jensen (1983a) "Separation of Ownership and Control," *Journal of Law and Economics* 26: 301–25.
—— (1983b) "Agency Problems and Residual Claims," *Journal of Law and Economics* 26: 327–49.
Hirshleifer, Jack (1976) "Comment," *Journal of Law and Economics* 19: 241–4.
Jensen, Michael C. and William H. Meckling (1976) "Theory of the Firm: Managerial Behavior, Agency Costs, and Ownership Structure," *Journal of Financial Economics* 3: 305–60.
Johnston, Jason (1993) "Notes on the Economic Theory of Legal Evolution," mimeo, Vanderbilt University.
Kalt, Joseph P. and Mark A. Zupan (1984) "Capture and Ideology in the Economic

Theory of Politics," *American Economic Review* 74: 279–300.

Kitch, Edmund W. (1981) "Regulation and the American Common Market," in *Regulation, Federalism and Interstate Commerce*, ed. Dan Tarlock. Cambridge, MA: Oelgeschlager, Gun and Hain.

Klausner, Michael (1995) "Corporations, Corporate Law, and Networks of Contracts," *Virginia Law Review* 81: 757–852.

Kobayashi, Bruce H. and John R. Lott Jr. (1993) "Judicial Reputation and the Efficiency of the Common Law," mimeo, George Mason University.

Landes, William M. and Richard A. Posner (1979) "Adjudication as a Private Good," *Journal of Legal Studies* 8: 235–85.

Levmore, Saul (1987) "Variety and Uniformity in the Treatment of the Good-Faith Purchaser," *Journal of Legal Studies* 16: 43–63.

Liebowitz, S. J. and Stephen Margolis (1990) "The Fable of the Keys," *Journal of Law and Economics* 33: 1–25.

—— (1994) "Network Externality: An Uncommon Tragedy," *Journal of Economic Perspectives* 8: 133–50.

Lott, John R., Jr. (1987) "Political Cheating," *Public Choice* 52: 169–87.

—— (1996) "When Does Political Reform Increase Wealth?," *Public Choice* forthcoming.

Lott, John R. and Michael Davis (1992) "A Critical Review and an Extension of the Political Shirking Literature," *Public Choice* 74: 461–84.

Lott, John R. and W. Robert Reed (1989) "Shirking and Sorting in a Political Market with Finite-Lived Politicians," *Public Choice* 61: 75–96.

Macey, Jonathan R. (1990) "Federal Deference to Local Regulators and the Economic Theory of Regulation: Toward a Public Choice Explanation of Federalism," *Virginia Law Review* 76: 265–91.

Macey, Jonathan R. and Geoffrey Miller (1987) "Toward an Interest-Group Theory of Delaware Corporate Law," *Texas Law Review* 65: 469–523.

Macintosh, Jeff (1993) "The Role of Interjurisdictional Competition in Shaping Canadian Corporate Law: A Second Look," University of Toronto Working Paper WPS-18.

Maloney, Michael T., Robert E. McCormick, and Robert D. Tollison (1984) "Economic Regulation, Competitive Governments, and Specialized Resources," *Journal of Law and Economics* 27: 329–38.

Manne, Henry G. (1967) "Our Two Corporation Systems: Law and Economics," *Virginia Law Review* 53: 259–84.

Miceli, Thomas J. and Metin M. Cosgel (1994) "Reputation and Judicial Decision-Making," *Journal of Economic Behavior and Organization* 22: 31–51.

Miller, Geoffrey P. (1992) "The Economic Efficiency of Close Corporation Law: A Comment," *Washington University Law Quarterly* 70: 399–408.

Nader, Ralph, Green, Mark J. and Joel Seligman (1976) *Taming the Giant Corporation*. New York: Norton.

Niskanen, William A. (1975) "Bureaucrats and Politicians," *Journal of Law and Economics* 18: 617–44.

Peltzman, Sam (1976) "Toward a More General Theory of Regulation," *Journal of Law and Economics* 19: 211–40.

Posner, Richard A. (1993a) *The Economic Analysis of Law*, 4th edn. Boston: Little Brown.

—— (1993b) "What do Judges and Justices Maximize? The Same Thing as Everyone Else Does," *Supreme Court Economic Review* 3: 1–42.

Posner, Richard A. and Kenneth E. Scott (1980) *Economics of Corporation Law and Securities Regulation*. Boston: Little Brown.

Priest, George (1977) "The Common Law Process and the Selection of Efficient Rules," *Journal of Legal Studies* 6: 65–82.

Ribstein, Larry E. (1992) "The Deregulation of Limited Liability and the Death of Partnership," *Washington University Law Quarterly* 70: 417–75.
—— (1993a) "Choosing Law by Contract," *Journal of Corporation Law* 18: 245–300.
—— (1993b) "The Mandatory Nature of the ALI Code," *George Washington Law Review* 61: 984–1033.
—— (1994) "Delaware Lawyers and Contractual Choice of Law," *Journal of Corporation Law* 19: 999–1025.
—— (1995a) "A Critique of the Uniform Limited Liability Company Act," *Stetson Law Review* 25: 311–88.
—— (1995b) "Statutory Forms for Closely Held Firms: Theories and Evidence from LLCs," *Washington University Law Quarterly* 73: 369–432.
—— (1995c) "Linking Statutory Forms," *Law and Contemporary Problems* 58: 186–220.
Ribstein, Larry E. and Robert Keatinge (1988) "An Applied Theory of Limited Partnership," *Emory Law Journal* 37: 835–95.
—— (1992) *Ribstein and Keatinge on Limited Liability Companies*. New York: Shepards–McGraw-Hill.
Ribstein, Larry E. and Bruce H. Kobayashi (1995) "Uniform Laws, Model Laws and Limited Liability Companies," *University of Colorado Law Review* 66: 947–99.
—— (1996) "An Economic Analysis of Uniform State Laws," *Journal of Legal Studies* 25: 131–99.
Romano, Roberta (1985) "Law as Product: Some Pieces of the Incorporation Puzzle," *Journal of Law, Economics and Organization* 1: 225–83.
—— (1992) "State Competition for Close Corporation Charters: A Commentary," *Washington University Law Quarterly* 70: 409–16.
Rose-Ackerman, Susan (1980) "Risk Taking and Reelection: Does Federalism Promote Innovation?," *Journal of Legal Studies* 9: 593–616.
—— (1981) "Does Federalism Matter? Political Choice in a Federal Republic," *Journal of Political Economy* 89: 152–65.
Rubin, Paul H. (1977) "Is the Common Law Efficient?," *Journal of Legal Studies* 6: 51–64.
—— (1982) "Common Law and Statute Law," *Journal of Legal Studies* 11: 205–24.
Scharfstein, David S. and Jeremy C. Stein (1990) "Herd Behavior and Investment," *American Economic Review* 80: 465–79.
Schelling, Thomas (1960) *The Strategy of Conflict*. Cambridge, MA: Harvard University Press.
Schwartz, Alan and Robert E. Scott (1995) "The Political Economy of Private Legislatures," *University of Pennsylvania Law Review* 143: 595–654.
Shapiro, Martin (1972) "Toward a Theory of Stare Decisis," *Journal of Legal Studies* 1: 125–34.
Shavell, Steven (1991) "Specific versus General Enforcement of the Law," *Journal of Political Economy* 99: 1088–108.
Shughart, William F., II and Robert D. Tollison (1985) "Corporate Chartering: An Exploration in the Economics of Legal Change," *Economic Inquiry* 23: 585–99.
Stigler, George S. (1971) "The Theory of Economic Regulation," *Bell Journal of Economics and Management Science* 2: 3–21.
Sugden, Robert (1986) *The Economics of Rights, Cooperation and Welfare*. New York: Basil Blackwell.
Tiebout, Charles M. (1956) "A Pure Theory of Local Expenditure," *Journal of Political Economy* 64: 416–24.
White, Michelle J. (1992) "Legal Complexity and Lawyers' Benefit from Litigation," *International Review of Law and Economics* 12: 381–95.
Winter, Ralph (1977) "State Law, Shareholder Protection, and the Theory of the Corporation," *Journal of Legal Studies* 6: 251–92.

4

WHY HOLD-UPS OCCUR

The self-enforcing range of contractual relationships*

Benjamin Klein

One of my most enjoyable intellectual experiences was working with Armen Alchian on the Klein *et al.* (1978) hold-up chapter. In this chapter I extend the basic framework presented in that paper, pointing out what I now consider to be its shortcomings and providing insights into the nature of hold-ups and the form of contracts chosen by transactors to avoid hold-ups. The major analytical extension entails combining hold-up analysis with my work on private enforcement. Because private enforcement capital is limited and written contract terms are necessarily imperfect, transactors must optimally combine court-enforced written terms together with privately enforced unwritten terms to define what I call the self-enforcing range of their contractual relationship. Hold-ups occur when unanticipated events place the contractual relationship outside the self-enforcing range. This probabilistic framework, where transactors enter contractual relationships knowing that a hold-up may take place (but believing that the expected gains from trade outweigh the expected rent-dissipating costs associated with the hold-up risk), is shown to have important implications for understanding the structure of contracts adopted by transactors in the marketplace.

WHY DO HOLD-UPS OCCUR?

I begin with a simple example that illustrates the basic economic forces involved in a hold-up. Assume that a builder constructs a house on a piece of land the builder does not own but, rather, only leases short term. After the initial land lease expires, the landowner could hold up the builder by raising the land rent to reflect the costs of moving the house to another lot. This example illustrates all the hold-up factors emphasized in Klein *et al.*: (1) the builder has made an investment that is highly specific to a particular

* I am grateful for comments from Armen Alchian, Harold Demsetz, Andrew Dick, Jon Karpoff, John Lott, Donald Martin, Kevin Murphy, and an anonymous referee.

piece of land and (2) the landowner has taken advantage of the incompleteness of the contract that governs the relationship (in particular, the fact that the lease does not cover future years) to (3) expropriate the quasi-rents on the builder's specific investment. The obvious question is why anything like this would ever occur; that is, why would someone be so naive as to build a house on land which they were only renting short term?

Our primary goal in Klein *et al.* was not to explain the existence of hold-ups, but rather the institutions adopted by transactors to avoid hold-ups. For example, we would expect that builders, anticipating a potential hold-up problem, would decide to own the land or at least to sign a long term ground lease before starting construction. However, we do present some examples in the paper of hold-ups that actually occurred. The implicit reason we give for the occurrence of these hold-ups is transactor ignorance. Apparently, transactors are not always smart enough to choose the contractual arrangement that would eliminate the hold-up problem.

Oliver Williamson provides a similar, but much more explicit, answer to the question of why hold-ups occur. When defining "opportunism" he states:

> By opportunism I mean self-interest seeking with guile. This includes but is scarcely limited to more blatant forms, such as lying, stealing and cheating. Opportunism more often involves subtle forms of deceit. . . . More generally, opportunism refers to the incomplete or distorted disclosure of information, especially to calculated efforts to mislead, distort, obfuscate, or otherwise confuse.[1]

For example, the hold-up may have occurred in our illustrative house construction example because the landowner deceived the builder with a low up-front land rental price and vague promises about the future.

Relying on the ability of one transactor to take advantage of the naiveté or ignorance of another transactor is a highly unsatisfactory way to explain the incidence of hold-ups we observe in the world. Simple examples of deception, such as a builder constructing a house on land that is only rented short term, rarely, if ever, occur. More complicated and less obvious examples of hold-ups may sometimes involve the deception of an imperfectly informed transactor. However, explanations of hold-up behavior that are based upon transactor deception are often not refutable. Moreover, the facts of some cases where hold-ups have occurred are clearly inconsistent with transactor deception. For example, the most extensively cited hold-up example presented in Klein *et al.* is the Fisher Body–General Motors case, a transaction between two large, sophisticated business firms with no evidence of any precontract deception on either transactor's part.

The Fisher Body–General Motors case concerned a contract signed by General Motors and Fisher Body in 1919 for the supply of automobile bodies by Fisher to General Motors.[2] Fisher Body, in order to produce the automobile bodies, had to make an investment in stamping machines and dies that was highly specific to General Motors. As a result, a significant potential was created for General Motors to hold up Fisher. After Fisher Body made the specific investment, General Motors could have threatened to reduce its demand for Fisher-produced bodies, or even to terminate Fisher completely, unless Fisher reduced its prices.

The Fisher–General Motors case appears analogous to our example of naive house construction on rented land. However, contrary to this house construction example, the transactors in the Fisher–General Motors case clearly recognized the hold-up potential and attempted to take account of it in their contract terms before any specific investments were made. In particular, to prevent General Motors from appropriating the quasi-rents from the Fisher investment by threatening termination, the contract included a ten-year exclusive dealing clause. This clause required General Motors to buy all of its closed metal automobile bodies from Fisher for a period of ten years. Obviously, such a contract had to set the price at which Fisher would supply bodies to General Motors. The transactors agreed upon a formula where the price was set equal to Fisher's "variable cost" plus 17.6 percent. An upcharge over variable costs, rather than a formula based on Fisher's total cost, was probably used because Fisher was selling automobile bodies to many different companies and it was difficult to isolate and measure the capital and overhead costs associated with General Motors' shipments. The 17.6 percent upcharge presumably was designed to cover Fisher's anticipated capital and overhead costs.

The Fisher–General Motors contract, therefore, was not totally unsophisticated, as was the short term land lease contract in our hypothetical house construction example. However, the Fisher–General Motors contract, as it turned out, was similarly inadequate in preventing a hold-up, albeit to the advantage of Fisher rather than General Motors. After the contract was signed, the demand for automobiles rose substantially. Fisher took advantage of the contract in the face of this large demand increase to adopt an inefficient, highly labor-intensive production process and to locate its body-producing plants far away from the General Motors assembly plant. From Fisher's point of view there was no economic reason to make capital investments when, according to the contract, they could instead hire a worker and put a 17.6 percent upcharge on the worker's wage. In addition, there was no economic reason for Fisher to locate their plant close to the General Motors assembly plant when, according to the contract, they could profit by locating their plant far away from the General Motors plant and put a 17.6 percent upcharge on their transportation costs. The result was automobile bodies that were very costly for General Motors to purchase and highly profitable for Fisher to produce.[3]

The Fisher–General Motors case illustrates why transactors are concerned about hold-ups. When automobile bodies are produced and sold inefficiently, as they were by Fisher, the total gains from trade are reduced. We can expect (and generally observe) in such cases that *ex post* renegotiation of the contract will occur so that, after a lump sum is paid to the transactor engaging in the hold-up, price and cost will return to the efficient level. In the Fisher–General Motors case the contract renegotiation took the form of a General Motors' side payment to the Fisher brothers along with purchase of the Fisher Body company. Since the probability of such *ex post* lump sum transfers will be taken into account by transactors in their *ex ante* contract terms, these hold-up lump sum transfers may appear to be of no significance if transactors are risk neutral. However, as the Fisher–General Motor case vividly illustrates, the transactor placed at a disadvantage during a hold-up does not immediately costlessly renegotiate the contract and make a lump sum payment to the transactor engaging in the hold-up. Real resources are wasted during the hold-up process, as transactors attempt to convince their transacting partners that a hold-up potential does exist and of its magnitude. It is these dissipative, purely redistributive costs associated with hold-up behavior, not the lump sum transfer itself, that are wasteful. Because of these costs it is efficient for transactors to design contractual relationships that reduce the likelihood of a hold-up occurring.

The obvious question in the Fisher–General Motors case is why a hold-up occurred; that is, why did General Motors use such an imperfect or incomplete contract which placed it in a position where it could be held up by Fisher in the way it was? It is much too unlikely an explanation to rely on General Motors' naiveté or on Fisher's deception. General Motors and Fisher were aware of the hold-up problems inherent in their relationship, and both Fisher and General Motors had to have been aware that the contract they adopted to solve their hold-up problem was "defective" in the sense that it contained obvious malincentives. Yet General Motors and Fisher adopted this incomplete and imperfect contract because they believed it would have been more costly to write a more complete and perfect contract.

THE USE OF INCOMPLETE CONTRACTS

General Motors and Fisher knowingly entered into their incomplete contract because they believed that this contract, while imperfect, was optimally designed to minimize the probability of a hold-up occurring. Unfortunately, conditions developed that permitted Fisher to use the contract to hold up General Motors. If General Motors and Fisher had known ahead of time what was to happen, no doubt they would have written their contract differently to take account of the problems that developed. In that sense the Fisher hold-up of General Motors was unanticipated. However, in an uncertain world where complete contractual specification is costly, transactors use incomplete contracts that deliberately do not take account of every contingency. As a result, transactors knowingly leave themselves open to the possibility of hold-ups.

The costs associated with contractual specification that lead transactors to use incomplete and imperfect contracts involve much more than the narrow transaction costs of writing down responses to additional contingencies. In addition to these extra "ink costs," complete contractual specification entails wasteful search and negotiation costs associated with discovering and negotiating prespecified contractual responses to all potential contingencies. Because most future events can be accommodated at lower cost after the relevant information is revealed, much of this activity involves largely redistributive rent dissipation with little or no allocative benefit. Transactors are merely attempting to obtain an informational advantage over their transacting partners, hoping to place themselves in a position where they will be more likely to collect on (and less likely to pay for) hold-ups.[4] Therefore, rather than attempting to determine all of the many events that might occur during the life of a contractual relationship and writing a prespecified response to each, the gains from exchange are increased by the use of incomplete contracts.

Transactors also use incomplete contracts because writing something down to be enforced by the court creates rigidity. Since contract terms are necessarily imperfect, once something is written down transactors can engage in a hold-up by rigidly enforcing these imperfect contract terms, even if the literal terms are contrary to the intent of the contracting parties. This is what occurred in the Fisher–General Motors case, where the written contract terms that were designed to prevent General Motors from holding up Fisher were actually used by Fisher to create a much greater hold-up of General Motors.

It may appear that this type of hold-up, where a transacting party uses the court and the threat of litigation to enforce an imperfect contract term that is contrary to the intent of the contracting parties, is different from the type of hold-up that occurred in our house construction – land rental example, where the landowner took advantage of the absence of a contract to hold up the builder after the short term land lease expired. We may wish to think of the court as unable to protect the builder in the house construction case, whereas actually the court is effectuating the hold-up by strictly enforcing the written contract terms in the Fisher–General Motors case. However, although this distinction may be important for contract law, the hold-ups are analytically similar. Both hold-ups are caused by a transactor using the court to take advantage of an imperfection in the contract that governs an economic relationship. In the Fisher–General Motors case, court enforcement of the imperfect cost-plus contract sanctions Fisher's attempt to charge General Motors arbitrarily high prices. Similarly, in the house construction–land rental example, court enforcement of the obvious imperfection in the contract (namely, that the contract is only short term) sanctions the landowner's attempt to charge the builder an arbitrarily high price after the short term land lease expires.

I am assuming in this discussion that the court only enforces written terms and does not enforce unwritten terms. This is, of course, an oversimplification. Courts interpret both written and unwritten terms when enforcing contractual agreements. However, we can assume that the amount of discretion exercised by the court with regard to unambiguous written terms is limited, and that as transactors add additional things to their contracts the likelihood that the court will effectuate a hold-up by rigidly enforcing these imperfect contract terms increases.

This does not mean that writing down contract terms is not beneficial to transactors. Writing down binding contract terms has the obvious benefit that the court can be used to enforce performance. The idea that court enforcement of explicit contracts may be the mechanism by which a transactor engages in a hold-up merely recognizes that contractual specification not only has benefits but also associated costs. For some elements of performance there may be no trade off in terms of added rigidity associated with writing down contract terms. For example, contractual specification is costless when desired performance is measured accurately by the contractually specified term and the term is costlessly observable by the court. However, when transactors must use a less than perfect proxy for performance in a contract there is a trade off. Including the proxy in the contract may help in enforcing the understanding but also may do harm by making the contractual arrangement more rigid.

It is the very benefit of contract specification, that is transactors' hands can be tied with respect to certain variables that might otherwise be used to effectuate a hold-up, that creates the harm of contractual rigidity. As the Fisher–General Motors case illustrates, once an agreement is formalized in a written contract, it cannot cheaply be breached if unanticipated changes occur in the market. The only limit on the cost to General Motors of not performing to the literal terms of the imperfect contract when market conditions deviated substantially from *ex ante* expectations was essentially General Motors' declaration of bankruptcy. If, on the other hand, a contractual understanding is not formalized in a written contract, transactors can more cheaply opt out of the agreement if subsequent market conditions deviate substantially from expectations. The understanding is much more flexible because, without the court forcing transactors to perform to the literal terms of the contract, transactors can renege and only lose the value of whatever transactor-specific investments are present in the relationship. Therefore, at some point transactors may decide to avoid the rigidity associated with court enforcement of written contract terms by intentionally leaving many elements of intended performance unspecified and enforcing these terms instead by a private enforcement mechanism.[5]

THE SELF-ENFORCING RANGE OF CONTRACTUAL
RELATIONSHIPS

The privately imposed sanction that permits transactors to enforce the unwritten terms of their contracts can be thought of as consisting of two parts. One part is the future loss that can be imposed directly on the transactor if the relationship is terminated. Given the presence of non-salvageable transactor-specific investments, the threat of termination of the relationship implies a potential capital loss equal to the discounted value of the quasi-rents from these investments. For example, if General Motors had terminated (or failed to renew) its relationship with Fisher, it could have imposed a capital cost on Fisher for non-performance equal to the specific investments made by Fisher in the General Motors specific tools and dies.

The other part of the private sanction that is imposed on a transactor who is engaging in the hold-up is the damage to the transactor's reputation in the marketplace. If the violation of the contractual understanding is taken account of by other transactors in their dealings with this transactor, the transactor engaging in the hold-up will face increased costs of doing business in the future. Potential trading partners will become less willing to rely upon the transactor's promises and demand more favorable and/or more explicit contract terms. For example, if General Motors had held up Fisher and this was communicated in the marketplace, General Motors would have found it more expensive to purchase inputs in the future.

Each transacting party compares the potential hold-up gain from breaching the contractual understanding with the capital loss from the private sanction. If the hold-up gain is less than the capital cost, then the transactor cannot credibly threaten breach of the contractual understanding. Therefore, although transactors could take advantage of the fact that all the elements of a contractual understanding are not included in the written contract, they will not do so and will instead perform in a manner that is consistent with the mutually understood contractual intent.

The magnitude of the private sanctions that can be imposed on each transactor who attempts a hold-up defines what can be called the self-enforcing range of the contractual relationship. The self-enforcing range measures the extent to which market conditions can change without precipitating a hold-up by either party. Changes in market conditions may alter the value of specific investments and, therefore, the hold-up potential, yet as long as the relationship remains within the self-enforcing range where each transactor's hold-up potential gain is less than the private sanction, a hold-up will not take place. Only when changes in market conditions move transactors outside the self-enforcing range so that the one-time gain from breach exceeds the private sanction will the hold-up threat (i.e. the threat of breach of the contractual understanding) become credible. When this occurs the transactor will not be deterred from breaching even if the transactor expects to be terminated and knows that everyone in the marketplace will think the transactor is a "cheat." This is what occurred in the Fisher–General Motors case. Fisher and General Motors found themselves outside the self-enforcing range because of a very large increase in demand by General Motors for Fisher-produced bodies. This increase in demand increased the Fisher hold-up potential so much that it became larger than the private sanction that could be imposed on Fisher by General Motors and Fisher found it profitable to violate the intent of the contractual understanding by taking advantage of imperfect terms of the agreement.

The change in market conditions that permitted Fisher to take advantage of General Motors in this way was presumably unanticipated. When the contract was entered into in 1919 the dominant production process for automobiles consisted of individually constructed, largely wooden, open bodies; the closed metal bodies supplied by Fisher were essentially a novelty. After 1919, demand for closed metal bodies grew dramatically, and by 1924 they accounted for about two-thirds of General Motors' automobile sales.[6] This unanticipated shift in demand increased the extent by which the contract forced General Motors to rely on Fisher and made it profitable for Fisher to take advantage of the contract to hold up General Motors. The large increase in demand increased Fisher's hold-up potential of General Motors so that it became greater than the private sanction that could be imposed on Fisher by the loss of new and future sales to General Motors and to others in the marketplace that learned about its behavior. If this large change in demand had not occurred, the Fisher–General Motors contract would have been self-enforcing. The malincentives associated with the cost-plus contract terms would not have mattered. Fisher would have known that it could not take advantage of the literal terms of the contract without being punished by General Motors and that the punishment would have been greater than its hold-up gain.

AN ILLUSTRATION: THE ALCOA–ESSEX CASE

The concept of the self-enforcing range of a contractual relationship can be further illustrated by the Alcoa–Essex case.[7] Essex, an aluminum cable manufacturer, located its cable fabrication plant adjacent to an Alcoa aluminum production facility, thereby permitting shipments of processed aluminum from Alcoa to Essex in molten form. While the Essex plant location lowered costs, it also created an Alcoa hold-up potential. Alcoa could threaten to hold up Essex by increasing the price of delivered aluminum, thereby expropriating the value of the Alcoa-specific element of Essex's investment, namely the added transportation cost of receiving aluminum from a more distant supplier and the increased cost of reheating cold ingots. To protect against such behavior Essex entered into a long term contract with Alcoa, in which Alcoa agreed to process alumina into aluminum for Essex at specified output rates and to be paid in accord with a predetermined price formula. The long-term pricing formula chosen by Alcoa and Essex tied the price Essex would pay over time to the increase in the wholesale price index for industrial commodities.[8] This prevented Alcoa from taking advantage of Essex by arbitrarily increasing the price after Essex had made its highly Alcoa-specific plant investment.

Unfortunately, the wholesale price index which the parties agreed to use in their contract turned out to be a very poor measure to rely upon. Although the wholesale price index had historically tracked Alcoa's costs, electricity costs (the principal non-labor cost in aluminum production) began to rise much more rapidly than the wholesale price index after the 1973 crude oil supply crisis. By June 1973 Essex was receiving aluminum from Alcoa at a net cost of less than one-half the contemporary market price of aluminum, resulting in what the judge asserted was an estimated windfall gain to Essex of more than $75 million over the life of the contract.[9] The enforcement by Essex of the literal terms of this imperfect contract can be considered a hold-up since it can be assumed to be contrary to the original intent of the contractual understanding. Like the Fisher Body–General Motors contract, the long term contract designed to protect Essex against a threatened expropriation of rents by Alcoa resulted, because of unanticipated changes in market conditions, in a much greater threatened shift of rents to Essex from Alcoa.

Figure 4.1 graphically illustrates the concept of the self-enforcing range of the Alcoa–Essex contractual agreement. The extent of unanticipated changes in market events is measured along the horizontal axis by the deviation of market prices, P_m, from contracted prices, P_c. For any deviation of market prices from contracted prices, the resulting associated potential hold-up (by the transactor who has gained by enforcing the literal terms of the agreement) is measured along the vertical axis. Let us assume for expositional simplicity that the contractually specified flow of goods implies that each $1 price deviation from the contract price along the horizontal axis creates a potential hold-up gain with a present value of $1 million. For example, if the market price rises above the contract price by $1, the potential hold-up gain to the buyer, Essex, of enforcing the literal terms of the agreement, which we denote by H_E, is $1 million; if the market price falls, say $2 below the contract price, the potential hold-up gain to the seller, Alcoa, of enforcing the contract agreement, denoted by H_A, is $2 million. The potential hold-up gain as market price deviates from contract price, therefore, is represented in Figure 4.1 by the 45 degree line HH.[10]

The self-enforcing range of contractual performance is determined by considering the transacting parties' private enforcement capital. Assume, for example, that Essex's private enforcement capital, which we denote by K_E, is $5 million (say $4 million from the capital depreciation of Essex's Alcoa-specific investments and $1 million from the future income loss to Essex of operating in the marketplace with a poorer reputation). Therefore, Alcoa

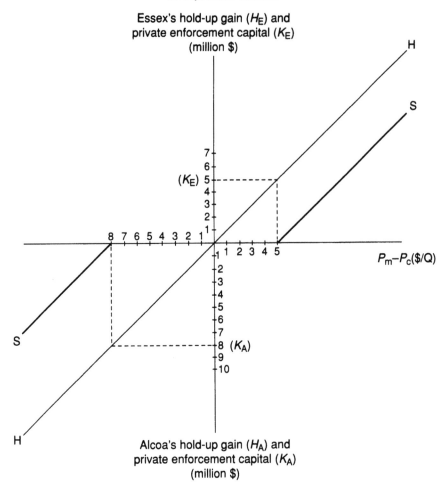

Figure 4.1 The self-enforcing range: potential hold-up gains (HH) and actual settlement payments made (SS) as market conditions deviate from contract terms

could impose a $5 million cost on Essex if it holds up Alcoa by insisting on delivery at contract terms when the value of aluminum has risen above contract terms. As a result, Essex cannot credibly insist on receiving the goods at the contracted price as long as the market price deviates from the contract price by less than $5. For example, if the market price increased, say, $3 from the contract price, the $3 million gain to Essex of such enforcement is less than the $5 million loss to Essex from termination of the relationship with Alcoa and communication to the marketplace of Essex's failure to adjust contract terms to market conditions.[11]

72

The analysis is symmetrical for the case of the potential Alcoa hold-up of Essex when the market price falls below the contracted price. If Alcoa's private enforcement capital loss, K_A, is, say, $8 million (consisting of, for example, a $2 million loss of Essex-specific investments and a $6 million loss of market reputation capital), the market price can, in principle, fall up to $8 below the contract price and the contract adjustment in price still be made by Alcoa. This is because of the now credible threat Essex can make to cut its losses by terminating its dealings with Alcoa and communicating to the marketplace the breach by Alcoa of the contractual understanding. The entire self-enforcing range, therefore, covers all market price deviations from the contract price between minus $8 and plus $5. Within this range of price deviations, represented in Figure 4.1 by the flat portion of the SS schedule between −$8 and +$5, contract terms will be "voluntarily" adjusted to the market price without any side payments being made by the transactors to one another.

More generally, the contractual understanding is not likely to require contractual adjustments of all deviations of P_m from P_c. Given costly information on changing market conditions, it will be wasteful for transactors to devote resources to search for information and negotiate changes for every small deviation of contract terms from market conditions. Consider, for example, a case of a contractor who, after agreeing to build an additional room on your home for $20,000, informs you at the start of construction that the contract price has to be adjusted upward from the agreed-upon price of $20,000.00 to $20,010.00 because of a change in the cost of nails which occurred in the two weeks since the contract was bid, negotiated, and agreed upon. You would, of course, not be aware of this cost change nor would it be practical for you to verify the claim. More importantly, you would, with good reason, wonder what kind of contractor you were dealing with – apparently one that intended to engage in significant rent-dissipating negotiating activities during the life of the contract. Analogously, we should not assume that Essex is holding up Alcoa if it enforces its contract with Alcoa when the market price exceeds the contracted price by a small amount. It is more likely that Alcoa would suffer reputational penalties if it seeks release from its contract with Essex unless a small upward adjustment in price were made. If contractual adjustment is part of the implicit contractual understanding, the understanding generally is that adjustments are not made unless some sufficiently large minimum disturbance occurs.[12] The contract terms that define the self-enforcing range can be thought of as a "contractual constitution" that is not anticipated to be frequently amended.[13]

Given the constitutional contractual understanding of the parties and the time necessary to negotiate contractual changes, transactors can find themselves outside the self-enforcing range if surprises take place – that is, if large and sudden unanticipated changes occur in market conditions. When this occurs a transactor's hold-up potential is greater than the transactor's private enforcement capital and threats to breach the contractual understanding and enforce the literal terms of the contract are credible. For example, if the positive deviation between market and contract prices is greater than the $5 given by Essex's reputation capital, Essex can credibly threaten Alcoa with litigation to enforce the literal terms of the contract if it does not receive a side payment in return for modifying the contractual arrangement to coincide with market prices.[14]

The magnitude of the necessary side payment settlement will be less than the potential transactor gain represented by the HH schedule in Figure 4.1. For example, if market prices move above contract prices so that (P_m-P_c) is $6, Alcoa need not pay Essex $6 million to force Essex to adjust the contract price up to the market price. In the real world we do not observe discontinuous behavior such as no side payment being made when the price deviation is $5.00, but a side payment of more than $5 million being made when the price deviation is, say, $5.10. Because of the presence of Essex's private enforcement capital, Alcoa can impose a $5 million loss on Essex. In the case of (P_m-P_c) equal to $6, if Alcoa and the market consider payment to Essex of any settlement greater than $1 million as a hold-up by Essex (i.e. as a breach of the implicit contractual understanding regarding settlements), then we can assume that Alcoa will be able to credibly impose the $5 million loss on Essex and Essex will willingly accept only $1 million to adjust the contract price up $6.00 before continuing the business relationship. The hold-up settlement payment schedule is, therefore, represented in Figure 4.1 by the schedule SS.[15]

This analysis suggests that when parties enter a contractual relationship they can be thought of as buying what amounts to an option, representing the probability of a hold-up occurring. In particular, Essex has purchased a call and has written a put, while Alcoa has purchased a put and has written a call. The defining points of the self-enforcing range can be thought of as the exercise prices of these put and call options that Essex and Alcoa have written and purchased along with their contract. As in standard options pricing theory,[16] the values of these options increase: (1) as the value of the ratio of the underlying asset price increases relative to the exercise price (in our case, as the value of the hold-up potential increases relative to the private enforcement capital), and (2) as the variance per period of the asset price multiplied by the number of period increases (in our case, as the variance of underlying market conditions and the length of the contract increases). Therefore, because hold-ups are costly, when the variance of (P_m-P_c) is high, transactors will require more reputational capital or reduce the length of their contract or the specific investments they make. The major difference between option analysis and our hold-up analysis is that by writing particular contract terms transactors can not only vary the exercise price but, as we shall see, they also can vary the underlying probability distribution that determines the value of their options.

THE ROLE OF CONTRACT TERMS

The role of contract terms within this framework is very different from the standard economic view of contract terms. The view of contract terms that underlies much of the principal–agent and mechanism design literature, for example, is that contract terms are used to create optimal incentives on some court-enforceable proxy for performance. Optimal but not perfect incentives are created by contract terms because the terms are only imperfect proxies for performance and are assumed to represent the sole elements of performance against which transactors maximize.[17] The problems that arose in the Fisher–General Motors case may be considered as an example of the type of imperfect incentives and associated inefficiencies created when imperfect contract terms are used. However, it is a mystery within this standard framework why Fisher and General Motors would have considered it optimal to choose such clearly imperfect contract terms to begin with.

The problem with the standard economic framework is that court enforcement and private enforcement are considered as alternatives – firms will rely upon one or the other, but never both. Principal–agent models, for example, formulate the contracting problem as if transactors do not possess any private enforcement capital. Therefore, it is not surprising that these models have limited predictive value in explaining real world contract terms. On the other hand, standard economic models of reputational enforcement provide no role for contractual specification.[18] However, given the fact that private enforcement capital is limited, transactors can be expected to use written contract terms and, hence, the assistance of the court, as a supplement to private enforcement.

Unlike standard economic models, the probabilistic hold-up framework presented here implies a fundamental complementarity between court enforcement and private enforcement. When employed together the mechanisms are substitutes in demand in the sense of a positive cross price effect (i.e. an increase in the price of one increases the demand for the other). For example, an increase in the cost of court enforcement increases investments in private enforcement capital. However, the two enforcement mechanisms are complements in production in the sense of a positive cross effect in production (i.e. an increase in the quantity of one increases the marginal product of the other). The two enforcement mechanisms work better together than either of them do separately.

Within this framework transactors use written contract terms not solely to create an incentive to perform with regard to some court-enforced, contractually specified proxy for performance. Rather, transactors use written contract terms to define optimally the self-enforcing range of their contractual understanding. The goal of contractual specification is to economize on the amount of private enforcement capital necessary to make a contractual relationship self-enforcing by merely "getting close" to desired performance in a wide variety of circumstances (without creating undue rigidity) and to let the threat of private enforcement move performance the remainder of the way to the desired level.

Contract terms can accomplish this goal of economizing on private enforcement capital in two fundamental ways. First of all, contract terms can operate directly to control non-performance. By defining performance with explicit court-enforceable contract terms, such as the quantity, quality, and price of a product that must be delivered, transactors control hold-up behavior by legally "tying their hands" with regard to variables that can be manipulated to expropriate rents from a transacting partner. In the Fisher–General Motors case, for example, these contractual restraints took the form of an exclusive dealing clause with a specified price formula.

This is illustrated in Figure 4.2, which presents the probability distribution of the hold-up potential in the General Motors and Fisher Body relationship, $f(H)$, which is assumed for expositional simplicity to be related to some scalar measure of *ex post* market conditions that can be measured along the horizontal axis, as in the Alcoa–Essex case.[19] Figure 4.2 measures General Motors' hold-up potential and private enforcement capital to the right of zero and Fisher's hold-up potential and private enforcement capital to the left of zero. (As illustrated, there is no reason that the probability distribution need be centered on zero.) The shaded area to the right of K_G defines the probability of a General Motors hold-up, the area to the left of K_F defines the probability of a Fisher Body hold-up, and the area between K_F and K_G is the probability that the General Motors–Fisher relationship remains within the self-enforcing range.

Panel A of Figure 4.2 represents the situation after Fisher has made its General Motors specific investment and a significant General Motors hold-up potential of Fisher has been created. Panel B represents the situation after Fisher and General Motors have negotiated a contractual arrangement which attempts to control the hold-up potentials of the parties. Assuming that the rent-dissipating costs associated with hold-ups are proportionately related to the magnitude of the hold-up, transactors will attempt to minimize these costs when setting contract terms by minimizing the expected value of the hold-up, that is the sum of the expected hold-up values associated with the tails of the probability distribution. Because the actual hold-up is assumed to be adjusted downward by the private enforcement sanction that can be imposed on the transactor engaging in the hold-up, General Motors and Fisher can be assumed to be minimizing

$$\int_{K_G}^{\infty} (H - K_G) f(H) \, dH + \int_{-\infty}^{K_F} (H - K_F) f(H) \, dH \tag{1}$$

Panel B illustrates that, although the contract terms substantially reduce the probability that General Motors will hold up Fisher for its specific investment, the contract terms also substantially increase the probability of

A. Fisher makes a General Motors specific investment

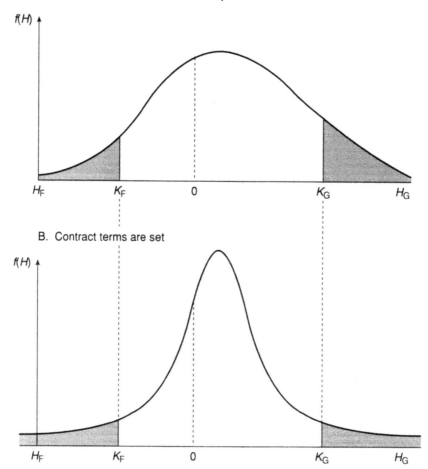

Figure 4.2 The hold-up probability distribution in the Fisher–General Motors case

a very large Fisher hold-up of General Motors if market conditions change dramatically. The contract decreases the probability of being outside the self-enforcing range, but also increases the far tails of the hold-up distribution. This corresponds to the rigidity costs associated with literal court enforcement of imperfect contract terms discussed above. It is because of these rigidity costs associated with contractual specification that, after some point, each contract term which the transactors decide to use involves a cost/benefit calculation. We can expect, therefore, that the degree of contractual specification will be lower the greater the private enforcement capital possessed by the transactors.

Where private enforcement capital is larger, contracts will be "thinner," with transactors writing out only the essential elements of the agreement, or perhaps even proceeding on the basis of a verbal understanding and a handshake; where private enforcement capital is smaller, written contracts will be "thicker," with transactors attempting to specify more elements of performance and provide for more contingencies. For example, contracts between Japanese companies can be expected to be much less completely specified than a similar contractual relationship between US companies. Japanese companies generally possess large amounts of private enforcement capital in transactions with one another because of the significant sharing of information regarding performance among Japanese companies and the large potential "loss of face" in the Japanese marketplace if it is perceived that one has engaged in a hold-up. When a large amount of private enforcement capital is present, there is a lower likelihood of being outside the self-enforcing range and, therefore, less need to bear the costs associated with contractual specification.

The second fundamental way in which contract terms can reduce the expected hold-up probability is by shifting private enforcement capital between transactors. Rather than directly attempting to reduce the hold-up potential, contract terms can shift the location of the self-enforcing range so that private enforcement capital coincides more accurately with the transactors' hold-up potentials under likely future conditions. By more closely relating actual private enforcement capital to likely requirements, transactors widen the *ex post* market conditions that are likely to fall within the range where performance remains assured.

This view of contract terms, as a way to increase the effectiveness of a self-enforcement mechanism by shifting private enforcement capital between transactors, has much greater predictive power in explaining the contract terms we observe in the world than the standard view of contract terms. For example, consider the grant by a franchisor to a franchisee of an exclusive territory. The standard economic view of contract terms would emphasize the effect of the exclusive territory in creating the correct incentive on the franchisee to perform due to the increased customer repeat sale created by the exclusive territory. The exclusive territory thereby reduces the franchisee's incentive to "free-ride" on other franchisees. However, the exclusive territory more importantly also creates a franchisee premium stream and, therefore, gives the franchisee something valuable to lose if it is terminated by the franchisor for non-performance.[20]

The exclusive territory and the associated payment of a premium stream from the franchisor to the franchisee can be thought of within our private enforcement framework as a shift of private enforcement capital from the franchisor to the franchisee. The franchisee now has more to lose if it is terminated, namely the franchisee loses the discounted value of the expected premium stream associated with the exclusive territory; and the franchisor

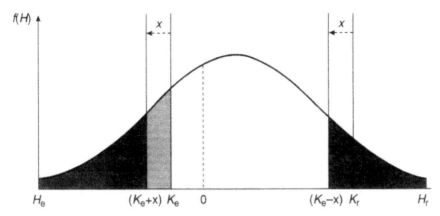

Figure 4.3 The shift of private enforcement capital from a franchisor to a franchisee

now has less to lose if it unfairly terminates the franchisee, namely the franchisor saves the discounted value of the larger expected premium stream that it no longer has to pay the franchisee.[21] This shift in private enforcement capital, because it more accurately aligns the transacting parties' enforcement capital with likely future franchisee hold-up possibilities, expands the self-enforcing range. That is, the exclusive territory increases the probability that *ex post* market conditions will fall within the range where performance can be privately enforced.

This example is illustrated in Figure 4.3 where, once again, we assume there is a market realization of a single hold-up potential, with H_e and H_r representing the franchisee and franchisor hold-up potential and K_e and K_r representing the franchisee and franchisor private enforcement capital, respectively.

If we assume that the shifts in private enforcement capital from the franchisor to the franchisee, represented by x in Figure 4.3, are dollar for dollar, in the sense that every dollar increase in the franchisor hold-up (in every *ex post* state where a franchisor hold-up occurs) implies a corresponding saving of one dollar in the franchisee hold-up (in every *ex post* state where a franchisee hold-up occurs), then this process of shifting private enforcement capital will occur until

$$d/dx \int_{K_r-x}^{\infty} (H - K_r - x) f(H) \, dH + \int_{-\infty}^{K_r+x} (H - K_e + x) f(H) \, dH = 0 \quad (2)$$

This implies that in equilibrium the probability of engaging in a hold-up will be the same for the franchisor and the franchisee, or

$$1 - F(K_r - x) = F(K_e + x) \quad (3)$$

Intuitively, if the probabilities are unequal, the overall probability of a hold-up occurring in the relationship could be reduced by shifting private enforcement

79

capital from the transactor with the lower probability to the transactor with the higher probability.[22]

Another example of contract terms efficiently shifting the self-enforcing range is the use of a contract to determine which transactor makes the transaction-specific investment. In general, the transactor who will make the specific investment is determined by comparing the likely future private enforcement capital requirements (i.e. the hold-up potentials) of each party under alternative likely contingencies with the amount of private enforcement capital that each transactor has available. Therefore, it is usually the transactor with the smaller private enforcement capital, such as Fisher Body, that will make the specific investment. The larger firm, because of its increased repeat transaction frequency, generally has more private enforcement capital and hence increased credibility that it will fulfill the contract.

Similar reasoning explains why many contracts may appear "one-sided" or "unfair."[23] For example, if General Motors possessed substantially more private enforcement capital than its suppliers, it could avoid the rigidity associated with contractual specification by not promising anything in writing in its supply contracts. The contracts would appear to be one sided, but this would not substantially increase the probability that it would hold up its suppliers. Another example is employee termination-at-will clauses. Because it is extremely difficult to specify in a court-measurable way all the conditions of adequate employee performance, and court enforcement of imperfect terms entails all the rigidity costs discussed above in addition to the costs of artificial record keeping, litigation expense, and time delay (during which the employee may impose additional costs on the firm), it may pay both parties to use a termination-at-will contract. Although such a contract may seem unfair, with the employee vulnerable to a potential hold-up by the employer, one cannot interpret such arrangements without recognizing that private enforcement capital, in addition to the explicit contract terms, also governs the relationship and that the employer may have sufficient private enforcement capital to define a sufficiently broad self-enforcing range.

A PROBABILISTIC VIEW OF HOLD-UPS

This analysis implies that contractual arrangements can only be understood if we recognize that transactors optimally design their contracts to combine court-enforced written contract terms with self-enforced unwritten terms. Given the particular contract terms they choose and the private enforcement capital they possess, transactors expect the relationship to remain within the self-enforcing range, where market conditions can change and the parties will perform as intended. However, transactors also know at the time they enter their contractual relationships and make their specific investments that their private enforcement capital is limited, that their written contract is imperfect and incomplete, and, therefore, that there is some probability of a hold-up occurring. In particular, transactors know that there is some probability that market conditions may change sufficiently (and the value of the quasi-rents accruing to one of the parties increase sufficiently) so that one party will find it in its interest to engage in a hold-up.

For example, the unanticipated change in market conditions that occurred in the Alcoa–Essex case was the 1973 crude oil "shock" which led to a quadrupling of the price of aluminum. This was a contingency that was not covered in the Alcoa–Essex contract and once this unanticipated event occurred, the short-run gain to Essex from the failure to adjust the price became greater than the depreciation of Essex's private enforcement capital. It became profitable for Essex to violate the intent of the contractual under-standing by demanding enforcement of the contract as written. The contrac-tual relationship had moved outside the self-enforcing range.

This probabilistic view of hold-ups should be contrasted with Williamson's view of opportunism which, he asserts, is equivalent to moral hazard behavior.[24] First of all, if moral hazard behavior is fully anticipated, it should be considered as merely part of the price. For example, if employees some-times take pencils home for their personal use, the pencils are part of the wage and working conditions of the job. (And if the value of the pencils to the employees exceeds their cost and employers do not expend resources to prevent the taking of them, there is nothing inefficient about this form of compensation.)

More importantly, identifying moral hazard behavior with a hold-up blurs a fundamental analytical distinction. Consider the example of the demand for medical services by individuals with health insurance, a commonly cited case where moral hazard behavior takes place. Health insurers, after writing the best contracts they can, knowingly accept the fact that their policy holders will take advantage of the low marginal price in these contracts to increase their demand for health services. In spite of this behavior, the transacting parties still find it in their interests to enter the relationship. It is true that the moral hazard behavior is "non-performance," in the abstract, ideal sense that if sufficient private enforcement capital existed or perfect contract terms could be written, the behavior would not exist. However, the behavior is fully expected and, I would maintain, has nothing to do with a hold-up.

A hold-up is a particular kind of transactor non-performance. Specifically, a hold-up, as opposed to moral hazard behavior, requires unanticipated events. It is true that a hold-up may be expected, in the sense that transactors may know ahead of time that if particular conditions develop, a hold-up will occur. However, hold-ups are always surprises in the sense that the particular conditions that will lead to the hold-up are considered unlikely and, because it is costly to negotiate and specify contract terms, these unlikely conditions are not taken account of in the contract. If the transactor being held up had anticipated that market conditions would develop to place the relationship outside the self-enforcing range, the transactor would have written a different contract or would not have made the specific investments to begin with. Moral hazard behavior, on the other hand, is fully anticipated; presumably transactors already have written their "best" contract. Moral hazard behavior is present not because of any unanticipated events, but merely because measurement and monitoring costs make it uneconomic for the transactors to write and enforce a perfect contract that would yield the idealized behavior that would exist in a costless contracting world.

CONCLUSION

The analytical framework I have presented here, like the framework originally presented in Klein *et al.*, should be judged by how much it assists us in explaining the particular contractual arrangements adopted by transactors in the marketplace. I believe that this framework provides an understanding of contracts which has much greater predictive power than the commonly accepted economic framework. Instead of thinking of contract terms as providing transactors with the correct incentives to perform with regard to particular contractually specified margins, this framework suggests that transactors choose contract terms, including vertical integration, in order to economize on their limited (and often unequal) amounts of private enforcement capital and thereby to define an optimal self-enforcing range for their contractual relationship. Rather than sharply distinguishing between two-party versus three-party enforcement mechanisms (i.e. between private reputational enforcement and court enforcement), contract terms can be explained as devices to assist transactors in assuring that sufficient private enforcement capital exists relative to the hold-up potential under the broadest range of likely *ex post* market conditions.

Finally, it may be argued that the framework presented here provides an economic justification for relational contract law. Because hold-ups are caused by rigid court enforcement of the imperfect and incomplete terms transactors choose to write in their contracts, it may be efficient for courts to use increased discretion in enforcing the terms. The court would appear to be able to provide an effective substitute for the transactors' limited private enforcement capital by taking more explicit consideration of the intent of the contractual understanding rather than merely rigidly enforcing the written terms of the contract. As a result, relational contract law, by leading courts to flexibly interpret contracts with the goal of avoiding hold-ups, could, in principle, expand the self-enforcing range of contractual arrangements.[25]

However, while flexible court interpretation may seem appealing in theory, in practice courts cannot employ increased discretion without losing some of the benefits associated with predictable court enforcement of written contract terms, namely the ability of transactors to tie one another's hands with respect to particular behavior and to create rental streams by shifting their private enforcement capital. Therefore, attempts to use increased court discretion to prevent hold-ups may, in fact, have the opposite effect of increasing hold-ups. It is difficult for judges, as it is for economists, no matter how smart and well intentioned they may be, to understand fully the economic intent and purpose of all the complex contractual terms transactors use in their contracts. Moreover, since many of these contract terms may appear superficially unfair or unconscionable, there may be a temptation not to enforce them. However, as noted above, these contract terms may be key elements of the transactors' joint attempt to define efficiently the self-enforcing range of their contractual relationship. Therefore, while contract law can, in principle, economize on transactors' limited private enforcement capital, one must proceed with caution down this road to avoid a narrowing of the self-enforcing range of contractual relationships.

NOTES

1 Williamson (1985: 47). Also see Williamson (1979: 234, n. 3).
2 The description of the Fisher–GM contract is taken from Klein *et al.* (1978: 308–10). The contractual agreement between Fisher Body and General Motors can be found in the minutes of the Board of Directors of Fisher Body Corporation for November 7, 1919.
3 See deposition testimony of Alfred P. Sloan, Jr., in *United States v. Dupont and Co.*, 366 U.S. 316 (1961), 186–90 (April 28, 1952) and 2908–14 (March 14, 1953).
4 These rent-dissipating costs during the contract negotiation process are analogous to the costs associated with the purely redistributive oversearching for an informational advantage analyzed in Kenney and Klein (1983).
5 The private enforcement mechanism upon which the following analysis is based is presented in Klein and Leffler (1981). Lott (1988) extends the Klein and Leffler model in the spirit of the present chapter by introducing random changes in cost or demand which alter the incentive of transactors to perform. A firm's decision to cheat is also considered to be stochastic in Darby and Karni (1973) and Karpoff and Lott (1993).
6 *Sixteenth Annual Report*, General Motors Corporation, year ended December 31, 1924.
7 *Aluminum Co. of America v. Essex Group, Inc.*, 499 F.Supp. 53 (W.D. Pa. 1980). This case is discussed in Speidel (1981) and Goldberg (1985).
8 The wholesale price index was chosen for this contract by Townsend–Greenspan (Federal Reserve Chairman Alan Greenspan's old consulting firm). The same index was also chosen for the contract litigated in *Missouri Pub. Ser. Co. v. Peabody Coal Co.*, 583 S.W. 2d 721 (Mo. App.), cert. denied, 444 U.S. 865 (1979).
9 The actual cost to Alcoa was substantially higher. The judge calculated the loss to Alcoa by considering Alcoa's accounting costs, including the cost to Alcoa of constructing the additional plant necessary to fulfill the Essex contract, over the period 1977–87. However, if we consider the opportunity cost to Alcoa by comparing what they could have sold the aluminum for in the marketplace with the price at which they were contractually bound to sell the aluminum to Essex, the amount is much higher. For example, in 1979, when Essex received aluminum from Alcoa under the contract at 36 cents a pound, Essex resold some of its aluminum in the open market at 73 cents a pound, for a difference of 37 cents

a pound. Multiplying this underpricing by the 75 million pounds Alcoa was committed to deliver to Essex annually yields an opportunity cost to Alcoa of nearly $30 million in 1979 alone.

10 We are assuming that the court will always enforce the written contract terms, not in the sense that the court would require specific performance, but that the court would award money damages to Essex (if market prices increased) or to Alcoa (if market prices fell) based on the written contract terms.

11 I am assuming that Alcoa can credibly threaten to terminate Essex in spite of the fact that it is costly for Alcoa to carry out such a termination threat because it has made Essex-specific investments. Alcoa can credibly threaten to terminate Essex when Essex threatens a hold-up within what Alcoa believed was the self-enforcing range either because of what Alcoa learns about Essex (that Essex has lower private enforcement capital) or because of what Essex and other buyers would learn about Alcoa if Alcoa failed to terminate Essex (that Alcoa has higher costs of imposing the termination sanction).

12 Some contracts explicitly formalize this by including reopener provisions, where the contract is opened for renegotiation after some market price index moves more than a minimum amount. See Goldberg and Erickson (1987). Crocker and Masten (1991) provide a general discussion of the contractual mechanisms employed by transactors to flexibly adjust prices in long term contracts.

13 Goldberg (1976: 428) has argued that it is useful to think of transactors designing a contractual arrangement as establishing a "constitution" to govern their ongoing relationship.

14 A relationship outside the self-enforcing range does not imply that litigation occurs. For litigation to take place it is necessary, in addition for the parties to be outside the self-enforcing range, for the parties to have sufficient informational differences regarding what they have at stake and what their probabilities of success in court are.

15 I am assuming for simplicity throughout the discussion a threshold model of private sanctions; that is, any and all types of hold-ups trigger the same lump sum private enforcement penalty.

16 See, for example, Brealey and Myers (1991: chapter 20).

17 A survey of the principal–agent literature is provided in Hart and Holmstrom (1987). The complex, contractually specified, incentive schemes that solve the agency problem in this literature are also generally claimed to be only second best because of the presence of transactor risk aversion, which creates a tension between the effect of a contract term in optimally rewarding productive work and in shifting unwanted risk to the agent.

18 See Kreps (1990) for a discussion of reputational enforcement models in non-cooperative game theory.

19 In reality there is unlikely to be market realizations that correspond to a single unique hold-up potential such that an increase in one transactor's hold-up potential necessarily implies a corresponding decrease in the other transactor's hold-up potential. Therefore, one may have to model the situation with a separate probability distribution for each transactor. However, the formulation presented here does illustrate the fundamental economic forces at work.

20 See Klein and Murphy (1988) and Klein (1995).

21 More completely, the franchisor's loss from terminating franchisees is the discounted value of its cost advantage of running the operation as a franchise arrangement compared to the next most efficient form of operation from which is netted out the premium stream the franchisor must pay the franchisee to assure franchisee performance. See Klein (1995).

22 This result assumes that the real costs associated with hold-ups are related to the magnitude of the hold-up and that this relationship is the same for both transactors. For example, the real costs may be proportional to the magnitude of the expected hold-up with both transactors having the same proportionality constant. This will not be the case, however, if any franchisee hold-up gains entail primarily distribution effects with relatively little real costs compared to franchisor hold-up gains of the same magnitude. For example, a franchisee hold-up may entail some costs associated with loss of product reputation on the part of consumers and the cost of replacing the franchisee, while a franchisor hold-up may entail much larger costs associated with the efficiency of the franchising arrangement compared to the next best alternative marketing arrangement. Since contract terms are set to minimize real costs (and not hold-ups), this would imply a higher probability of a franchisee hold-up than a franchisor hold-up in equilibrium.

23 See Klein (1980).

24 Williamson (1985: 51, n. 8). Considering moral hazard behavior as opportunism is inconsistent with Williamson's definition of opportunism in terms of deception and guile (n. 1 above). Williamson attempts to reconcile this inconsistency by claiming that one should consider deception broadly.

25 This provides an economic foundation for the relational contract law analysis in Macneil (1978), Muris (1981), Goetz and Scott (1981), and Schwartz (1992).

REFERENCES

Brealey, Richard A. and Stewart C. Myers (1991) *Principles of Corporate Finance*, 4th edn. New York: McGraw-Hill.

Crocker, Keith J. and Scott E. Masten (1991) "Pretia Ex Machina? Prices and Process in Long-term Contracts," *Journal of Law and Economics* 34: 69.

Darby, Michael R. and Edi Karni (1973) "Free Competition and the Optimal Amount of Fraud," *Journal of Law and Economics* 16: 67.

Goetz, Charles J. and Robert E. Scott (1981) "Principles of Relational Contracts," *Virginia Law Review* 67: 1089.

Goldberg, Victor P. (1976) "Toward an Expanded Theory of Contract," *Journal of Economic Issues* 10: 45.

—— (1985) "Price Adjustment in Long-Term Contracts," *Wisconsin Law Review* 3: 527.

Goldberg, Victor P. and John R. Erickson (1987) "Quantity and Price Adjustment in Long-Term Contracts: A Case Study of Petroleum Coke," *Journal of Law and Economics* 30: 369.

Hart, Oliver and Bengt Holmstrom (1987) "The Theory of Contracts," in *Advances in Economic Theory*, ed. Truman F. Bewley. Fifth World Congress, Cambridge: Cambridge University Press, pp. 71–155.

Karpoff, Jonathan M. and John R. Lott, Jr. (1993) "The Reputational Penalty Firms Bear from Committing Criminal Fraud," *Journal of Law and Economics* 36: 757.

Kenney, Roy W. and Benjamin Klein (1983) "The Economics of Block Booking," *Journal Law and Economics* 26: 497.

Klein, Benjamin (1980) "Transaction Cost Determinants of 'Unfair' Contractual Arrangements," *American Economics Review* 70: 356.

—— (1995) "The Economics of Franchise Contracts," *Journal of Corporate Finance* 20: 9.

Klein, Benjamin and Keith Leffler (1981) "The Role of Market Forces in Assuring Contractual Performance," *Journal of Political Economics* 89: 615.

Klein, Benjamin and Kevin M. Murphy (1988) "Vertical Restraints as Contract Enforcement Mechanisms," *Journal of Law and Economics* 31: 265.

Klein, Benjamin, Robert G. Crawford, and Armen A. Alchian (1978) "Vertical Integration, Appropriable Rents, and the Competitive Contracting Process," *Journal of Law and Economics* 21: 297.

Kreps, David (1990) "Corporate Culture and Economic Theory," in *Perspectives on Positive Political Economy*, ed. James Alt and Kenneth Shepsle. Cambridge: Cambridge University Press, pp. 90–143.

Lott, John. R., Jr. (1988) "Brand Name, Ignorance, and Quality Guaranteeing Premiums," *Applied Economics* 20: 165.

Macneil, Ian R. (1978) "Contracts: Adjustments of Long-Term Economic Relations Under Classical, Neoclassical, and Relational Contract Law," *Northwestern University Law Review* 72: 854.

Muris, Timothy J. (1981) "Opportunistic Behavior and the Law of Contracts," *Minnesota Law Review* 65: 521.

Schwartz, Alan (1992) "Relational Contracts in the Courts: An Analysis of Incomplete Agreements and Judicial Strategies," *Journal of Legal Studies* 21: 271.

Speidel, Richard E. (1981) "Court-Imposed Price Adjustments Under Long-Term Supply Contracts," *Northwestern University Law Review* 76: 369.

Williamson, Oliver E. (1975) *Markets and Hierarchies: Analysis and Antitrust Implications*. New York: Free Press.

—— (1979) "Transaction Cost Economics: The Governance of Contractual Relations," *Journal of Law and Economics* 22: 233.

—— (1985) *The Economic Institutions of Capitalism*. New York: Free Press.

5

ARMEN ALCHIAN'S CONTRIBUTION TO MACROECONOMICS

Jerry L. Jordan and William T. Gavin*

Armen Alchian's contributions to macroeconomics forged important paths that are still crucial to the understanding of monetary theory and monetary policy. The authors outline Alchian's examination of the fundamental role of money in society and his work (with Benjamin Klein) on the measurement of inflation. They also detail how, in research with Reuben Kessel, Alchian brought insight into the problems that followed the erratic inflation policies of the 1960s and 1970s, explained the effects of anticipated and unanticipated inflation on the real economy, and described the difficulty of identifying the effects of monetary shocks in macroeconomic data.

INTRODUCTION

This essay examines Alchian's contribution to the theory and practice of macroeconomics. We have the task of reviewing Alchian's contributions in an area that represents only a tiny fraction of his body of work. Citations to his work on the theory of the firm greatly outnumber those on money and inflation. Nevertheless, we find that many of the major developments in macroeconomics in the last two decades follow paths that were pointed out in the late 1950s and early 1960s by Armen Alchian, much of the work being in collaboration with Reuben Kessel. Alchian's ideas about macro-economics were developed in a fertile environment at UCLA in conversations with colleagues such as Karl Brunner and Jack Hirschleifer, as well as with graduate students such as Allan Meltzer and Rachael and Ted Balbach.

A signature of Alchian's work was his great ability to clarify the issues. He was careful to distinguish the effects of money versus real shocks, of anticipated

* President and Chief Executive Officer, Federal Reserve Bank of Cleveland, and Vice President and Research Coordinator, Federal Reserve Bank of St Louis. This chapter was originally presented as a paper at the 69th Annual Western Economics Association International Conference in Vancouver, British Columbia, on July 2, 1994.

versus unanticipated inflation, and to work through the impact of an event to the general equilibrium consequences. He understood that real-world problems such as incomplete information might explain apparently non-economic behavior, but unlike many macroeconomists of that time, he did not abandon microeconomic principles when explaining nominal/real interactions. Alchian's views were a clear contrast to those of prominent macroeconomists of the day who argued that aggregate monetary policies could not be used to stabilize the price level at full employment because of asymmetric rigidities in markets that prevented the downward adjustment of any nominal price as part of the process of adjusting relative prices.[1]

The conventional wisdom of the day led to policies that ultimately caused two decades of accelerating and costly inflation. Both the rational expectations revolution and developments in modeling the microfoundations of business cycles were a reaction to this experience and to the apparent failure of standard macroeconomic analysis. Alchian's 1970 work on the effect of private information was one of the original articles in this microfoundation literature. Although he used a narrative approach rather than the highly structured mathematical models available to researchers today, Alchian was more than two decades ahead of the real business cycle economists in asking researchers to explore economic explanations fully before adopting explanations based on market failure, money illusion, and irrational behavior.

This chapter is organized in four parts. The first part describes Alchian's work involving the fundamental role of money in society. King and Plosser (1986: 93) wrote

> But in the explosion of formal modeling of monetary economies in the postwar period, Brunner and Meltzer (1971) and Alchian (1977) stand nearly alone in stressing ... the idea that monetary arrangements economize on the information production that would otherwise be necessary to mitigate problems of moral hazard in the exchange of commodities.

The second part discusses Alchian and Klein's work on the measurement of inflation. This measurement problem appears to be more obvious when inflation is low and the variance of price indexes is dominated by real factors. This work was generally neglected at the time it was written, perhaps because inflation accelerated so rapidly that the real factors became less important. Now that inflation has declined to moderate levels, the measurement problems are resurfacing.

The third part of the chapter documents Alchian's insight into the problems and intellectual developments that followed the erratic inflation policies of the US government in the 1960s and 1970s. In a 1962 article in the *Journal of Political Economy*, he and Reuben Kessel set forth a description of the events that occur as an economy shifts from one steady-state inflation regime to another. This work revealed an understanding of the importance of credibility for the policy maker that was missing from much of the writing about macro policy making in the subsequent three decades. In recent years, economists have worked out computable general equilibrium models that include financial sectors.[2] Yet, we still do not have a satisfactory model of the transition from one inflation regime to another. Alchian and Kessel described a learning process in which asset markets adjusted immediately to revised expectations regarding monetary policy. Developing models of this learning process is one of the promising fields of research in monetary economics today.

The fourth part documents Alchian's insight into the problem of understanding how nominal policies can have real effects. In "The Effects of Inflation," he and Kessel explained how anticipated and unanticipated inflation could affect the real economy through wealth redistribution, our nominal tax code, and the tax effect on nominal balances. Even more important, Alchian and Kessel described how difficult it would be to identify the effects of monetary shocks in macroeconomic data. They clearly understood the identification problem that plagues almost all macroeconometric studies. Furthermore, methods they used three decades ago are once again being used at the frontier of monetary and macroeconomic research, although in a more rigorous mathematical setting.

WHY MONEY?

Any attempt to understand money must address the question of what it is and why it exists. Armen Alchian provided the starting point in "Why Money?"[3] He argued that only by understanding the important functions of money could one fully understand how to formulate and evaluate monetary policy. In "Why Money?" Alchian outlined his intuition about why money evolved and why it matters.[4] The ideas in this short article were passed around among UCLA students and faculty for many years before being published in the *Journal of Money, Credit and Banking* (JMCB) in 1977. It is an excellent example of Alchian's ability to clarify issues and make complicated ideas intelligible to the rest of us.

A society will use as money that commodity which economizes best on the use of other real resources in gathering information about relative prices and conducting transactions. Alchian said that "low recognition cost" is the key attribute of the entity that comes to serve as money. The ability to recognize the characteristics and quality of a good facilitates trade in that good. His simple example showed how the idea of money evolved as a way of reducing information costs in exchange.

In "Why Money?" Alchian explained how incomplete information, search costs, and heterogeneous goods may give rise to the use of a particular commodity as money. Indeed, he defined money as a commodity used in all, or in a dominant number of, exchanges. Alchian developed a numerical example to illustrate how information costs create an opportunity for specialists in trading. These specialists will have good information about traded goods and profit from the use of that information in facilitating exchange. Alchian demonstrated that if there is some good about which everyone is informed, then everyone will be a specialist in that good and it will be used as money.

The intuitive aspects of Alchian's analysis were illustrated in "Why Money?" This intuition is similar to that used by a variety of researchers in seeking a more fully developed theory of money. Ostroy and Starr (1990), for example, surveyed this literature, and Kiyotaki and Wright (1989) developed a theory of money based on search costs, emphasizing the role of money in reducing storage costs. Following the Alchian (1977) suggestion, Williamson and Wright (1994) built a search model of money with private information and goods with quality differences.

MEASURING INFLATION

"Price stability" or "zero inflation" is not as far out of our reach as it may have seemed fifteen years ago. The question then arises, how do we know when we have price stability? Exactly that question was asked by Charles Goodhart (1993) at a Bank of Japan conference in Tokyo. Goodhart based his entire paper on a two-decades-old study by Alchian and Klein (1973). There, Goodhart asserted

> It is remarkable that, at a juncture when so much of macro and monetary economics has been recast in terms of dynamic *intertemporal* utility maximization (e.g. Sargent 1993), that the same has rarely been done for the analysis of price inflation.[5] This is so *despite a cogently argued plea for this to be done in an excellent, but rarely referenced, article by Alchian and Klein.*

(emphasis added)

Goodhart concludes that monetary policies in several industrialized countries in recent years have been flawed because policy makers were wrong in "ignoring the message about inflation given by asset prices."[6] Goodhart's goal of increasing understanding of the relation between inflation and the booms and busts in real estate finance would have been improved by digesting the analysis in Alchian and Kessel, discussed in the next section.

Goodhart quoted extensively from Alchian and Klein (1973) in order to establish the theoretical framework for his attempt to determine the appropriate deflator for permanent income. In their article "On a Correct Measure of Inflation," Alchian and Klein discussed which measure of inflation is appropriate for use by the monetary authorities when intertemporal exchange is important.

The basic idea is simple, yet profound. If most exchange were in goods to be consumed in the current period (in an agrarian, near-barter economy), the intertemporal value would not be important. As transactions in claims to future consumption increase, the intertemporal dimension becomes of interest. What is difficult to recognize is the future purchasing power of a currency.

The equation of exchange, $MV = PT$, has long been a useful way to organize our thoughts about money and prices. For issues involving intertemporal decisions, the right-hand side, PT, should be a measure of permanent income. Alchian/Klein and Goodhart argue that the answer to the question, "What is the appropriate deflator for permanent income?," is that it must include a complete set of asset prices – the present price of future consumption rights as well as of current consumption.

As Alchian (1977) argued, an entity must first become a commonly used medium of exchange in transactions involving current consumables before it takes on the characteristics of a unit of account or standard of value for contracts involving intertemporal exchanges. The process by which a monetary unit makes the transition to becoming a generally recognized numeraire for transactions including long-lived assets is not well understood. A problem in assessing the purchasing power of money exists because price indexes measure the price of current consumption – the ideal price index would also include the current price of future consumption.

When inflation is high and rising, almost any measure of inflation will serve policy makers' needs. There is a very high correlation among available measures of inflation and measures of money growth when the inflation rate is high. When output prices are changing very little, much less correlation is evident. Recently, as inflation has fallen to a steadily lower trend, measurement problems have become more obvious, and it is not surprising that we see a resurgence of interest in Alchian's work on this topic. In addition to Goodhart's paper, which includes references to work from the Bank of Japan, Wynne (1994) and Santoni and Moehring (1994) also build on the framework developed by Alchian and Klein (1973).

THE EFFECTS OF INFLATION

In the late 1950s and early 1960s, Armen Alchian and Reuben Kessel produced a variety of papers on the effects of inflation. Today, we tend to think about the US inflation problem as something that began in the mid-1960s, worsened through the 1970s, and began to be cured in the 1980s. The goal for the 1990s is to take the inflation rate to zero, which has heightened interest in knowing how close or far away we are. Much of the analysis that Kessel and Alchian presented about the redistributional effects of inflation was written at a time when most price indices suggested that little inflation was occurring. "The Effects of Inflation," published in the *Journal of Political Economy* in 1962, contains many ideas that subsequently became conventional wisdom as experience with inflation worsened.

Kessel and Alchian begin with a discussion of inflation and money demand in which they outline the problems that inflation will cause for economists who want to measure the demand for money. They noted that people would shift out of non-interest-bearing money and into close substitutes that provided both an investment return and some monetary services. Kessel and Alchian (1962: 523) provided a clear description of the rationale for Barnett's (1980) construction of the weights in the Divisia monetary index:

the use of money in modern societies is a result of cost advantages, and . . . the ratio of money to other assets held, particularly money substitutes, will change with these costs . . .

[A]t the margin, the difference in the yield between an interest-bearing security and money represents an equalizing difference that measures the difference in the money services of the two assets. A change in this difference attributable to changes in the yield of physical capital implies a change in the demand for money.

Kessel and Alchian understood that inflation expectations *per se* were important. They emphasized the difference between the effects of anticipated and unanticipated inflation. The authors (1962: 524) clearly anticipate ideas developed later by Friedman (1977), Lucas (1972), and Barro (1977):

the state of expectations about inflation is crucial for predicting the effects of inflation. If inflation is unanticipated, that is, if the holders of cash balances on the average expect the contemporaneous level of prices to persist, then one set of implications is generated. These are the economics of unanticipated inflation. But, if the holders of cash balances taken as a group expect the general level of prices to rise, then a second and quite different set of implications follow. These constitute the economics of anticipated inflation.

They go on to discuss in detail the economics of both anticipated and unanticipated inflation. A particularly interesting section in this article is a discussion of the transition from a steady state with price stability to a steady state with anticipated inflation. They were quite explicit in suggesting a procedure for modeling this problem (1962: 528):

For a non-commodity money, short-run equilibrium conditions are non-existent. The stock of real balances adjusts, once a tax on money is recognized, to long-run equilibrium conditions.

This quote suggests that economists should model people's beliefs about current and prospective monetary policies. Recently, Sargent (1993) suggested that the profession has finally developed the models and technology to address this learning problem in a useful way. There is also practical work being developed along these lines at the Bank of Canada.[7]

Clearly, Kessel and Alchian were not the first economists to remark on the differential effects of anticipated versus unanticipated inflation. Indeed, they cite Irving Fisher (1930) on the subject. It is interesting to note, however, that while most members of the profession were using the assumption of rigid wages and prices to understand the real effects of nominal policies, Kessel and Alchian were approaching the problem in a way that has survived the rational expectations and microfoundation revolutions.

With the experience of a long period of accelerating inflation, followed by a disinflation policy, we are able to see more clearly not only the effects of inflation, but also the transition from a world where people expected and experienced price stability, to a world with persistently higher-than-expected inflation. In 1962 (fn. 19), Kessel and Alchian could write:

> The sequence in which this analysis is developed, in particular present-ing the economics of unanticipated inflation before that of anticipatory inflation, corresponds to the temporal sequence of economic events during an inflation. In this light, the inflations of the United States during the last century failed to reach the anticipated stage whereas the German inflation following World War I went through all three stages.

THE REAL MACROECONOMIC EFFECTS OF INFLATIONARY POLICY

Even though Alchian recognized why price theory was inadequately developed to understand the welfare consequences of inflationary policies, he also main-tained that it was important to use price theory to understand why monetary forces may not be the only or even the most important cause of fluctuations in real variables. This is a major theme of current research in macroeconom-ics. Perhaps three of the most important developments in macroeconomics over the last two decades have been (1) the realization that we should reject non-economic explanations for macro phenomena until we have exhausted the price-theoretic explanations; (2) the focus on identification in macroeco-nometrics; and (3) the use of historical episodes to reexamine price-theoretic explanations of macroeconomic phenomena. The first of these points is made quite explicitly in Alchian (1970: 27), in which he showed how the presence of information costs could lead optimizing agents to choose unemployment.

> And macroeconomic theory does not explain why demand decreases cause unemployment rather than immediate wage and price adjust-ments in labor *and* non-human resources. Instead, administered prices, monopolies, minimum wage laws, union restrictions, and "natural" inflexibilities of wages and prices are invoked.

This chapter attempts to show that economic theory is capable of being formulated – consistently with each person acting as an individual utility, or wealth, maximizer without constraints imposed by competitors, and without conventions or taboos about wages or prices – so as to imply shortages, surpluses, unemployment, queues, idle resources, and non-price rationing with price stability.

In even earlier work with Kessel, Alchian was well ahead of his time in promoting all three of these ideas.[8]

Data and price theory

The hypothesis that monetary inflation raised output prices before wages, thereby raising profits, was conventional wisdom in 1960. It was grounded in a widespread acceptance of the notion that the labor market did not work like other markets. This wage-lag hypothesis was the forerunner of the Keynesian Phillips Curve. In the late 1950s, Armen Alchian, working with Reuben Kessel, wrote two papers showing that there was scant empirical evidence supporting this wage-lag hypothesis. After reviewing six episodes that were considered evidence in favor of the wage-lag hypothesis, they found only two in which the raw facts concurred: the North and the South in the period covering the Civil War. They wrote (1960: 58):

> For these (two) cases, the wage-lag hypothesis has to compete with price theory. For the one case that has been studied in great detail, that of the North during the Civil War, price theory offers a more satisfactory explanation.

Kessel and Alchian criticized the use of non-economic ideas to explain phenomena when a price-theoretic explanation is at hand. They clearly advocated starting with microeconomic principles in order to understand macroeconomic phenomena (1960: 56):

> The acceptance by Lerner of the wage-lag explanation of the fall in real wages is inconsistent with another interpretation of the events of the time that may be found in his own papers. He indicates that much of Southern capital was highly specialized to the production of cotton for an international market and that the Northern blockade sharply reduced the productivity of this capital. Lerner also reports that excises, either in the form of taxes or payments in kind, constituted an important means of war finance. In fact, Lerner implicitly presents a hypothesis that explains the fall in real wages by nonmonetary phenomena, but he explicitly accepts the thesis that the fall in real wages is attributable to inflation.

As economists have developed more detailed economic models for the purpose of explaining macro phenomena, the data requirements have become more demanding. Kessel and Alchian (1960: 57) demonstrated the importance of being careful about the use of macro data, both in their criticism of existing work and in producing new evidence:

These data of Hansen's contain an unfortunate bias in favor of the wage-lag hypothesis for the entire time interval with which he was concerned. Starting with 1890, Hansen uses weekly earnings rather than hourly earnings. If leisure is a superior good, and if the real hourly earnings per capita rise, then weekly earnings understate real wages because of the substitution of leisure for income from work.

Kessel and Alchian concluded this paper by offering new evidence. They examined the wage bills and equity values of US firms during the inflationary period from 1940 to 1952. They showed that the average equity value for a firm rose faster, the lower its ratio of wages to equity. They also provided evidence that the inflation was not fully expected. They sorted the firms by net monetary debtor status and found that those with relatively more monetary debt had the greatest rise in equity value. In a multiple correlation analysis in which they controlled for the presence of net monetary debt, they again found a negative relation between the wage intensity of a firm and the change in its equity value over this period of rising inflation.

This work was important because it presented evidence that inflation did not necessarily benefit firms at the expense of workers, a common misconception associated with the belief that inflation reduced real wages. It also showed that managers did not have systems in place to protect their firms from the high and variable inflation that occurred during this period. Many new developments in cash and portfolio management have emerged since this paper was written. One of the things we have learned is that it is difficult, if not impossible, for firms to hedge completely against the costs of inflation.

Econometric practice and the Phillips Curve

The growing acceptance of these three developments – the use of price theory, careful identification, and use of historical episodes – in modern macro research may have been driven by a reaction against the continued use of the Phillips Curve as a framework for setting monetary policy. As mentioned above, the wage-lag hypothesis is a forerunner of the modern Phillips Curve hypothesis. It is interesting to note that in two recent presentations of evidence in favor of the latter, well-known economists repeated some of the very mistakes that Kessel and Alchian warned against over thirty-five years ago.

Blinder (1987) attempted to measure the output loss associated with the decision to lower inflation in the early 1980s. He attributed all of the increase in unemployment above the 5.9 percent rate in 1979 to the disinflation policy. Even though he was aware of the expected real effects of the structural adjustments occurring at the time, he chose to ignore them. In another recent study, Princeton economist Laurence Ball did much the same thing, attributing all of the decline in output during recessionary periods to the reduction of inflation.[9]

The Kessel/Alchian criticism of evidence in favor of the wage-lag hypothesis applies with equal force to such recent evidence in support of the Phillips curve hypothesis. In 1960 (p. 44), they wrote:

> For any time series of real wages, there exists a fantastically difficult problem of imputing changes in the level of real wages to one or the other of two classes of variables, i.e. real or monetary forces. Only if one is able to abstract from the effects of real forces can one determine the effect of inflation upon an observed time series of real wages.

Compare this statement to a comment by Stephen Cecchetti (1994: 189) on Larry Ball's paper, "What Determines the Sacrifice Ratio?":

> Ball assumes that a monetary shock induces the recessions that he observes, and that the path of output and inflation declines during each of the episodes he examines are caused solely by the shift to tight money. But in order to measure the impact of monetary policy, we need to identify the policy shocks.

CONCLUSION

On occasions throughout his career, Armen Alchian turned his attention to applying fundamental economic principles to issues in the realm of macroeconomics. Some of the topics he addressed are still the most important issues in monetary theory and monetary policy. He asked the essential question, "Why Money?" He worked through clear examples showing how money would arrive endogenously in a world with private information and heterogeneous goods.

Having shown how information costs defined money and its role in society, he moved on to policy questions involving the effects of inflation. He and Kessel challenged the conventional wisdom that workers were systematically underpaid during inflations. They were careful to distinguish between anticipated and unanticipated inflation. They accurately described the transition from a regime of relative price stability to a regime of ongoing inflation. This analysis was done in the early 1960s, well before most Americans were aware that the US government had embarked on a sustained devaluation of the dollar. As we return to the moderate inflation rates of that era, Alchian's questions about the role of asset prices in measuring the purchasing power of money are once again of considerable interest.

Today, policy makers are actively engaged in research that Armen Alchian began more than thirty years ago. For several years now, both central bank and academic economists have been involved in attempts to restore the application of microeconomic theory to macro policy issues. We have sought "correct" measures of inflation, and we continue to investigate and challenge

the conventional wisdom that discretionary monetary policy can have systematic and welfare-enhancing effects on real output.

Empirical research in economics is difficult even when grounded in good
theory. Policy makers often ask questions that are beyond the scope of existing
methods. Sometimes economists have responded by changing the questions
– asking only those for which the models and data seem to provide answers.
Alchian always started with careful formulation of the questions, and then
challenged us to continue developing models and methods so that we can
answer the questions that matter.

NOTES

1 For example, in analyzing the causes of and cures for the 1955–7 inflationary
period, Charles L. Schultze (1959) wrote:

> Excess aggregate demand has been the basic cause of all of our major infla-
> tions, including the postwar conversion inflation. And for a short while in
> late 1955 there seemed to be some excess aggregate demand. But the major
> thesis of this study is that the creeping inflation of 1955–57 is different in
> kind from such classical inflations, and that mild inflation may be expected
> in a dynamic economy whenever there occur rapid shifts in the mix of final
> demands. It is, in effect, a feature of the dynamics of resource adjustment
> where prices and wages tend to be rigid downward. Moreover, it gives a
> secular upward bias to the price level so long as the major depressions which
> "broke" the ratchet in the past are avoided in the future.

Another prominent Keynsian, Otto Eckstein (1958), voiced similar ideas:

> Turning to the inflation of the last three years, which was largely caused
> by the investment boom, we find that the incidence of the inflation was
> very uneven. The rise in the Consumer Price Index was largely due to the
> rising cost of services, caused by such long-run factors as the lack of produc-
> tivity rise in this sector, the rising cost of medical care, and so on. But
> there also was substantial inflation in the wholesale prices of finished goods.
> These rises were concentrated in the steel industry, in some branches of
> the machinery industry and 1 or 2 other fields, where prices rose by about
> 30 percent from 1953 to 1957, while finished goods prices of manufac-
> turing as a whole only rose by 10 percent. This suggests that a considerable
> part of the inflation can be blamed on specific shortages. There was
> certainly no general state of excess demand, since unemployment never
> reached particularly low levels, and the utilization rates in many industries
> were below levels desired by the industries.

2 See, for example, Fuerst (1992) and Christiano and Eichenbaum (1992).
3 See Alchian (1977).
4 Brunner and Meltzer (1971) formalized the idea and extended it in a simple
general equilibrium framework.
5 Goodhart (1993: fn. 1) cites Shibuya (1992) as "the main recent exception" to
this generalization, and notes that Shibuya cites earlier works by Pollak (1975),
Carlson (1989), and Shigehara (1990).
6 Goodhart (1993: 31).

7 See Ricketts *et al.* (1993) for the work being done at the Bank of Canada, and Bullard and Duffey (1994) for an application to US policy.
8 See Kessel and Alchian (1960).
9 See Ball (1994) and comment following by Cecchetti.

REFERENCES

Alchian, Armen A. (1970) "Information Costs, Pricing, and Resource Unemployment," in *Microeconomic Foundations of Employment and Inflation Theory*, ed. E. Phelps. New York: Norton, pp. 27–52.
—— (1977) "Why Money?," *Journal of Money, Credit and Banking* 133–40.
Alchian, Armen A. and Reuben A. Kessel (1956) "How the Government Gains from Inflation," proceedings of the Thirtieth Annual Conference of the Western Economics Association (1955), Salt Lake City, pp. 13–16.
—— (1959) "Redistribution of Wealth through Inflation," *Science* 4: 535–9.
Alchian, Armen A. and Benjamin Klein (1973) "On a Correct Measure of Inflation," *Journal of Money, Credit and Banking* 183–91.
Ball, Laurence (1994) "What Determines the Sacrifice Ratio?," in *Monetary Policy*, ed. N. Gregory Mankiw. Chicago: University of Chicago Press, pp. 155–82.
Barnett, William A. (1980) "Economic Monetary Aggregates: An Application of Index Numbers and Aggregation Theory," *Journal of Econometrics* 11–48.
Barro, Robert J. (1977) "Unanticipated Money Growth and Unemployment in the United States," *American Economic Review* 101–15.
Blinder, Alan S. (1987) *Hard Heads, Soft Hearts: Tough Minded Economics for a Just Society*. Reading, MA: Addison-Wesley.
Brunner, Karl, and Allan H. Meltzer (1971) "The Uses of Money: Money in the Theory of an Exchange Economy," *American Economic Review* 784–805.
Bullard, James and John Duffey (1994) "A Model of Learning and Emulation with Artificial Adaptive Agents," Federal Reserve Bank of St Louis, Working Paper 94–014B.
Carlson, Keith (1989) "Do Price Indexes Tell Us about Inflation? A Review of the Issues," *Federal Reserve Bank of St Louis, Review* 12–30.
Cecchetti, Stephen G. (1994) Comment on "What Determines the Sacrifice Ratio?," in *Monetary Policy*, ed. N. Gregory Mankiw. Chicago: University of Chicago Press, pp. 188–93.
Christiano, Lawrence J. and Martin Eichenbaum (1992) "Liquidity Effects and the Monetary Transmission Mechanism," *American Economic Review Papers and Proceedings* 82: 346–53.
Eckstein, Otto (1958) "Statement of Otto Eckstein," in *The Relationship of Prices to Economic Stability and Growth*, Compendium of papers submitted by panelists appearing before the Joint Economic Committee, Congress of the United States, pp. 249–50.
Fisher, Irving (1930) *The Theory of Interest*. New York: Macmillan.
Friedman, Milton (1977) "Inflation and Unemployment," the 1976 Alfred Nobel Memorial Lecture, first published by the Institute of Economic Affairs.
Fuerst, Timothy S. (1992) "Liquidity, Loanable Funds, and Real Activity," *Journal of Monetary Economics* 29: 3–24.
Goodhart, Charles (1993) "Price Stability and Financial Fragility," paper presented at the Sixth International Conference of Financial Stability, Bank of Japan, October, pp. 28–9.
Kessel, Reuben A. and Armen A. Alchian (1959) "Real Wages in the North during the Civil War: Mitchell's Data Reinterpreted," *Journal of Law and Economics* 95–113.

—— (1960) "The Meaning and Validity of the Inflation-Induced Lag of Wages behind Prices," *American Economic Review* 43–66.

—— (1962) "The Effects of Inflation," *Journal of Political Economy* 521–37.

King, Robert G. and Charles I. Plosser (1986) "Money and the Mechanism of Exchange," *Journal of Monetary Economics* 93–115.

Kiyotaki, Nobuhiro and Randall Wright (1989) "On Money as a Medium of Exchange," *Journal of Political Economy* 927–54.

Lucas, Robert E. (1972) "Expectations and the Neutrality of Money," *Journal of Economic Theory* 103–24.

Ostroy, Joseph M. and Ross M. Starr (1990) "The Transactions Role of Money," in *Handbook of Monetary Economics*, Vol. 1, ed. Benjamin M. Friedman and Frank H. Hahn. Amsterdam: North-Holland, pp. 3–62.

Pollak, Robert (1975) "The Intertemporal Cost-of-Living Index," *Annals of Economic and Social Measurement* 4: 1.

Ricketts, Nicholas, David Rose, and Douglas Laxton (1993) "Uncertainty, Learning and Policy Credibility," paper presented at a Bank of Canada Conference, *Economic Behavior and Policy Choice under Price Stability*.

Santoni, Gary J. and H. Brian Moehring (1994) "Asset Returns and Measured Inflation," *Journal of Money, Credit and Banking* 232–48.

Sargent, Thomas J. (1993) *Bounded Rationality in Macroeconomics*. New York: Oxford University Press.

Schultze, Charles L. (1959) *Recent Inflation in the United States*. Washington, DC: US Government Printing Office.

Shibuya, Hiroshi (1992) "Dynamic Equilibrium Price Index: Asset Price and Inflation," *Bank of Japan Monetary and Economic Studies* 95–109.

Shigehara, Kumiharu (1990) *Shisankakaku No Hendo To Infureshon (Asset Price Movement and Inflation)*. Kinyu Kenkyu.

Williamson, Steve and Randall Wright (1994) "Barter and Monetary Exchange under Private Information," *American Economic Review* 104–23.

Wynne, Mark A. (1994) "An Intertemporal Cost-of-Living Index," Federal Reserve Bank of Dallas, manuscript.

6

APPROPRIABLE RENTS FROM YELLOWSTONE PARK
A case of incomplete contracting

Terry L. Anderson and Peter J. Hill*

INTRODUCTION

Though the general populace accepts that national parks are and should be the domain of government, the history of our first national park, Yellowstone, reveals that from the beginning private entrepreneurs were actively involved in preserving the amenity values and capturing the amenity rents. To appropriate the rents from Yellowstone, the early entrepreneurs had to carve the amenity values from the common domain or see them dissipated through open access. Without private ownership of the land, this was accomplished through vertical integration of complementary inputs, namely transportation services and tourist facilities, necessary for the enjoyment of the natural amenities.

The extent of private sector success or failure in the history of Yellowstone can be best understood in the context of the theory of the firm as developed by Armen Alchian. His work with Demsetz (1972) and with Klein and Crawford (1978) expands our understanding of how firms contract to appropriate rents and prevent postcontractual opportunism. Klein *et al.* (1978: 300) distinguish between two reasons for vertical integration, both of which apply to private firms operating in Yellowstone at the time of its creation. The first is the successive monopoly problem which occurs when two monopolists supply inputs into a final product or service, and the second is postcontractual opportunism.

Our purpose here is to apply these two important threads from the firm's contractual tapestry to the formation and operation of Yellowstone National

* Professor, Montana State University, Bozeman, and Professor, Wheaton College, Wheaton, Illinois. Anderson and Hill are Senior Associates of the Political Economy Research Center (PERC), in Bozeman, Montana. We wish to thank Dan Benjamin, Richard Erickson, Ron Johnson, Randy Rucker, and participants in workshops at the University of Chicago, the University of Illinois, Northwestern University, and California Institute of Technology.

100

Park. The central theme is that amenity rents associated with the Yellowstone region either could be dissipated through open access and the ensuing "tragedy of the commons" or appropriated through contractual arrangements that limited entry to the commons. The former occurred until the Northern Pacific Railroad with its monopoly on transportation services vertically integrated with monopoly suppliers of tourist facilities and operated the park as if it were privately owned.[1] However, the potential for rent dissipation still existed because the railroad did not own the park itself and could not effectively contract with the federal government to restrict entry. Therefore, when the federal government opened the park to automobiles in 1915, the railroad's monopoly was eliminated and rent dissipation occurred through congestion.

A BRIEF HISTORY OF YELLOWSTONE

The natural features of the area that is now Yellowstone National Park were well known by 1860. Following John Colter's exploration of the area in 1807, numerous other trappers and later prospectors explored "Colter's Hell." In 1865, 1870, and 1871, the first formal explorers, financed in part by Congress, were sent to Yellowstone. These explorers provided scientific information, photographs, and paintings that increased the awareness in the East about the Yellowstone area.

This awareness culminated in the creation of Yellowstone National Park by an Act of Congress on March 1, 1872, making it the first national park (though Yosemite had been established as a state preserve in 1864). Early administration of the park was haphazard because the federal government provided no funds for operating expenses. Indeed many of Yellowstone's natural features were being defaced until, in 1886, the US Army assumed administrative responsibilities, stationing a cavalry troop there. The Army stayed until 1918.

At the time of Yellowstone's creation, the region was relatively inaccessible and sparsely settled, but railroads changed this. The Northern Pacific Railroad completed its transcontinental line in 1883 and immediately added a sixty-mile spur from Livingston, Montana, to Yellowstone's northern entrance. In 1903, the Chicago, Burlington, and Quincy Railroad gained access to Yellowstone through Cody, Wyoming, and in 1907 the Union Pacific arrived at West Yellowstone, Montana. Finally, in 1915 the park was opened to automobile traffic.

VERTICAL INTEGRATION AND APPROPRIABLE RENTS

We would expect the allocation of the amenity rents from Yellowstone measured in terms of numbers of visitors to vary depending on the ownership of the land itself and on the industry structure of complementary inputs such as transportation to the park. If the land were an open access resource, standard economic theory shows that the rents would attract entry, creating a congestion externality that would ultimately dissipate the value of those rents, as in Cheung (1970).[2] On the other hand, if the land were privately owned, the owner would restrict congestion and capture the amenity rents.

Monopolistic pricing of a specialized asset necessary for final consumption or production of the commonly owned amenity resource would lead to the same rent maximization as would private ownership.[3] This result follows because the monopolistic supplier of a specialized asset is in a position to capture quasi-rents from joint production. When the specialized asset is supplied monopolistically, the congestion externality is effectively internalized by the monopolistic supplier. Therefore the specialized asset owner will restrict entry and capture the amenity rents in the price of the specialized input.

The successive monopoly problem occurs if another specialized input is also supplied under monopoly conditions. In this case, too little of the final product is supplied, and herein lies one incentive for vertical integration between the monopolistic suppliers of the complementary inputs. As shown by Blair and Kaserman (1985), internalization of the true marginal revenue and marginal costs of production through vertical integration of firms will increase the level of production. Hence resolution of the successive monopoly problem in the presence of an open access amenity resource returns the system to an efficient equilibrium with rents maximized.

The successive monopoly problem is only one reason firms vertically integrate; Klein *et al.* (1978: 300) explain that the other reason is to avoid "postcontractual opportunistic behavior that occurs when specialized assets and appropriable quasi rents are available." The postcontractual opportunism problem is costly to overcome even when ownership of inputs can be transferred among private owners, but when the government is involved and cannot transfer ownership, the problem is even worse. Long term contracts or franchising provide a possible solution to this problem, but contracting with the sovereign ultimately means that the sovereign can renege and capture quasi-rents.[4]

Let us summarize the implications of this theory for Yellowstone National Park. With open access, the amenity values of Yellowstone would be dissipated through the "tragedy of the commons." However, monopolistic supply of a specialized asset such as the rail link to the park would put the supplier of rail services in a position to capture the amenity rents. Unlike the typical textbook example of monopoly which yields under production, the combination of open access and monopolistic supply of the specialized input promotes rent maximization. The successive monopoly problem arises because final enjoyment of Yellowstone's amenities required specialized tourist facilities as well as transportation services. By vertically integrating into the supply of internal tourist facilities, the railroad should have been able to solidify its monopoly position, avoid the successive monopoly problem, and prevent postcontractual opportunistic behavior. Ultimately, however, the government as sovereign owner of the park was in a position to redistribute the quasi-rents by allowing competing transportation and regulating the prices charged for rail services and tourist facilities.[5]

CONTRACTING FOR YELLOWSTONE'S RENTS

Recognition of rents and creation of Yellowstone

It is often assumed that amenities like Yellowstone National Park were saved from commercial exploitation and despoliation only because, to quote historian John Ise (1979: 1), "a few farsighted, unselfish, and idealistic men and women foresaw the national need and got the areas established and protected in one way or another, fighting public inertia and selfish commercial interests at every step." This implies either that only those farsighted few recognized the unique amenity values of the resource while others could only see value in more traditional extractive uses, or that the amenity values could not be captured by a private owner through a market process. Both of these implications are not consistent with the history of Yellowstone.

It was obvious to the earliest explorers, as trapper Osborne Russell noted in his journal in 1835, that Yellowstone had special amenity values:

> There is something in the wild romantic scenery of this valley which I cannot ... describe. ... For my own part I almost wished I could spend the remainder of my days in a place like this where happiness and contentment seemed to reign in wild romantic splendor.
> (quoted in Haines, 1977: I, 49)

The reputation of the region grew and finally culminated in three more formal expeditions in 1869, 1870, and 1871.

This recognition suggests that there would be competition to capture the amenity rents. While the area was so remote in the first half of the nineteenth century that few dreamed the rents would ever be positive, Jackson (1957: 56) describes how two individuals were cutting poles to fence off the geyser basins in 1870, and how two other men attempted to privatize 320 acres encompassing Mammoth Hot Springs under the Preemption Act in 1871. Another entrepreneur, C. J. Baronett, captured a share of the rents in 1871 by building and maintaining a toll bridge across the Yellowstone River just above its junction with the Lamar River. And "Yankee Jim" and his partners Bart Henderson and Horn Miller built a toll road through a narrow canyon along the Yellowstone River just north of Mammoth Hot Springs. Yankee Jim squatted on the land necessary for construction of the road in 1871, twelve years before the land was surveyed, and opened his National Park Toll Road in July 1873.[6]

These piecemeal efforts, however, proved to be insignificant in comparison to the efforts of the most active private interest in the region, the Northern

Pacific Railroad, chartered by Congress on July 2, 1862. Given the proximity of the railroad's transcontinental route to Yellowstone, it could naturally capture some of the rents by bringing passengers to this remote area. Because the main line came within sixty miles of Mammoth Hot Springs, the Northern Pacific actively supported exploration of the region. It also sponsored publicity campaigns extolling the scenic wonders of the upper Yellowstone valley. Clearly the Northern Pacific recognized the aesthetic value of the region and its potential for generating passenger traffic for the railroad.

In light of this recognition, one might think that the railroad would attempt to establish private ownership of the region rather than support legislative efforts to establish Yellowstone National Park. Surely private ownership of the land area encompassing the major attractions in the Yellowstone region would have given the railroad a more secure claim on the amenity rents, but US public land policy made the establishment of property rights virtually impossible. The Homestead Act of 1862 was geared to a particular type of land use, namely agriculture. It and subsequent land acts including the Mining Act (1872), the Timber Culture Act (1873), and the Timber and Stone Act (1878) made provision for farming, timber harvest, and mining, but no consideration was made for establishing private ownership for amenity values that did not require cultivation or extraction. If the railroad had engaged in farming, timber harvesting, or mining to establish rights, amenity rents would have been reduced rather than maximized. Moreover, the acreage limitations for each claim (initially 160 acres but subsequently raised to 640 acres) mitigated against railroad ownership of a sufficiently large area to prevent congestion externalities.[7] Had other individuals been able to establish small claims to the Mammoth Hot Springs or to Old Faithful, rents available to the Northern Pacific would have been reduced because a portion of the total rents would have gone to the owners of the specific sights.

The Northern Pacific realized that it would have a far greater chance of controlling access and capturing rents if Yellowstone was managed as a contiguous unit even if under governmental ownership. Indeed, the railroad may well have been the originator of the idea of making Yellowstone a government preserve. The first contemporary record of the suggestion is found in a letter dated October 27, 1871 from the Northern Pacific's publicity man, A. R. Nettleton, to Ferdinand Hayden, leader of the 1871 expedition:

> Judge Kelley has made a suggestion which strikes me as being an excellent one, viz. Let Congress pass a bill reserving the Great Geyser Basin as a public park forever – just as it has reserved that far inferior wonder the Yosemite Valley and the big trees. If you approve this, would such a recommendation be appropriate in your final report?
>
> (quoted in Bartlett, 1985: 206–7)

The judge, William Darrah Kelley, was a Republican Congressman from Pennsylvania and a business associate of Jay Cooke, the principal financier of the Northern Pacific. Just three days after the letter was written, Cooke wrote to his aid in Montana, W. Milner Roberts:

> We are delighted to hear such good accounts of the Yellowstone expedition from both ends. Gen. Hancock and Gen. Sheridan have both telegraphed that the report will be a splendid one from the expedition at this end. . . . It is proposed by Mr. Hayden in his report to Congress that the Geyser region around Yellowstone Lake shall be set apart by government as park, similar to that of the Great Trees and other reservations in California. Would this conflict with our land grant, or interfere with us in any way? Please give me your views on this subject. It is important to do something speedily, or squatters and claimants will go in there, and we can probably deal much better with the government in any improvements we may desire to make for the benefit of our pleasure travel than with individuals.
>
> (quoted in Bartlett, 1985: 208)

W. Milner Roberts responded from Helena, Montana, on November 21, 1871: "Your October thirtieth and November sixth rec'd. Geysers outside our grant advise Congressional delegation be in East probably before middle December" (quoted in Bartlett, 1985: 208).

The Northern Pacific's interest in preserving the amenity values in Yellowstone is clear from this statement from a representative of the company:

> We do not want to see the Falls of the Yellowstone driving the looms of a cotton factory, or the great geysers boiling pork for some gigantic packing-house, but in all the native majesty and grandeur in which they appear today, without, as yet, a single trace of that adornment which is desecration, that improvement which is equivalent to ruin, or that utilization which means utter destruction.
>
> (quoted in Runte, 1990: 23)

Thus the officials of the Northern Pacific recognized the amenity value of Yellowstone and were instrumental in passage of the legislation establishing it as a national park. The railroad made sure Hayden's report included the suggestion that the area be set aside as a government preserve. Bartlett (1985: 208) notes that the railroad hired Nathaniel P. Langford to lobby for the legislation and paid to have a collection of William Jackson's photographs placed on the desk of every member of Congress and for some of Thomas Moran's watercolors to be distributed to the especially influential senators and representatives.[8] The lobbying efforts were successful; the Forty Second Congress passed legislation establishing the park in February of 1872, and on March 1 President Ulysses S. Grant signed it into law. Runte (1979: 91) contends that the lobbying efforts of the Northern Pacific and other railroads with an interest in the region were not driven by "altruism or environmental concern; rather the lines promoted tourism in their quest for greater profits."

In establishing the park, Congress did not provide funding for operations nor did it offer guidance as to how the resource should be managed. According to Haines (1977: I, 212 and 242), Nathaniel P. Langford was appointed the first Superintendent of Yellowstone but was expected to serve without salary. Langford only entered the park twice during his five-year term. Initial appropriations for park operation were not made until 1878 and even then were only for $10,000. There were no rules or regulations posted for tourists who numbered 500 by 1873 and 1,000 by 1877.[9]

Under these circumstances the tragedy of the commons resulted, not so much from congestion but from despoliation. In the fall of 1873 an article in a Bozeman, Montana, paper described mutilation of the park's "curiosities."[10] Captain William Ludlow led an army expedition into the park in 1875 and reported that during the winter of 1874–5 from 1,500 to 2,000 elk were slaughtered for their skins within fifteen miles of Mammoth Hot Springs. He also commented on the destruction of certain geyser formations:

> The ornamental work about the crater and pools had been broken and defaced in the most prominent places by visitors. ... The visitors prowled about with shovel and ax, chopping and hacking and prying up great pieces of the most ornamental work they could find; women and men alike joined in the most barbarous pastime.
>
> (quoted in Hampton, 1971: 40–1)

In the 1880s protection of Yellowstone improved with the arrival of the railroad and its potential to capitalize on the amenity rents.[11] Railroad employees monitored visitor activities around geysers, guarded against poaching, and generally protected the environmental qualities that people came to see. Not surprisingly, the Northern Pacific lobbied for congressional funding for these protection efforts. Congress increased its annual appropriations from $15,000 to $40,000 in 1883, including an appropriation for compensating ten assistants who would reside continuously in the park. The Northern Pacific also supported putting the Army in charge of enforcing rules and regulations to prevent desecration of the park's resources. The lobbying efforts were successful, and on August 17, 1886 the first troops arrived to establish Fort Yellowstone at Mammoth Hot Springs. For the next thirty years, the Army patrolled the park, enforced regulations, designed roads and other improvements, and battled fires.

The success of the railroad in cornering a large share of the market for transportation to the park is shown in Table 6.1. Once the Northern Pacific established itself as a main carrier from the East, it carried 46 percent of all visitors to the park between 1890 and 1900. Thereafter, its share declined slightly due to competition from the Union Pacific that arrived in 1903 and the Chicago, Burlington, and Quincy that arrived in 1908. Even after that, however, the three railroads cooperated in offering combined packages to carry passengers from the East and in operating businesses providing internal transportation.

Table 6.1 Visitations to Yellowstone Park, 1890–1903

Year	Visitors to Yellowstone	Visitors carried by Northern Pacific
1890	7,808	3,904
1891	7,154	3,577
1892	7,290	3,645
1893	6,154	3,076
1894	3,105	1,635
1895	5,438	2,866
1896	4,659	2,427
1897	10,825	4,872
1898	6,534	2,207
1899	9,579	3,217
1900	8,928	3,785
1901	10,769	2,991
1902	13,433	4,209
1903	13,165	5,611

Source: Haines (1977: II, 478) and various annual reports of the Northern Pacific Railroad

Vertical integration to prevent rent dissipation

The Northern Pacific was concerned about the successive monopoly problem from the beginning. When the park was established, Secretary of Interior Carl Schurz said that he would not "grant to any person or firm, exclusive privileges" to operate facilities in the park (quoted in Bartlett, 1985: 123). But this stance changed as a result of the railroad's effort to further secure its monopoly position and guard against successive monopolies.[12] The *New York Times* reported on January 16, 1882 that a syndicate had been formed "of wealthy gentlemen, more or less intimately connected with the Northern Pacific to build a branch tourist's line . . . to the heart of Yellowstone National Park, and erect there a large hotel for the accommodation of visitors." The syndicate would enjoy "exclusive privileges in the Park" (quoted in Bartlett, 1985: 124). Congress did not allow the railroad to extend rail service from its terminus into Yellowstone, but long term exclusive leases were granted for hotel service to the Yellowstone National Park Improvement Company (YNPIC) and for other internal transportation services.

For all intents and purposes, the railroad and YNPIC were fully integrated. At the outset the relationship between the two companies was not clear, although Carrol T. Hobart, one of the founders, had been a section superintendent of the railroad. However, in 1884 the railroad loaned $20,000 in working capital to the receiver of the financially distressed YNPIC, and in 1885 the railroad purchased the property of the defunct concern. Bartlett (1985: 152) notes that most of the investors in the new Yellowstone Park Association incorporated on April 15, 1886 "were directly involved with the Northern Pacific, or were among its heavy investors." As the concessionaire expanded its

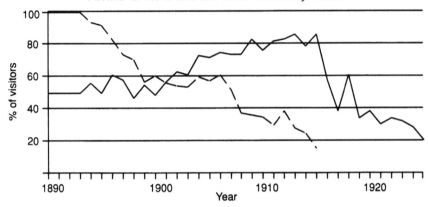

Figure 6.1 Yellowstone visitors carried by internal transportation companies

Source: Haines (1977: II, 484–5): and various annual reports of the Northern Pacific Railroad

Notes:

—— curve: Park visitors carried by internal transportation companies as a percentage of all park visitors

- - - - curve: Park visitors carried by the Yellowstone National Park Transportation Company as a percentage of those using internal transportation companies

services over the next several years, the railroad made no attempt "to keep secret its interest in park concessions or its role as a silent partner. Certainly its cooperation with the big park concessionaires was widely known," according to Bartlett (1985: 170). Over the remainder of the nineteenth century, the Northern Pacific retained firm control of the Yellowstone Park Association (later merged with the Yellowstone National Park Transportation Company), continually contributing capital so that additional properties could be purchased and facilities built.[13] When the Northern Pacific Railroad Company went into receivership for the second time in 1895, Haines (1977: II, 48) says its stock in the Yellowstone Park Association was valued at $372,550, and "the gross passenger receipts from the Yellowstone Park business had averaged $92,357 annually between 1890 and 1896."

By vertically integrating to overcome the successive monopoly problem, the Northern Pacific captured an even larger share of the rents. The dashed line in Figure 6.1 shows park visitors carried by the Yellowstone National Park Transportation Company (a subsidiary of the Northern Pacific) as a percentage of all those using internal transportation companies. During the early period most visitors to the park availed themselves of public transportation, and the Northern Pacific's subsidiary carried a majority of those people until 1907. Thereafter competition from the Frank J. Haynes' company backed by the Union Pacific chipped away at the internal traffic market. Finally in 1917, the three railroads joined together in a cooperative agreement to help finance a single transportation company with an exclusive franchise. Unfortunately for the railroads, as the solid line in Figure 6.1 shows, the percentage of visitors using internal transportation companies plummeted with the arrival of automobiles in Yellowstone in 1915.

The railroads also tried to ensconce their monopoly profits from internal services through a series of long term contracts between concessionaires and the federal government. In 1894, the first of these granted concessionaires up to ten acres at a site and up to twenty acres total. Grants at a single site were increased to twenty acres in 1906. Franchises were extended to twenty years, and franchisees were given the right to mortgage their grants in order to raise capital. At least during the early years, vertical integration along with these franchises and grants gave the Northern Pacific enough control to solve the successive monopoly problem and to reduce rent dissipation through congestion.

Creating a commons

But troubles for the Northern Pacific and its associates began in the late nineteenth and early twentieth centuries as the federal government increased its regulatory authority over transportation. The beginning of regulatory control of the Northern Pacific and its subsidiaries arose because of competition from the new permanent camps that were springing up in Yellowstone. Visitors were always able to camp on their own, but in 1897 William W. Wylie applied for and obtained permission to operate "semi-permanent camps" at numerous locations in the park. This designation meant that the camps were to be removed after the summer season and hence did not violate the terms of other franchisees. Haines (1977: II, 136) explains that Wylie also offered alternative transportation services, with the total package costing $35, in contrast to the $50 charged by the Yellowstone Park Association.

The railroad responded with a pricing scheme that made its package cheaper than Wylie's. It offered a package arrangement whereby one could purchase rail transportation along with a five and a half day tour of the park for a single price. The package charged more for the transportation to the park, however, if the tour was not purchased. This arrangement scheme reduced the marketability of the Wylie tour and led Wylie to protest the pricing scheme.

In 1905 the Interstate Commerce Commission found:

> In other words, the railway company gets $45.00 on a ticket to Gardiner and return, and only $30.50 on a ticket which includes stage transportation through the park, and only $28.50 on a ticket which includes the same stage transportation and entertainment at the hotels of the association.[14]

The Commission also charged that the Northern Pacific was engaging in unfair competition:

> The defendant railway refuses to make any arrangement with complainant for a joint service or to sell at any place coupons or other tickets for the transportation and entertainment which he provides. . . . It is apparent that he is an active competitor of the transportation company and the association and the only inferable motive for any discrimination against him is the desire of the defendant railway to favor the agencies which it controls and in which it is largely interested.[15]

The ICC decided

> the Northern Pacific has no right to make one rate for passengers whose journey ends at the terminus of its branch line and a lower rate for passengers who travel beyond that point by the stage of the transportation company or who patronize the hotels of the association.[16]

This decision to regulate railroad pricing of tourist services and to allow competition for internal services reduced the monopoly power of the railroad, weakened its position as a residual claimant, and increased the potential for rent dissipation through the tragedy of the commons.

The real death knell for the railroads' monopoly position came on August 1, 1915 when the first private automobiles were allowed into Yellowstone. Initial requests to allow automobiles into the park came in 1902, and pressure increased every year thereafter. Of course, the interior transportation companies and the railroads opposed such action and succeeded in prohibiting automobiles even after they were allowed in other national parks. Finally Congress brought pressure to bear on the Secretary of Interior, and Yellowstone was opened to motorized travel.

The reason for opposition from the railroad and the internal transportation companies is obvious: without complete ownership, they stood to lose rents. However, if the railroad had owned the land itself, it might well have allowed autos into the park. As a landowner and hence residual claimant, the Northern Pacific would have had an incentive to consider the rents associated with automobile entry and could have captured those rents through higher entry fees. In the absence of landownership, however, the facility suppliers and the railroad could not capture the rents associated with auto transportation.

Not only did the automobile mean that people could get to the park without the train, it meant that they could take day excursions into Yellowstone and return to the gateway cities for many of their services. The result was a precipitous drop in the percentage of visitors carried by public transportation after 1915, obvious in Figure 6.1. Haines (1977: II, 273–4) notes that the

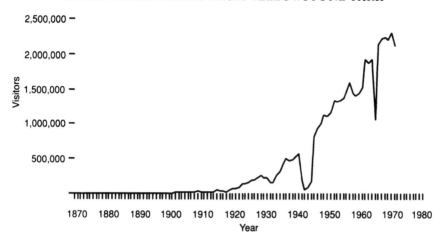

Figure 6.2 Visitors to Yellowstone National Park
Source: Haines (1977: II, 478–9) and various annual reports of the Northern Pacific Railroad

motorization of park transportation eliminated the need for many of the intermediate stopping places and led to abandonment of a number of facilities in the Park. . . . A further casualty of the reorganization was the boat operation on Lake Yellowstone; transportation across the lake was rendered unprofitable by the automobile.

As the railroad faced increasing competition in providing transportation to and within the park, its interest in Yellowstone waned. Initially automobiles mostly provided local visitors a means of transportation to the park, but Yellowstone's distance from major population centers and a dearth of good roads meant most transcontinental passengers continued to arrive by rail until the 1920s. In 1924 the Northern Pacific still conveyed 35 percent of the total visitors. As more roads were built and automobiles improved, however, the railroad's share declined dramatically to under 7 percent by 1929 according to Bartlett (1985: 95). Haines (1977: II, 372) concludes that from then on the Northern Pacific's interest in Yellowstone slowly declined as it

found Yellowstone Park tourism less profitable than it had been in earlier times and soon decided to give up its postwar (World War II) effort to reestablish the former pattern of passenger traffic to the Park. Thus, the hauling of tourists to Gardiner by rail ended with the 1948 season.

With the park gates opened to autos in the absence of any residual claim on gate fees, the potential for a congestion externality arose. The data presented in Figure 6.2 show the dramatic impact the automobile had on

111

visits to Yellowstone. An *F*-test on these data shows that the visitor trend prior to 1915 was significantly different from that after (i.e. there is no possibility these two data sets were drawn from the same sample).[17] Keep in mind that this increase in visitors was not just a move to a competitive optimum. Given open access to the park, the previous monopoly position of the railroad and concessionaires tended to promote rent maximization. Opening the park to autos simply created the "tragedy of the commons."[18]

Rent dissipation was not total as long as internal facility suppliers maintained some market power. Hotels, stores, and other facilities were definitely specific assets that could capture a share of the amenity rents from Yellowstone. Moreover, the government had to have a way to ensure that these facilities were supplied to the visitors. To guarantee the concessionaires a return and provide an incentive to make investments, the federal government entered into long term service contracts with monopoly concessionaires. As noted above, these contracts began with an act in 1897 granting acreage to concessionaires. Bartlett (1985: 179) believes these grants along with exclusive franchises to provide services "greatly aided the concessionaires in raising money." To mitigate the last-period problem which reduces the incentive of franchisees to maintain capital if they are going to lose their franchise, there was continued pressure by the concessionaires for early renewals. "Usually these legal agreements were for twenty years but it was not unusual for a concessionaire to request a renewal before even five years of the current one had elapsed," says Bartlett (1985: 201–2). For example, a twenty-year franchise of the Yellowstone Park Association signed in 1917 was canceled six years later and a new one granted because park superintendent Albright felt "that a little more protection, by virtue of the extension of the term of the franchise, might be given" (quoted in Bartlett, 1985: 202).

Bartlett (1985: 202) emphasizes the importance of these long term contracts to both sides of the agreement:

> The reasons for these requests are apparent to any business-oriented person. It was easier to obtain loans, and when obtained, at lower interest, the longer the contract had to run. Moreover, both the Park Service and concessionaires became dissatisfied with contract provisions as times changed.

The "apparent" benefits of altering long term contracts, however, become blurred when the potential for postcontractual opportunism is introduced, especially when one party to the contract is the sovereign government represented by bureaucratic agents as described by Haddock (1994). On the one hand, because there is no residual claimant on the governmental side of the contract, franchisees may be able to capture a disproportionate share of the rents. According to Bartlett (1985: 202), "Again and again incidents appear indicating Park Service cooperation with the concessionaires that seems to place consideration for these businesses above the public welfare." Indeed the criticism is that monopoly privileges granted by the Park Service allow the franchisees to capture rents from Yellowstone by charging high prices without maintaining their capital investment and services.

But franchisees facing a sovereign have little recourse if the government decides to act opportunistically. In particular after World War II when the country was facing inflation, the Park Service would not allow concessionaires to raise prices. The rental rate for rooms was held at depression level prices, leaving concessionaires with little incentive or desire to upgrade facilities. In the absence of a normal contractual regime, concessionaires had little confidence in their ability to capture a return on investment. If the Park Service was putting "businesses above the public welfare" during the first fifty years of Yellowstone's history, its recent emphasis on regulating concessionaire profits and on limiting construction of tourist facilities has placed concessionaire investments in a precarious political position. Bartlett (1985: 376) captures the problem: "The thirty-five or so concessionaires possess an overriding fear: that the Park Service will eliminate them, purchase their facilities, and, after public bidding, lease the facilities on a short-term basis – five years is a commonly mentioned period." Such potential opportunism is hardly conducive to long term joint production that maximizes rents.

CONCLUSION

The policy of the national parks with respect to private interests continues to be controversial. There is continuous political pressure to keep entrance fees low and to allow unrestricted entry. The main private aspect of park operations is concessionaires who have a long term contract guaranteeing exclusive rights to operate in the parks in return for a fee paid to the government. Many argue that these monopolies should not be allowed and that the fees paid by concessionaires are too low. Understood in the context of the potential for postcontractual opportunism, however, such long term contracts represent a way of trying to avoid opportunism when vertical integration is not possible and when the land cannot be privately owned. Nonetheless, the sovereign is in a position to appropriate quasi-rents by unilaterally changing the terms of the contract.

Indeed the history of Yellowstone is best understood in the contractual context. Pressure to establish Yellowstone emanated from the Northern Pacific Railroad because it was in a position to capture rents by combining its transportation services with the amenity values. To avoid the successive monopoly problem and further secure its monopoly position, it vertically integrated into the supply of internal services, but it could not vertically integrate totally by owning the land. Without owning Yellowstone, the railroad could not completely control entry as it found when automobiles were allowed into the park in 1915. As result, the tragedy of the commons ensued and rents were dissipated instead of maximized.

NOTES

1 Because the Northern Pacific was the main line to the park, we refer to "the railroad" throughout the chapter. We recognize, however, that there were three railroads with access to Yellowstone and that all had some role in the park's operation.

2 This result assumes an elastic supply of inputs necessary to capture the rents, but as Libecap and Johnson (1982) have shown, an upward-sloping supply of inputs can allow some input owners to capture rents.

3 For a more complete discussion of the impact of monopolistic supply of a complementary input and of the successive monopoly problem see Blair and Kaserman (1985).

4 For a more complete discussion of the problems associated with contracting with the sovereign see Haddock (1994).

5 We use the term redistribute rather than appropriate because it is not clear who appropriates rents captured by the sovereign. For example, when the park was opened to automobile traffic, railroad rents went down, but they were not all appropriated. Rather they were partially dissipated through the tragedy of the commons.

6 For a colorful discussion of Yankee Jim's toll road see Whithorn (1989).

7 See Libecap and Johnson (1979) for a discussion of how acreage limitations raised the costs of acquiring land for timber companies.

8 Both Jackson and Moran accompanied early expeditions to the area as photographer and landscape artist, respectively, with the Northern Pacific paying Moran's expedition expenses.

9 See Haines (1977: II, 478).

10 See Hampton (1971: 35) for a complete discussion.

11 The Northern Pacific had been scheduled to complete its transcontinental line in the early 1870s, but a financial panic in 1873 put the railroad into bankruptcy and delayed the line for a decade.

12 For a more complete discussion of rent-seeking activities by providers of resources complementary to a government-owned facility see Benson and Mitchell (1988).

13 Initially the subsidiary was the Yellowstone National Park Improvement Company that later became the Yellowstone Park Association. However, with the threat of competition by the Yellowstone National Park Transportation Company chartered in 1892, the Northern Pacific merged the companies to restrict competition. Haines (1977: II, chapter 13) discusses the details of these efforts to cartelize internal transportation.

14 *Wylie v. Northern P.R. Co. et al.*, 11 I. C. C. Rep. 145, 151 (1905).

15 *Wylie v. Northern P.R. Co. et al.*, 11 I. C. C. Rep. 145, 152–3 (1905).

16 *Wylie v. Northern P.R. Co., et al.*, 11 I. C. C. Rep. 145, 154 (1905).

17 The F-statistic is 138.044 and the likelihood ratio is 135.478.

18 For a more complete discussion of the problem of overexploitation of the park once it became an open access resource in 1915, see Anderson and Hill (1994).

REFERENCES

Alchian, Armen and Harold Demsetz (1972) "Production, Information Costs, and Economic Organization," *American Economic Review* 62: 775–95.

Anderson, Terry L. and Peter J. Hill (1994) "Rents From Amenity Resources: A Case Study of Yellowstone National Park," in *The Political Economy of the American West*, ed. Terry L. Anderson and Peter J. Hill. Lanham, MD: Rowman and Littlefield.

Bartlett, Richard A. (1985) *Yellowstone, A Wilderness Besieged.* Tucson, AZ: University of Arizona Press.

Benson, Bruce L. and Jean M. Mitchell (1988) "Rent Seekers Who Demand Government Production: Bureaucratic Output and the Price of Complements," *Public Choice* 56: 3–16.

Blair, Roger D. and David L. Kaserman (1985) *Antitrust Economics.* Homewood, IL: Richard D. Irwin.

Cheung, Steven N. S. (1970) "The Structure of a Contract: The Theory of a Non-exclusive Resource," *Journal of Law and Economics* 13: 49–70.

Haddock, David D. (1994) "Foreseeing Confiscation by the Sovereign: Lessons From the American West," in *The Political Economy of the American West*, ed. Terry L. Anderson and Peter J. Hill. Lanham, MD: Rowman and Littlefield.

Haines, Aubrey L. (1977) *The Yellowstone Story: A History of Our First National Park*, 2 vols. Boulder, CO: Yellowstone National Park and Museum Association with Colorado Associated University Press.

Hampton, H. Duane (1971) *How the U.S. Calvary Saved Our National Parks.* Bloomington, IN: Indiana University Press.

Ise, John (1979) *Our National Park Policy.* New York: Arno Press.

Jackson, W. Turrentine (1957) "The Creation of Yellowstone National Park," *Montana, The Magazine of Western History* 7,3: 52–65.

Klein, Benjamin, Robert G. Crawford, and Armen A. Alchian (1978) "Vertical Integration, Appropriable Rents, and the Competitive Contracting Process," *Journal of Law and Economics* 21,2: 297–326.

Libecap, Gary D. and Ronald N. Johnson (1979) "Property Rights, 19th Century Federal Timber Policy, and the Conservation Movement," *Journal of Economic History* 53: 129–42.

Libecap, Gary D. and Ronald N. Johnson (1982) "Contracting Problems and Regulation: The Case of the Fishery," *American Economic Review* 72: 1005–22.

Runte, Alfred (1979) *National Parks: The American Experience.* Lincoln, NE: University of Nebraska Press.

—— (1990) *Trains of Discovery.* Niwot, CO: Roberts Rinehart.

Whithorn, Doris (1989) *Yankee Jim's National Park Toll Road and the Yellowstone Trail.* (No publisher.)

7

CULTURAL EVOLUTION AND CONSTITUTIONAL PUBLIC CHOICE

Institutional diversity and economic performance on American Indian reservations

*Stephen Cornell and Joseph P. Kalt**

INTRODUCTION: EVOLUTIONARY REASONING AND CONSTITUTIONAL POLITICAL ECONOMY

In a major contribution to social science reasoning, Armen Alchian set forth in "Uncertainty, Evolution, and Economic Theory" an alternative to neo-classical economic mechanisms of change and equilibration in individual and organizational behavior (Alchian, 1950). Alchian's mechanism – what he called "environmental adoption" – replaced orthodox utility maximization and profit maximization with agents that draw on suites of adaptive, imitative, trial and error, lucky, and goal-directed strategies. With conscious use of Darwinian language, Alchian defines success in terms of survival, and sur-viving strategies are selected on the basis of their relative performance (fitness) in an environment in which resource constraints mean that not every strategy can survive. Rationality, in the usual sense of informed transitive choice over more or less complete preference orderings under conditions of scarcity, remains standing only as a special case of models that produce downward-sloping demand schedules and (relatively) efficient outcomes.

Those of us fortunate to have become students of Armen Alchian recognize his characteristic intellectual trait in his pioneering of evolutionary approaches to economic problems.[1] There is a methodological preacher in Armen Alchian.

* Cornell is Professor of Sociology, University of California, San Diego, and Kalt is a professor at the John F. Kennedy School of Government, Harvard University. This publication was made possible through support provided by the U.S. Agency for International Development under Cooperative Agreement No. DHR-0015-A-00–0031–00 to the Center on Institutional Reform and the Informal Sector (IRIS) and administered by the Office of Economic and Institutional Reform, Center for Economic Growth, Bureau for Global Programs, Field Support, and Research.

The message is at the heart of the UCLA school that stands as his legacy: economics is a *social* science. The goal of economics is not to test economic models, as the range of "economic" may be defined by the sociology of the profession at any particular time. The goal is to understand society – why it is like it is, why it changes as it does. With appropriate deference to Occam's razor and the "as-if" Popperian positivism of the Chicago school, there remains in Alchian's message a methodologic questioning: be careful with any single set of axioms and theorems; there might be some, or whole ranges of, interesting social phenomena that your model won't be able to capture. And, infused in this verifiable proposition, there is the philosopher's benevolent advice to probe the methodologic edges of social science inquiry.

The introduction of evolutionary modes of reasoning into analysis of economic problems is, indeed, methodologically stretching in at least several notable ways. First, it turns attention away from motive and intention in human behavior. In particular, invisible hand mechanisms for explaining the position and movement of such social phenomena as the state of the economy and the operation of political institutions become truly impersonal; that is, not necessarily choice theoretic in even their microfoundations. Second, evolutionary modes of reasoning draw attention away from stasis, homogeneity, and equilibrium, focusing scholarly attention on change, heterogeneity, and disequilibrium. Finally, when the evolutionary reasoning of the biologic sciences is applied to social phenomena as not mere metaphor, but as a competing substantive paradigm, it pulls analysis away from models of human behavior as individual optimization subject to constraints. Even if such models remain valid and useful in their own realm (in which questions such as "why those tastes?" are off limits), the evolutionary perspective seems pregnant with the promise of more complete explanations of social phenomena in which diversity (and perhaps, mutability) of individuals, groups, and institutions seems to be pervasively at the heart of outcomes,[2] and actual behavior is undertaken in the messy environment of uncertainty, luck, and learning that Alchian investigated in his seminal piece.[3]

Alchian introduced the case for evolutionary modes of reasoning in the context of familiar market institutions such as firms. At the present time, however, the call for such modes of analysis is nowhere more pressing than in the investigation of non-market behavior and institutions. Public choice economics and the related subfields of other social sciences have pushed themselves up against the very difficult problem of understanding the origins, change, and sustainability of the collective institutions that devise, implement, and enforce a society's crucial "rules of the game." This study presents the outlines of an interdisciplinary model of at least part of the problem: the embeddedness of individuals as social animals in implicit, extra-choice social contracts.[4] We draw on the results of research we have been conducting over the last seven years on a particularly fruitful sample of several hundred (recently) self-governing mini-nations which are struggling with the problems of launching and sustaining productive economic systems – contemporary American Indian reservations in the United States. We argue that: (1) the evidence strongly supports the key hypothesis that a form of implicit social contract founded on durable cultural norms of political propriety undergirds the formal institutions of successful societies, and (2) this finding is consistent with a model of cultural conventions shared over a network of socially constructed rational individuals.

THE WEALTH OF NATIONS AND THE SEARCH FOR THE SOCIAL CONTRACT

Evolutionary modes of reasoning hold particular attraction at the present time for social scientists interested in economic development. Hard theoretical and empirical research, as well as recent world events, continue to drive home the point that the formal and informal institutions by which people govern themselves hold the necessary, if not sufficient, keys to the wealth of nations. From the kind of theoretically informed search for generalizable paradigms represented by North (1981, 1990), Ostrom (1990, 1992), Putnam (1992), Olson (1982), and Bates (1988), to concrete case studies and everyday reports from the World Bank (e.g. 1991, 1994), to the "natural" experiments such as East/West Germany and North/South Korea, a central lesson of the post-World War II period seems to be that it is institutions and the policies that flow from them that determine at least whether a society is able to move close to the production possibility frontier defined by its resources, or whether it will be consigned to poverty far off the frontier.

The almost cliché advice of economists to the effect that economic development "requires getting price signals right and creating a climate that allows businesses to respond to those signals in ways that increase the returns to investment" (World Bank, 1994: 61) has been vindicated as a general matter. But "getting prices right" (i.e. establishing and sustaining markets) and creating an environment that channels rent seeking into productive endeavors requires a whole panoply of formal and informal social institutions that set down the "rules of the game." Formal institutions range from courts and constitutions to laws and regulations. Informal institutions range from norms regarding whether it is proper to vote to standards of on-the-job behavior. Getting prices and incentives "right" requires getting institutions "right."

North (1990; and, of course, many others) must have the basic story of the primacy of institutions down right: (1) *Specialization* is productive, apparently reflecting diseconomies of scope in (at least) human capacities. (2) Successful specialization requires a certain amount of *coordination* (so that an appropriate mix of desired goods and services is produced within a group) and *exchange* (so that members of a group are not stuck solely with the particular item they produce). (3) Coordination and exchange require *enforce-*

118

able and stable rules of allocation and dispute resolution. (4) Rules of allocation and dispute resolution require *third-party enforcement* by parties restricted in their ability to wield enforcement powers for self-aggrandizing rent seeking.

The ability to create a list like the foregoing oversimplifies the challenge of economic development. In point of fact, there cannot be much of the world that has not been exposed to some version of the "get prices and institutions right" advice. Yet, in society A the advice takes hold, and in society B it does not. More generally, notwithstanding the change in political and market affairs occasioned by the collapse of the Soviet Union, it is hard to argue that there are invisible-hand-like forces compelling convergence of political and economic systems on an optimum – at least not at a rate sufficient to make convergence a more interesting topic than the diversity of systems that seems to predominate.

The challenging problem for human beings that is embedded in the New Institutionalist description of the foundations of economic development (and social success, more generally) is that the rules of the game, and the institutions through which those rules are devised, implemented, and enforced, are classic shared public goods. As such, their creation and maintenance present self-interested individuals with Prisoners' Dilemmas, rife with defection and free-riding opportunities. Ordinary, self-interested rationality by utility-maximizing humans gives the invisible hand fits under such conditions, and the provision of mutually beneficial rules of the game and associated institutions, much less their optimal provision, is problematic in the extreme. How many groups of humans succeed in getting out, and staying out, of the Hobbesian world?

In one form or another, this question is now at the heart of burgeoning research efforts among social scientists (of all subdisciplines), biologists, psychologists, and neurophysiologists. There is a logic to the convergence of disciplines on the matter. Beginning with economics, the search for some original voluntary binding of economically rational individuals to a formal or informal constitution by which they agree to coordinate, legislate, adjudicate, and enforce mutually beneficial rules of the game has proven illusory. The problem is not the collective consumption attribute of rules and institutions as public goods; invisible hands can supply public goods when would-be free riders can be compelled to reveal and pay for their demands by exclusion devices (Demsetz, 1970). The analytic problem for economic models of governing social rules and institutions arises from their non-excludability. As Hirshleifer (1976), North (1990), Buchanan (1972), and others have stressed, there is no meta-enforcer of contracts and constitutions by which we can bind ourselves to abide by laws and constitutions, or by which those individuals who control the instruments of governance at any particular time can be held to the role of the disinterested third-party enforcer. Contractarian theories of public choice are incomplete: we cannot write a

119

contract or constitution to abide by our constitution without falling into an infinite regress of such contracts. Within a Contractarian framework, formal institutions of social control should be archetypically subject to defections and free riding. If such institutions should somehow arise, ruling cliques should overthrow (or at least whittle away at) them, otherwise well-meaning citizens should wait for their neighbors to bear the costs of policing such usurpers, and innumerable scofflaws should cheat on their taxes and run traffic lights.

The game theoretic approach to the problem of the genesis and maintenance of the rules and institutions of social control has taken as a major piece of its research agenda the discovery of the genesis and sustainability of cooperative behavior in Prisoners' Dilemma settings in which defection from cooperation with one's fellow members of society might readily seem individually rational (Axelrod, 1984; Maynard Smith, 1982). As Binmore's (1994) comprehensive survey and analysis make clear, the results of the game theory search for cooperation out of conflict might best be described as a set of "partial possibility" results. In the long run in the infinitely repeated Prisoners' Dilemma with a fixed number of players who make no mistakes, equilibria can exist in which players cooperate. An infinite number of paths of intermediate play, however, can end up in this long run state; at any point in time, observed equilibrium strategies can be expected to be mixed strategies of cooperation and defection. The workings of economic rationality do not promise to eliminate "nasty" strategies, and both "nice" strategies of readily established cooperative behavior and "nasty" strategies may be upset by invasion by players entering from outside (Binmore, 1994: 192–203). In fact, no strategy is stable in the face of invasion by outsiders in the infinitely repeated Prisoners' Dilemma (1994: 198).

Anything approaching *guarantees* of stable cooperative behavior requires, at a minimum, shared common knowledge – knowledge not that everyone is rational, but commonly understood conventions about how behavior is to be coordinated (Binmore, 1994: 5–6 and 139–40; also Aumann, 1976). Explanation of how people coordinate and cooperate that makes reference to commonly shared conventions, however, takes game theory approaches outside the realm of own-utility-maximizing automatons and begins to embed them in socially constructed shared histories and contexts. That is, such explanation starts down the path toward something like a social contract as the source of sustained cooperative behavior in models of human interaction and as the undergirding of formal institutions of social control in real societies.

In fact, that is exactly where we are headed. As Hirshleifer (1980: 655) summarizes: "There is no doubt that, from the most primitive to the most advanced stages of society, a higher degree of cooperative interaction . . . takes place than can be explained simply as a pragmatic option for totally egoistic man." As each of the social science disciplines, using its own terminology and arriving at key conclusions at its own speed, turns its research skills to the questions of why some societies are successful and others are not, the existence of extra-constitutional informal shared conventions and perceptions is more or less being deduced as a necessity: If invisible hand mechanisms emanating from the choice theoretic microfoundations of economics cannot adequately explain the genesis and life histories of societies' crucial institutions of collective action, what else is left? With formal institutions written on perishable paper, people must come to the game every day with informal constraints on their free riding and defection and informal prods toward cooperative outcomes – constraints and prods that are not the product of neoclassical economic behavior. When a Buchanan (1972) confronts the "paper" foundations of Contractarianism and a Tullock (1993) asks "Why so much stability?," the economist starts looking for an understanding of shared "ideologies" (North, 1981, 1988, 1990), the rational choice brand of political scientist advises turning to our "sociologically-minded brethren" (Bates, 1988), more traditionally originating political scientists start investigating "social capital" (Putnam, 1992), sociologists and anthropologists reinvigorate models of "cultural norms" (Coleman, 1990; Elster, 1989), and historians find explanations for social and economic decay in mismatches between societies' sociopolitical cultures and their formal institutions (Davidson, 1992). Indeed, a new imperialist appears on the scholarly scene – sociobiology, threatening to send all of the social scientists off to work on other problems (Wilson, 1975, 1978).

As the New Institutionalism, with its property rights, public choice, and Contractarian antecedents, gives way to what we might as well call the New Social Contract Theory, it is not the case that the Stiglerian chant of "no testable implications" can be used to protect the walls of economics. Neoclassical, choice theoretic economic models are not the only testable models of individual and social human behavior. In fact, that is what Alchian's foray into evolutionary modes of reasoning demonstrates.[5] Evolutionary modes of reasoning are likely to stand at the center of the New Social Contract Theory, putting evolutionary selection mechanisms in the place that individual-level utility maximization and social-level invisible hand theorems might otherwise occupy. This is clearly the case when biologic explanations enter the Theory. But it is also likely to be the case when the Theory makes reference to such concepts as common knowledge, shared ideologies, cultural norms, and social capital. As the "ideational" (as opposed to the genetic; Durham, 1991) prechoice genesis of human behavior, their nature seems to call for models of mutation, invasion, dispersion through populations, and success-as-reproduction.

We now turn to outlining a version of a New Social Contract Theory. For purposes of drawing out testable implications, we focus in particular on the position within this Theory of what can be called the socially constructed rational individual. To provide empirical context, and some tests of hypotheses, we embed our discussion in the results of our research on the performance of self-government on contemporary American Indian reservations in the United States.

SUCCESS, FAILURE, AND INSTITUTIONAL DIVERSITY AMONG AMERICAN INDIAN NATIONS

Institutional setting

As a result of a series of US Supreme Court decisions over the last two decades and the Indian Self-Determination and Education Assistance Act of 1975, American Indian tribes on US reservations have a very high degree of political sovereignty.[6] Tribes generally have rights of self-government exceeding a state's, with the ability to establish their own courts, police, legislatures, bureaucracies, business and environmental codes, tax systems, civil and criminal procedures, and most of the other functions of sovereign polities.[7] Most tribes operate under constitutions that were drafted by the US Government in the 1930s, pursuant to the Indian Reorganization Act (IRA) of 1934. IRA constitutions were modelled after business or social club boards of directors. They typically provide for: (1) a representative tribal council of (commonly) 7–20 members with legislative powers; (2) a tribal chairperson or president selected in parliamentary fashion by the council or in US executive fashion by direct popular election; (3) little or no provision for judicial institutions or functions; (4) little enumeration of powers of the various parts of the tribal government; and (5) a requirement that the US Secretary of the Interior approve of any changes in the tribal constitution. Even tribes without IRA constitutions often had their constitutions drafted by others (e.g. at the time of a treaty), and non-IRA constitutions often follow the foregoing enumerated structure.

We believe that the particular history of the origins of the formal institutions by which contemporary American Indian reservations today are governed provides hard-to-find "torque" to research questions of the kind raised here. Because tribal constitutions were effectively imposed on tribes in most cases (and changes in those constitutions were and are often made subject to control by an outside power through Secretarial approval), and tribes demonstrably differ a great deal in their present and historic sociopolitical cultures, the Indian context affords the possibility of observing mismatches between "social contracts" and formal institutions. The public goods theory of such institutions reviewed in the preceding section directly yields the hypothesis – testable because of the torque of the Indian setting – that a mismatch between the underlying social contract and the formal institutions of a self-governing society should lead those formal institutions to perform relatively poorly. Moreover, because we have tribes with the same formal institutions (derived from the IRA), but with different sociopolitical cultural settings (contracts), the Indian context provides some prospect of isolating the social contracts as undergirding determinants of social success. Lastly, because American Indian societies are relatively homogeneous within tribe and heterogeneous across tribe, and because within-tribe homogeneity is much clearer than in larger nations such as the US (where it may be harder to conclude that a particular cultural attribute is widely shared), it may be possible to generate observable paths of cultural evolution within Indian societies.

Economic and social conditions on reservations

As a general matter, American Indian reservations are quite poor communities. Reservation Indians are the poorest minority in the US, with average unemployment across all reservations typically around 50 percent (even without adjusting for the not-surprising large discouraged worker effects on officially defined Bureau of Labor Statistics unemployment). Average social conditions are correspondingly unsatisfactory, with rates of social pathologies (e.g. suicide, crime) far above the rates for the US as a whole.

Such "average" images of struggling and underdeveloped economies mask diversity in reservation performance (Table 7.1). Some reservations appear to be almost pure transfer and grant economies with little on-reservation economic productive activity and most employment in social service sectors. The Pine Ridge reservation in South Dakota, for example, is the poorest community in the United States, according to the US Census. At Northern Cheyenne in Montana, the Tribe reports that approximately 95 per cent of all reservation income is derived from federal and state programs, with the remaining small amount of income coming from on-reservation agricultural production. At the neighboring Crow reservation, on paper, the Tribe is one of the wealthiest societies in the world as a result of extremely rich endowments of coal and agricultural lands, with measured per capita wealth exceeding $3,000,000 as of 1988; yet, the effective rate of income generation off of this wealth amounts to an annual rate of return of approximately 0.01 percent (Cornell and Kalt, 1991). As at a number of reservations, Crow unemployment adjusted for discouraged workers is in the range of 80–90 percent.

In contrast, some reservations have been booming economically and rapidly progressing in terms of social conditions. This holds even outside of the much-publicized cases of successful gaming tribes (which have been able to capitalize on their sovereignty and capture niches in the gambling market). The Flathead reservation in Montana, for example, is the site of an extremely healthy private sector economy based on agriculture and tourism, with real incomes growing and unemployment appearing to be at the economist's "natural rate" (Cornell and Kalt, 1996). With a different strategy (i.e. tribal ownership of enterprises) the Mississippi Choctaw have made the Tribe the fourth or fifth largest employer in the State of Mississippi, and the traffic

Table 7.1 Economic performance and institutional forms on American Indian reservations

	Change in income 1977–89	1989 BLS employ- ment[1]	Employment rel. to fitted expectation[2]	Governmental form[3]	Indepen- dent judiciary	Cultural "match"[4]
Flathead	16 %	80 %	+11 %	Parliamentary	Yes	Yes
White Mtn Apache	12 %	89 %	+23 %	Executive	No	Yes
Cochiti Pueblo	10 %	90 %	+20 %	Theocracy	No	Yes
Mescalero Apache	9 %	80–90 %	+33 %	Executive	No	Yes
Muckleshoot	6 %	74 %	+5 %	Parliamentary	No	Yes
Pine Ridge Sioux	-1 %	50 %	-20 %	Executive	No	No
San Carlos Apache	-7 %	49 %	-15 %	Executive	No	No
Rosebud Sioux	-10 %	10 %	-38 %	Executive	Yes	No
Hualapai	-11 %	26 %	-18 %	Executive	No	No
Yakima	-12 %	39 %	-1 %	Athenian	Yes	No
Crow	-12 %	33 %	-7 %	Athenian	No	No
Northern Cheyenne	-15 %	52 %	-4 %	Executive	No	No
All reservations	-1 %	60 %	0 %	–	–	–

Sources: Bureau of Indian Affairs, US Department of the Interior, *Indian Service Population and Labor Force Estimates*, various issues
Notes:
[1] BLS employment is 100 percent minus the BLS unemployment rate (with the latter measuring the percent of the workforce actually looking for employment and not finding it)
[2] Employment rel. to fitted expectation represents the difference between actual employment levels and the employment levels predicted by a model of sixty-seven reservations, controlling for reservation governmental form, local economic conditions in surrounding counties, human and resource capital endowments, and on-reservation property rights structures. This model is presented and estimated in Cornell and Kalt (1991)
[3] Parliamentary refers to governments in which the tribal chief executive is selected by the representative tribal council. Executive refers to governments in which the tribal chief executive is directly elected by the tribe's reservation citizens. Theocracy indicates that the tribal religious leader(s) appoints the key tribal authorities and establishes central tribal policies. Athenian refers to democratic decision-making authority being vested in a tribal council in which all adult members of the tribe serve on the tribal council
[4] Cultural match refers to possible congruence between historical self-selected governmental form and modern (largely imposed) governmental form (see Cornell and Kalt, 1991, 1993)

flow at morning rush hour is *onto* the reservation as non-Indians commute to work at the Tribe's automobile subassembly plant, its industrial park, its greeting card factory, its shopping centers, and its tribally run schools and other social service organizations. The White Mountain Apaches in Arizona have followed a similar organizational strategy to build a natural-resource-based economy that is the economic base for Indians and non-Indians in its region. With a tribal membership of 12,500, the White Mountain Apaches operate tribal enterprises with revenues of $80–$100 million per year, including a major logging and sawmill industry, a ski resort, the premier for-fee sport hunting business in the United States, and an aerospace manufacturing subcontractor.[8]

Explaining cross-tribe differences in performance

With tribes operating in a common policy environment vis-à-vis federal and state authorities, and with all tribes being turned loose to pursue self-government in approximately the same way at approximately the same time, what explains the fairly sharp differences in their economic performance since the start of the self-determination period? The answers to this question of the origin of the wealth of Indian nations are, of course, multi-layered and incomplete. We believe the evidence is strong, however, at a number of layers of inquiry.

First, it is clear that formal institutions matter in precisely the "get the institutions right" sense. In previous research, we have reported cross-sectional analyses of the sixty-seven largest tribes (populations over 700) for which data on economic performance and plausible explanatory variables are available (esp. Cornell and Kalt, 1991). These analyses indicate with quite strong degrees of statistical confidence that, holding constant variables suggested by neoclassical growth theory (including human capital endowments, natural resource endowments, marketplace opportunities, and the like), constitutional forms add significantly to the explanation of cross-tribe differences in economic performance. The relevant results are shown in Table 7.2, which reports the *ceteris paribus* contribution to the level of tribal employment of alternative formal governmental institutions.

Over the sample, the combination of a directly elected chief executive and an independent judiciary adds the most to tribal economic performance – raising employment almost 20 (19.9) percentage points relative to a tribe governed by an "athenian" democracy with no independent judiciary. The

Table 7.2 Contributions of alternative governmental forms to reservation employment levels

	General council	Parliamentary system	Independent chief executive
No independent judiciary	–	10.8 %	14.9 %
Independent judiciary	5.0 %	15.8 %	19.9 %

Source: Cornell and Kalt (1991)

Note: Contributions at mean sample values, as determined by the model estimated in Cornell and Kalt (1991). The effects of resource endowments and adjacent non-reservation economic conditions, human capital (education and labor force experience), and degrees of mixed jurisdiction re on-reservation property rights due to allotment history are held constant. Contributions are measured relative to a reservation with a general council form of government, with no independent judiciary latter is the poorest-performing form of formal government in Indian Country. "Athenian" democracies (known as general councils in Indian Country) make every voting age member of the tribe a member of the tribal council. In so doing, they turn the political arena into a tragedy of the commons for rent-seeking political factions and individuals (Cornell and Kalt, 1991, 1992a, 1992b). Directly-elected chief executives and independent judiciaries, on the other hand, provide countervailing power bases that serve as checks and balances on rent seeking through political action.

At a second layer of inquiry, we believe the evidence is compelling that there is, indeed, a social contract that undergirds successful formal institutions of self-government and, thereby, social and economic success at the level of Indian nations. The foregoing description of the contributions of various forms of formal governmental structures does not explain all of the variation in the performance of cross-reservation economies. As shown in Table 7.1, tribes differ sharply in the economic performance (the first and second columns of figures), and such differences persist when performance is measured (conceptually) as distance from the production possibility frontier defined over resource endowments and governmental form (third column of Table 7.1). In particular, holding constant production possibility frontiers (as given by resource endowments, etc.) *and* holding constant governmental form, there remain sharp differences in tribal economic performance. In Table 7.1, for example, the White Mountain Apache and the Pine Ridge (Oglala Lakota) Sioux have very similar strong-chief-executive/no-independent-judiciary IRA governments from the 1930s. Yet, the Apaches are performing more than 20 percentage points (in terms of employment) higher than would be predicted by neoclassical growth theory mediated by the New Institutionalism, and the Sioux are performing 20 percentage points more poorly than predicted (third column, Table 7.1).

In previous research, we have hypothesized that such differences arise as a result of mismatches between indigenous tribal sociopolitical norms regarding the location, scope, source, and structure of political authority, on the one hand, and the (imposed) formal institutions of tribal government, on the other (Cornell and Kalt, 1991, 1995). It is relatively easy to document the immediate (commonly in the second half of the 1800s) pre-reservation governmental systems of a number of tribes. As self-governing societies that had passed the test of environmental adoption to that point in time, such systems were embedded in the indigenous, diverse cultures of tribes. In some cases, the basic structure of a tribe's contemporary government accords well with the historic structure of that tribe's government; in other cases, the mismatch is stark. Thus, for example, the quite successful Cochiti Pueblo has never given up its traditional theocracy, has no written constitution, and operates a highly productive tourism and retirement home economy; Cochiti shows a "match" in Table 7.1 (Cornell and Kalt, 1996). On the other hand, the current Crow government of undifferentiated athenian democracy bears little or no resemblance to the hierarchical and two-branch governmental structure of pre-reservation Crow society; Crow is a "no match."

Applying pseudo-regression Boolean procedures to the sample of twelve tribes for which data on current and prior governmental systems are obtainable and which are shown in Table 7.1 permits testing as to whether a "match" between the current governmental system and the indigenous sociopolitical culture adds significantly to our ability to explain and predict the relative economic performance of tribes. As we report in Cornell and Kalt (1991), the results are very interesting. Our tests indicate that economic success (defined either as the ability to sustain growth in the present period of self-determination, or as the ability to simply sustain more than a grants and transfers economy) is undergirded by a set of jointly necessary and sufficient conditions. Economic success requires (1) the willingness to specialize and engage in trade with the broader off-reservation economy; (2) a non-trivial stock of at least one resource (e.g. human capital, natural resources); (3) a formal governmental structure that provides some mechanism of confining the government to the third-party enforcer role;[9] and (4) a match between indigenous cultural norms governing political affairs and the present formal governmental institutions.[10]

In Cornell and Kalt (1995), we show that a detailed dissection of Apache and Sioux societies reveals that the pre-reservation Apache produced notably hierarchical governing structures with authority (including legislative and judicial) centered in single, charismatic chieftains. Among the Oglala (Sioux), on the other hand, single autocratic chieftains were seldom created, and executive functions were performed by multiple individuals selected, parliamentary style, by a sitting legislature. In a sense, it appears that the White Mountain Apaches got "lucky." The IRA constitution, with its directly elected chief executive and absence of an independent judiciary, which was essentially imposed on both White Mountain and Pine Ridge, "matched" the Apaches' indigenous norms of political legitimacy relatively closely. As shown in Table 7.1, the Apaches have begun to prosper in the era of self-determination, while the Pine Ridge reservation remains desperately poor. In fact, the mismatch of formal governmental institutions and cultural norms of political legitimacy appears to be a recipe for defection and the breakdown of cooperation in the extreme: Pine Ridge tribal government is extremely unstable, with only one tribal president being reelected to the office's two-year term since elections began in 1937; and the single reelected individual emerged as the faction leader favored by US federal officials during the armed Wounded Knee civil war in 1973.

Summary

In short, the evidence derived from contemporary American Indian reservations is supportive of the conclusions that: (1) economic and social success require "getting institutions right" in the way that the preceding section implies; (2) formal institutions of social control and organization are shared public goods for which no meta-enforcer exists to shut down defections and free riding; and (3) successful formal institutions of governance are founded upon on informal, shared systems of coordinating norms and conventions that we can call a social contract. Having set forth evidence that seems to support the logical deductions (as discussed in the preceding section) that lead to the existence of a social contract as the glue of society in an otherwise Hobbesian world, the question of how this contract "works" – its genesis and evolution – remains. To this point, we have said nothing of particular force that would explain how the social contract comes about and how it operates.

CULTURAL NORMS AND NETWORKS OF SOCIALLY CONSTRUCTED RATIONAL INDIVIDUALS

The American Indian cases exhibit a number of attributes that appear to be more generally applicable to the evolution of societies. Beyond the mere existence of a social contract that supports and sustains the viability of effective institutions of social control and organization, the evidence from Indian Country indicates a great deal of diversity in institutional form and economic development strategies. From the theocracy of Cochiti to the autocracy of White Mountain Apache to the parliamentary democracy with a strong judiciary at Flathead, a variety of structures and strategies are succeeding. If there is a process of equilibrating homogenization going on, it is not yet evident. Diversity seems to pervade culture and institutions. Moreover, the historical cultural roots of conventions and norms of political legitimacy that underlie both cases of success (as at White Mountain) and failure (as at Pine Ridge) appear to be quite durable.[11]

These generalizations suggest the questions that a theory of the social contract ought to be able to address. How does the process of generating and sustaining the coordinating conventions and norms of a society – the social contract (Binmore, 1994) – work? What makes agreement, for example, on the propriety and authority of a strong chief executive less susceptible to defection among the White Mountain Apache than among the Pine Ridge Sioux? What makes it possible for a group of senior males at Cochiti, peacefully and with authority, to remove a rent-seeking theocrat, who, in turn, can have the authority to appoint all tribal officials and direct overall resource allocation so long as he stays away from rent seeking (Cornell and Kalt, 1996)? Why are at least some shared conventions and norms so durable? What is the source of evident diversity in social contracts and the formal institutions of social control that they apparently support? Under what conditions do conventions and norms change?

To get at questions of the foregoing type, we propose a model which consider the following points:

1 *Rationality*: Individual human beings are self-interestedly rational (at least in the presence of sufficient information), seeking to make themselves as well off as possible given their tastes and resource constraints.

The selfishness hypothesis is, perhaps, the most readily established link between biology and choosing behavior; its fitness value is undeniable. Indeed, a great deal of research has gone into the question of whether there is any room at all for altruism or some form of other-regardingness in human behavior (Wilson, 1978; Becker, 1976). It seems fair to summarize this research as indicating that instrumental altruism or other-regardingness can be one equilibrium outcome of evolutionary processes, where "instrumental" refers to the concept that own well-being may be set aside when assisting the well-being of others capable of replicating and propagating one's own traits (e.g. in genetic kin) is sufficiently enhanced (Becker, 1976; Pollock, 1991a, 1991b).

That human beings are calculating, reasoning entities is self-evident (to be Cartesian about the matter). This conclusion is not altered by the fact that this trait is grounded in physiological mechanisms that may or may not make human rationality strictly logical (Barkow *et al.*, 1992). In fact, rationality may be limited by both genetic hard-wiring (restricting the amount of information that can be processed, if nothing else) and pervasive uncertainty. As Heiner (1990), Denzau and North (1993), and others demonstrate, the problem of choice in such circumstances makes shorthand rules and conventions, imperfectly matched to reality at any point, productive in the effort to promote self-interest. Of particular relevance here, these authors also demonstrate that such "imperfect choice" (in Heiner's terms) generates diversity in decision rules, and this is a source of durable diversity within evolutionary systems that deprives such systems of optimality properties.

2 *Hard-wired social sentiments*: Individuals are hard-wired by genetic evolu-
tion with capacities for specific tastes. As a social animal, among these capacities are the capacities for *social* sentiments. These may include, with accompanying neurophysiological effects in the brain, emotional affects such as guilt, belonging/loneliness, self-righteousness, and sympathy. Because human beings are social animals, social sentiments are triggerable by messages sent and received in interaction with other human beings.

While there is controversy among evolutionary biologists over the extent to which humans are hard-wired by evolution to behave in cooperative (and especially altruistic) ways, there is little controversy that we are hard-wired to be sociable. In fact, researchers studying the brain and intelligence report strong evidence that even the logical structure of the brain is constructed to acquire information and solve problems of social coordination. Barkow *et al.* (1992) and Cosmides and Tooby (1989), for example, find a mental mechanism apparently functioning to monitor and detect defectors in potentially

cooperative settings. Even if it takes linguistic construction to label the sensation of mental activity accompanying mental functioning of this type as a social sentiment or emotion (Binmore, 1994), the existence of inter-personal triggering mechanisms labeled isolation and loneliness, sympathy, guilt, and so on seems compelling from this and other research.

Whether or not these emotional capacities have evolved for the purpose of solving interpersonal coordination problems (per Frank, 1988) may be debated, but the biological basis for such social sentiments in humans seems conclusive (see also Durham, 1991; Hirshleifer, 1980). Cosmides, Tooby, and others at the forefront of evolutionary psychology, in fact, see the familiar economic concepts that specialization is productive and that specialization requires coordination as the keys to the process of environmental selection over human fitness – what has made the human animal so evolutionarily successful is the notable ability to solve the problems of coordination and cooperation (Allman, 1994). Their experiments demonstrate that taking a given set of problems with identical logical structures, human reasoning capability increases dramatically when the problems are posed as the task of detecting defectors within a group seeking a shared cooperative solution. Cosmides concludes:

> Many of the most important problems our ancient ancestors had to face were social. They needed to know how to cooperate, how to respond to threats, how to participate in coalitions, how to respond to sexual infidelity, and so on. The result is that the human mind contains a number of specific mechanisms that were specially designed by evolu-tion for processing information about the social world. One of these mechanisms is a "cheater detector."
>
> (Allman, 1994: 39–40)

3 *Social construction of specific tastes*: The capacities for social sentiments are given specific ideational content by processes of acculturation. These processes attach specific tastes to the hard-wired capacities for social sentiments.

While it seems incontrovertible that there is a biological basis (if not an evolutionary explanation) for social sentiments such as affection, loneliness, guilt, and the like (see above, as well as Fisher, 1992), the range of specific ideational constructs that attach themselves to what can be called "primary values" (Durham, 1991: 200–1) is astonishing. In one society, successful behavior leading to belonging and social inclusion may require eating one's fellows, while in another the same act is cause for the most extreme ostracism. From gambling to abortion, from individual accumulation of wealth to inviolate obligations toward the less fortunate, the specific tastes that fill up the human capacities for social sentiments seem virtually unbounded (except by the biologically unsustainable). The reason for the wide range of feasible tastes may have been identified by Becker (1962): there is no crisp invisible hand mechanism for weeding out more or less optimal tastes; indeed, the economic concept of tastes contains no criteria for choosing over specific tastes.

The huge range of specific tastes that humans attach to the social sentiments belies a genetic explanation for those tastes. A more cogent explanation lies in the workings of the cultural environment in which individuals grow up and function. Social interaction is the key to acculturation, the process by which social sentiments take specific ideational form. The conceptual information that, once shared, constitutes culture is communicated between individuals in what we call cultural messages. These messages may take a variety of forms, may or may not be explicit, may be targeted or broadcast, and may or may not be intentionally sent. The mechanisms of cultural transmission or acquisition vary widely, from imitation to direct instruction, conditioned upon the individual's stage of cognitive development (Denzau and North, 1993). The result at the individual level is the socially constructed person.

The socially constructed rational individual is in no way inconsistent with economic conceptions of the individual, since the economic approach takes the individual to be represented by the bundle of tastes that are brought to choice contexts. Economic models do not care directly about the process by which the chooser acquired his or her tastes. Of course, economics *qua* economics is uncomfortable with worrying itself about the origins of tastes. The combination of the first three propositions set forth here, however, yields tastes over dimensions of social interaction that are analytically no different, for purposes of economic reasoning, from the other tastes that economists assume exist when, for example, investigating demand behavior. We can analogize to a taste for, say, chocolate candy. Arguably, the energy payoff to sugars has manifested itself as a genetic basis for the human attraction to what we label linguistically as "sweet." Much like the social construction of the specific tastes that trigger the social sentiments, a process of acculturation fills up the capacity for pleasurable responses to "sweet" with specific attributes – chocolate candy in one culture, and a multiplicity of alternatives in other cultures (Douglas and Isherwood, 1979).

Whatever the mechanism involved, cultural transmission is not the same as precise replication. Messages may be ambiguous, and reception is affected by the preexisting conceptions and capacities of receivers. Furthermore, transmission is not simply a matter of adoption. Messages move in two directions; senders are also receivers and vice versa. Conceptual information is not only transmitted through communication, but is transformed through debate and analysis as individuals exchange messages and, in effect, reason with themselves and each other (Douglas, 1992). The implied "mutation" in cultural messages is a source of variation in cultural conventions that societies throw up for potential adoption or rejection by the environments they face.

4 *Culture as positive and normative conventions*: Culture consists of shared conceptual, or "ideational," information that in fact or potentially guides behavior by providing (1) positive descriptions of the individual's context, identity, constraints, and opportunities for action, and (2) normative rules for action.

The process of acculturation or social learning described above provides individuals with both positive and normative constructs. Across the positive dimension, individuals acquire mental models of how the world is, and of how to negotiate effectively within it (Swidler, 1986). Research indicates, for example, that the perception of colors and the ability of individuals to work with them is dependent on the linguistic cultural repertoire acquired by individuals, notwithstanding common genetic capacities to perceive color (Durham, 1991). Closer to the topics at hand, Douglas and Wildavsky (1982; and seconded by many others) argue convincingly that perceptions of risk that form part of individuals' representations of their opportunity sets are socially constructed. As they relate to issues of institutional design for political affairs among people, cultural conventions are inputs to the cognitive definition of the boundaries of the feasible set of social institutions; the concept of a hierarchical theocracy may seem wholly functional to one society, and inconceivable to another.

As normative information, cultural conventions include conceptions of the desirable (ends or wants statements) and norms (should statements). Normative cultural conventions provide definitions of the proper, the fair, the just, and the normal. In so doing, they serve as the substance of the tastes that fill up the capacities for social sentiments. They provide the cultural messages by which responses of guilt, self-righteousness, morality, and the like are communicated within society. In so doing, normative cultural conventions (potentially) provide mechanisms by which defectors may be punished (i.e. through the triggering of appropriate sentiments in potentially free-riding individuals).

5 *Individuals as nodes in a network*: Individuals socially constructed in this way constitute sending and receiving nodes in networks of associated individuals. Interactions with others trigger the emotional hard-wiring that causes a message with cultural content to be sent or received by the nodal individual.

While the goal here is to understand the genesis and evolution of a shared social phenomenon – the social contract – methodologic individualism remains at the heart of the analysis. Individuals reason, respond, make choices, cooperate, and defect. The social contracts that might emerge from their doing these things as social animals living in interaction with other individuals arise as the result of the individuals' behavior. Conceiving of individuals as nodes in a network respects methodologic individualism while recognizing

132

that humans really are connected to each other in society. This connection arises, at least in part, because we have the ability to affect each other. We send affective messages to each other. In part, we do this with offers of material payoff through exchange or coercion. But we also "say" things to each other – linguistically, symbolically, attitudinally, representationally (Fisher, 1992). We threaten, cajole, sanction, praise, debate, admonish, encourage, etc. – and thereby trigger the social sentiments. We do this within a social context in which each pairwise sender and receiver are participants in a network operating according to shared conventions of meaning and process.

Interestingly, Ostrom (1994) reports that, in her experiments on the emergence of cooperation in tragedy-of-the-commons games, cooperation is very hard to achieve at all in the absence of communication among players. When the opportunity for linguistic communication (as messages within the computer network of the experimental game) is opened up, however, efficiency-enhancing cooperation is sharply increased, and this is achieved by the exchange of moral sanctions against defectors that take the form of simple attacks: "You scumbag."[12]

6 *Cultural conventions as public goods*: The set of cultural conventions that come to be shared and sent as messages over a social network, along with the conventions for communication that allow a network to operate, constitute shared public goods and, together, make up the social contract.

Coordinating cultural conventions that propagate and replicate within a society are collective goods in the classic Samuelsonian sense. Whether they produce "goods" by productively solving problems of cooperation, or "bads" by destroying prospective cooperative solutions, the results are shared by the members of the network. If our network can sustain a norm, for example, which constrains rent seeking by political leaders, we may be able to sustain formal institutions that provide *third*-party enforcement services; we will share in the raising (other things equal) of our material well-being. At least in the pre- or extra-constitutional setting, cultural conventions are non-excludable; and to the extent that every member of society grows up in an acculturating environment, no matter what formal and informal institutions exist, cultural conventions of the type set forth in Proposition 4 above are inherently non-excludable. As the next proposition argues, the behavioral mechanism underlying the production of cultural conventions as public goods is the equivalent of a system of private Olsonian side payments.

7 *Node participation as a private good*: The sending and receiving of cultural messages is economically experienced as a private good by the nodal individual, as the sending or receiving of a message triggers pleasurable or unpleasurable hard-wired feedback to the extent affected tastes are satisfied or contradicted.

Social interaction through networks is the route to the triggering of the social sentiments. Whatever the physiological manifestations of such triggering, they are experienced as private goods and bads (in the Samuelsonian collective/private sense) by affected individuals. As such, the triggering of the social sentiments as cultural messages on the network operates on socially constructed specific tastes as Olsonian side payments. These can hold individuals in the public goods production process of message replication and transmission that network participation entails. In extremely dysfunctional societies, the net of increments and decrements to privately experienced well-being may be negative (in the expected present value sense), and individuals may then exit a network by migrating out. When this is a widespread response, networks break down as coordinating mechanisms and cease to survive. Successful (or "fit") networks, on the other hand, have the property that they sustain shared cultural conventions (social contracts) that hold individuals as nodes.[13]

The triggering of privately experienced responses to actual or potential acts of defection or cooperation in social interaction may occur as result of actual communication over the network, as when a receiver receives normative messages ("You scumbag") or positive messages ("You're wrong"), or a sender, A, receives such normative or positive messages from another sender, C, upon A's delivery of messages to a receiver, B.[14] Triggering may also arise as the consequence of the apparently hard-wired human capacity for "internalization" so much studied by developmental and child psychologists (see also Elster, 1989). As a learning and reasoning entity, humans can anticipate what kinds of messages their actions in a particular context might trigger, and such anticipation or "imagination" is sufficient to trigger emotional responses in the individual. In addition, it may be that the entity is hard-wired with logical capacities for detecting contradictions between prospective actions and identity-creating conceptions of the positive and normative dimensions of "self" – with contradictions triggering internally felt responses of their own (Cancian, 1975).

A stylized illustration may help here. The relatively successful Apaches discussed above are somewhat surprising in their attitudes toward higher education. Relative to a number of other, less successful tribes, there appears to be little or negative cultural support for higher education. The Apaches show rates of educational attainment that are well below national Indian averages, while tribes such as the Crow show the opposite. Consider this representation of a network communication story for the Apache case: Despite the fact that niece Jane is the best student at the local high school, with all sorts of offers for minority scholarships to college, Uncle John sends her the message that she will not be a good Apache and may be shunned in the future if she is so uppity as to go to college. This interaction takes the following notional form: Actor A (Jane) potentially violates cultural norm N1 (good Apaches shouldn't go off to college). This is consumed as a private good by Actor B (John), taking the form of internalized self-righteousness upon B's sending A the message of ostracism and guilt in consonance with Apache conventions. Actor A consumes this message as a subtraction to her private well-being as the message triggers the social sentiments attached to guilt and ostracization; this raises the cost of going to college and tends to maintain Apache coordination around the issue of out-migration for purposes of education. Apache Actors C, D, . . . send their own supportive messages to Actor B for being a good Apache for reasons that mirror B's. The result is a network of reinforcing communication, held together by the privately rational behavior of each socially constructed individual.

8 *Sources of cultural variation*: Variations of cultural messages within the social contract arise from the acquisition by individuals of potential cultural conventions by imitation, trial and error, rational calculation, cultural drift, and perhaps changes in hard-wiring.

Within any process of cultural evolution, variation in cultural messages provides the raw material over which processes of environmental adoption or selection operate (Durham, 1991: 21–2). Culture, however, consists of ideational, rather than genetic, material – material that Dawkins (1976) has termed "memes" to distinguish it from "genes." This ideational material is acquired and communicated by individuals, and the corresponding sources of cultural variation include: imitation as a method of learning in a social animal, trial and error by individuals confronting uncertainty and imperfect information, rational calculation and observation in the Kantian and Popperian senses, cultural drift in which rarely used conventions fail to replicate, and (perhaps) slow processes of ongoing genetic variation affecting learning and mental capacity (Boyd and Richerson, 1985; Durham, 1991). As individuals learn in these ways, they impart variations in the messages that they send over the networks they participate in, creating the possibility of new messages that may propagate and replace old messages. If new messages take hold, the social contract changes.

9 *Mechanisms of environmental adoption*: Variations in the cultural messages that make up social contracts are successful, in the fitness sense, to the extent that they propagate through a network and are sustained in a process of environmental adoption. Success in these terms depends, in general, on compatibility with such factors as other norms, biological and physical constraints, rationality and preexisting knowledge, market and political environments.

As variation in cultural material is thrown up by the foregoing mechanisms, they are subjected to a process of environmental adoption or selection. The relative fitness value of alternative cultural conventions applicable to a given area of human behavior (such as the design of third-party enforcement mechanisms and court systems) will in general be determined by their assistance in promoting the reproductive effectiveness of the individuals that carry them and send them as messages on the network. In a social animal where specialization and exchange are productive, environmental adoption can select for *shared* cultural conventions that promote the success of groups of individuals (Pollock, 1991a, 1991b). As described above, this can occur when a particular cultural convention that promotes the well-being of others sufficiently enhances an individual's own prospects of replication and propagation (Becker, 1976; Pollock, 1991b).

This last finding is of particular relevance to the evolution of cultural conventions as we have described them here. Cultural conventions provide guides to both public (civic) and private behaviors. That is, cultural conventions not only arise as behavioral guides in coordination contexts such as the design and implementation of political institutions; they also arise as guides in private activities from the mundane (cooking food) to the complicated (predicting outcomes of career choices). In fact, many cultural conventions have mixed public/private attributes. A norm regarding the proper number of children to have seems to possess much more privateness than a norm regarding the independence of the judiciary. This leads to the potentially testable prediction that a norm of the former type is much more instrumental and subject to invisible hand and relative price effects. On the other hand, norms which are primarily collective in their payoffs might be predicted to be less subject to invisible hand forces that weed out inefficiency, particularly when highly collective norms are produced by tying them (per Propositions 1, 2, and 6 above) to the selective incentives of the perfectly rational private consumption of triggered social sentiments. Thus (from the Jane/John illustration above), Apache elders may be paying some private cost as their sanctions against higher education hold down future contributions from students who might return after college and contribute to tribal development. Compared to the immediate private payoffs from their production of sanctioning messages (upon receipt of pleasing internalized and external messages from others participating in the current norms of "proper Apacheness"), the future and necessarily shared improvements in wealth that more college education in the Tribe's capital stock might produce provide a relatively weak fitness test of current norms.

The description of the process of environmental adoption is fairly abstract to this point. What we have in mind is that the fitness of a particular cultural convention is dependent upon how it performs in the face of: biological and physical constraints (e.g. a norm urging a group to consider wholesale infanticide to be proper will not be replicable beyond one generation); imposition, invasion, or removal of nodes in the network (e.g. the killing off of indigenous leaders sanctioned as "supernodes" within the culture may change the balance of cultural variation within a path-dependent system and put the society on a different path as substitute messages take hold); consistency/inconsistency with rationality and preexisting knowledge among learning individuals (e.g.

a positive cultural convention promoting divine rights for rulers may be "unfit" as the new potential political convention is checked against other positive conventions in a culture that is already far down the path of secularism in its religious affairs); and market and political environments (e.g. a cultural norm that urges resistance to trade and interaction with outsiders in an increasingly internationalized economy and political system is likely to be relatively unfit, even if such a norm had been adopted in a prior setting before the market and political environment changed).

This process of environmental adoption suggests a high degree of path dependence and serendipitous predisposition in social contract options. For instance, picking up the example above of divine rights of rulers, the survivability of such a convention at Cochiti (where theocracy has realized a surprisingly unbroken history) in no way suggests that a theocracy would work at Flathead (where an amalgam of historically unaffiliated tribes were forced onto a common reservation – see Cornell and Kalt, 1996). Similarly, serendipitously preadaptive paths to fitness are suggested by the White Mountain Apache case, where sustainable conventions supporting autocratic central chieftains in the pre-reservation environment turned out to be relatively well adapted when the environment changed and the US government "invaded" and imposed its IRA constitutions. In other words, the pairwise comparison of the histories of White Mountain Apache and Pine Ridge Sioux described in the preceding section provides a test of at least this mechanism of the theory of cultural evolution and environmental adoption set forth here.

CONCLUSION

The model of cultural evolution developed here seems to be ripe with additional testable implications. At this stage, however, we would say only that the model is consistent with key characteristics of the evidence on institutional forms and economic development in Indian Country. Specifically, the model describes cultural conventions as shared public goods transmitted in a network of socially constructed rational individuals interested in the private payoffs from social participation as nodes in that network. This is consistent with the evident durability of highly public conventions regarding the design, implementation, and maintenance of the institutions of governance. The path dependence of evolutionary models of the type developed here is likewise consistent with the durability of the diversity of social contracts and attendant formal institutions in Indian Country.

NOTES

1 Among the two of us, Kalt is a 1980 UCLA Ph.D., in economics, with an unpayable debt to Armen Alchian for his teaching, advising, and mentoring. As

a University of Chicago trained sociologist, Cornell is not so fortunate, but has been privileged to spend several hundred man-days in the field, mostly on long drives through rural America, over the last seven years, listening to and challenging the methodologic speculations of one of Alchian's students.

2 Consider, for example, the explanatory fate of neoclassical economics in the face of the following (somewhat) stylized facts. Holding constant the effects of price, income, expected criminal penalties, and other monetizable determinants of demand, per capita consumption of cocaine in New York City is much, much higher than in Salt Lake City, Utah. Heuristically, the demand curve for cocaine in Salt Lake City lies much closer to the price axis than the demand curve of the representative individual in New York. Neoclassical theory is relatively powerful in predicting that both cities' demand schedules are negatively sloped, but quite poor at explaining the positions of the respective schedules. For many questions (such as how much consumption will be reduced if supply interdiction by law enforcement authorities succeeds in raising price), the neoclassical perspective may indeed be potent. Yet, for other questions that are arguably much more interesting questions (such as why the cocaine business is so much bigger in New York City than in Salt Lake City), neoclassical analysis is of little help. It seems obvious that religious beliefs in the two populations have more than a little to do with the phenomenon, and the neoclassical approach might find ways to describe the effects of religion in choice theoretic terms – with reference to the relative size of the penalties for illicit drug use that participation in a particular religion (e.g. Mormon) might entail. Going down this path, however, is largely a linguistic exercise in saving the discipline. It begs the question of why the constraints of religion that are holding back the choices of residents of Salt Lake City took hold and persist. The Stigler and Becker (1977) offer to explain present heterogeneity of tastes (i.e. the positions of demand schedules) by reference to past differences in experience with the good at hand in a population of originally homogeneous individuals offers no particular assistance. It means that particular phenomena of interest, such as why cocaine use is so much higher in New York City than in Salt Lake City, are extremely path dependent and, thereby, largely immune from economic analysis. In fact, such path dependence suggests the need to turn to modes of explanation that worry themselves with matters such as why particular traits successively disperse themselves throughout a population, while other traits remain confined or are eliminated. The very language here suggests the usefulness of evolutionary models.

3 The "messiness" referred to here gives rise to what Alchian suggests in his analysis. Namely, processes of "environmental adoption" (read *evolution*) provide room for survival of multiple phenotypes (e.g. types of firms in a given industry) within a given system at any point in time and over time, and no individual type can be said meaningfully to be optimally adapted (particularly when dynamic environmental change makes success in subsequent periods dependent on present-period traits).

4 As made clearer below, we are using "extra-choice" here to capture the idea that the process of embeddedness is not logically representable in the terms of standard neoclassical economic choice theory, but is, instead, a process of learning and acculturation.

5 Alchian's insights are echoed by Becker's (1962) demonstration that the central tools of economic reasoning (including the laws of demand) can be derived through a process equivalent to Alchian's "environmental adoption" without reference to the (within field) untestable axioms of neoclassical utility theory.

6 A word of caution and perspective: the use of terms such as evolution, cultural norms, customs, etc., in a study that focuses on "tribes" might conjure up the image of a long tradition of anthropological research which concerns itself with

preindustrial peoples. Our research is not in that tradition. "American Indian" and "Tribe" are the self-designations of American Indian polities in the US (in Canada, both terms are politically incorrect). Images of primitivism, however, have no relevance to the current state of reservation life. In terms of daily *activity* American Indian reservations are modern societies, with factories, schools, bureaucracies, businesses, social clubs, and so on. As with other societies (e.g. many holidays and customs in the US trace back to primitive European practices), activity is conducted within the context of highly path-dependent custom and convention with deep historical roots. What perhaps does distinguish such contextual settings in Indian Country is that the particular military, social, and political histories of most tribes bring issues of temporal continuity in tribal cultures to center stage in discussion and debate.

7 While the boundaries between tribal sovereignty and federal and state authority are contentious and somewhat unstable, the key elements are that tribes are subject to US civil rights laws (including the Bill of Rights), tribes and tribally owned enterprises (but not private Indian enterprises or individuals) are free of non-tribal taxation, state governments have very little regulatory authority on reservations, and congressionally mandated federal regulatory authority is often subject to lax enforcement or exemption. See Cornell and Kalt (1994).

8 The willingness of the Apaches to "marketize" their forest-based resources prompted us to write a section of a recent study entitled "Was Ronald Coase an Apache?" Based on analysis of the economic and ecological impact of Apache management (e.g. tribal members would have to pay the going market price of $15,000–$20,000 to hunt the Tribe's trophy elk), the answer, heuristically, is "yes" (Cornell and Kalt, 1994).

9 Note that there is huge diversity in this regard. The Flathead reservation has opted for a highly developed US-style judicial system, including participation in a third-party intertribal appeals court. At Cochiti, with its traditional theocracy, when asked what prevents the extremely powerful theocrat from moving from third-party to interested party, senior tribal leaders report (paraphrasing): "He wouldn't do that, but if we did catch him with his fingers in the pie, a group of the senior males would get together and declare him senile, thereby removing him from power." In fact, this group of senior males is made up of appointed War Captains, which the traditional theocracy at Cochiti continues to vest with impeachment powers. See Cornell and Kalt (1996).

10 Note that these conditions do not imply a naive view that tribes could all perform well if they could just go back to their traditional ways. For example, a tribe with a traditional government of the athenian form would not be expected to succeed in the environment of the 1990s. A tribe that may have survived without significant "international" trade in a pre-reservation period could not expect to succeed with that strategy now. Furthermore, it is reasonable to conclude that, in the course of things and absent federal imposition, tribes' pre-reservation governmental forms would have continued to evolve, albeit in diverse and path-dependent ways.

11 Our general finding that cultural norms from the pre-reservation period of the second half of the 1800s are durable and affect performance of tribal institutions in the second half of the 1900s is consistent with the durability found by Putnam (1992) for Italian villages under central-government-mandated changes in institutional form, and the durability described (from another viewpoint) by Davidson (1992) for the case of recently decolonized African countries.

12 As reported by Elinor Ostrom (1994) "Frontiers of Research into the Design of Institutions," Seminar in Political Economy, John F. Kennedy School of Government, Harvard University, April.

13 It is interesting to speculate on the evolutionary origins of the apparent universality of denying sociality as a method of punishment for extreme "defectors" (deviants and criminals). From Sioux banishments (Hassrick, 1964) to contemporary systems of solitary confinement and imprisonment, exile is punishment to a social animal.

14 On senders' benefits, see Coleman (1990).

REFERENCES

Alchian, Armen A. (1950) "Uncertainty, Evolution, and Economic Theory," *Journal of Political Economy* 58: 211–21.
Allman, William F. (1994) *The Stone Age Present*. New York: Simon and Schuster.
Aumann, R. (1976) "Agreeing to Disagree," *The Annals of Statistics* 4: 1236–9.
Axelrod, Robert M. (1984) *The Evolution of Cooperation*. New York: Basic Books.
Barkow, Jerome, Leda Cosmides, and John Tooby (eds) (1992) *The Adapted Mind*. New York: Oxford University Press.
Bates, Robert (1988) "Contra Contractarianism: Some Reflections on the New Institutionalism," *Politics and Society* 16: 387–401.
Becker, Gary S. (1962) "Irrational Behavior and Economic Theory," *Journal of Political Economy* 70: 1–13.
—— (1976) "Altruism, Egoism, and Genetic Fitness: Economics and Sociobiology," *Journal of Economic Literature* 16: 817–26.
Binmore, Ken (1994) *Game Theory and the Social Contract: Playing Fair*. Cambridge, MA: MIT Press.
Boyd, Robert and Peter J. Richerson (1985) *Culture and the Evolutionary Process*. Chicago: University of Chicago Press.
Buchanan, James M. (1972) "Before Public Choice," in *Explorations in the Theory of Anarchy*, ed. G. Tullock. Blacksburg, VA: Virginia Polytechnic Institute.
Bureau of Indian Affairs, US Department of the Interior. *Indian Service Population and Labor Force Estimates*, various issues.
Cancian, Francesca M. (1975) *What Are Norms? A Study of Beliefs and Action in a Maya Community*. Cambridge: Cambridge University Press.
Coleman, James S. (1990) *Foundations of Social Theory*. Cambridge, MA: Belknap Press of Harvard University Press.
Cornell, Stephen and Joseph P. Kalt (1991) "Where's the Glue?: Institutional Bases of American Indian Economic Development," Harvard Project on American Indian Economic Development, Kennedy School of Government, Harvard University.
—— (1992a) "Culture and Institutions as Public Goods: American Indian Economic Development as a Problem of Collective Action," in *Property Rights and Indian Economies*, ed. Terry L. Anderson. Lanham: Rowman and Littlefield.
—— (1992b) "Reloading the Dice: Improving the Chances for Economic Development on American Indian Reservations," in *What Can Tribes Do? Strategies and Institutions in American Indian Economic Development*. Los Angeles: University of California at Los Angeles.
—— (1994) "The Redefinition of Property Rights in American Indian Reservations: A Comparative Analysis of Native American Economic Development," in *American Indian Policy and Economic Development*, ed. Lyman H. Legters and Fremont J. Lyden. Westport, CT: Greenwood Press.
—— (1995) "Where Does Economic Development Really Come From? Constitutional Rule Among the Contemporary Sioux and Apache," *Economic Inquiry* 33: 402–26.

—— (1996) "Successful Economic Development and Heterogeneity of Governmental Form on American Indian Reservations," in *Getting Good Government: Capacity Building in the Public Sectors of Developing Countries*, ed. Merilee S. Grindle. Cambridge, MA: Harvard Institute for International Development.

Cosmides, Leda and John Tooby (1989) "Evolutionary Psychology and the Generation of Culture, Part II: A Computational Theory of Social Exchange," *Ethology and Sociobiology* 10.

Davidson, Basil (1992) *The Black Man's Burden: Africa and the Curse of the Nation-State*. New York: New York Times Books.

Dawkins, Richard (1976) *The Selfish Gene*. New York: Oxford University Press.

Demsetz, Harold (1970) "The Private Production of Public Goods," *Journal of Law and Economics* 13: 295–306.

Denzau, Arthur T. and Douglass C. North (1993) "Shared Mental Models: Ideologies and Institutions," Center for the Study of Political Economy, St Louis (unpublished), p. 3.

Douglas, Mary (1992) *Risk and Blame: Essays in Cultural Theory*. New York: Routledge.

Douglas, Mary and Baron C. Isherwood (1979) *The World of Goods*. New York: Basic Books.

Douglas, Mary and Aaron Wildavsky (1982) *Risk and Culture*. Los Angeles: University of California Press.

Durham, William H. (1991) *Coevolution: Genes, Culture and Human Diversity*. Palo Alto, CA: Stanford University Press.

Elster, Jon (1989) *The Cement of Society: A Study of Social Order*. Cambridge: Cambridge University Press.

Fisher, Helen E. (1992) *The Anatomy of Love*. New York: Norton.

Frank, Robert H. (1988) *Passions Within Reason*. New York: Norton.

Hassrick, Royal B. (1964) *The Sioux: Life and Customs of a Warrior Society*. Norman, OK: University of Oklahoma Press.

Heiner, Ronald A. (1990) "Rule-Governed Behavior in Evolution and Human Society," *Constitutional Political Economy* I: 19–46.

Hirshleifer, Jack (1976) "Comment," *Journal of Law and Economics* 19: 241–4.

—— (1980) "Privacy: Its Origin, Function, and Future," *The Journal of Legal Studies* 9: 649–64.

Maynard Smith, J. (1982) *Evolution and the Theory of Games*. Cambridge: Cambridge University Press.

North, Douglass C. (1981) *Structure and Change in Economic History*. New York: Norton.

—— (1988) "Ideology and Political/Economic Institutions," *Cato Journal* 8: 15–28.

—— (1990) *Institutions, Institutional Change and Economic Performance*. Cambridge: Cambridge University Press.

Olson, Mancur (1982) *The Rise and Decline of Nations*. New Haven, CT: Yale University Press.

Ostrom, Elinor (1990) *Governing the Commons*. Cambridge: Cambridge University Press.

—— (1992) *Crafting Institutions for Self-Governing Irrigation Systems*. San Francisco: ICS Press.

—— (1994) "Neither Markets Nor States: Linking Transformation Processes in Collective Action Arenas," in *The Handbook of Public Choice*, ed. Dennis C. Mueller. New York: Basil Blackwell.

Pollock, Gregory B. (1991a) "Crossing Malthusian Boundaries: Evolutionary Stability in the Finite Repeated Prisoner's Dilemma," *Journal of Quantitative Anthropology* 3: 159–80.

—— (1991b) "Personal Fitness, Altruism, and the Ontology of Game Theory," *Journal of Quantitative Anthropology* 3: 65–81.

Putnam, Robert D. (1992) *Making Democracy Work: Civic Traditions in Modern Italy.* Princeton, NJ: Princeton University Press.

Stigler, George and Gary S. Becker (1977) "De Gustibus Non Est Disputandum," *American Economic Review* 67: 76–90.

Swidler, Anne (1986) "Culture in Action: Symbols and Strategies," *American Sociological Review* 51: 273–86.

Tullock, Gordon (1993) "Public Choice: What I Hope for the Next Twenty-Five Years," *Public Choice* 77: 9–16.

Wilson, Edward O. (1975) *Sociobiology: The New Synthesis.* Cambridge, MA: Harvard University Press.

—— (1978) *On Human Nature.* Cambridge, MA: Harvard University Press.

World Bank (1991) *World Development Report 1991: The Challenge of Development.* New York: Oxford University Press.

—— (1994) *Adjustment in Africa: Reform, Results, and the Road Ahead.* New York: Oxford University Press.

8

ENVIRONMENTAL DEGRADATION UNDER EAST EUROPEAN STATE SOCIALISM

*Benjamin Zycher**

INTRODUCTION

The modern theory of property rights yields important and familiar implications for preservation of such environmental commons as air and water. The absence of enforceable property rights renders even land a "common" in this sense, since the benefits of actions taken or forgone in efforts to enhance the quality of the common resource are transformed into a public good, with an attendant free-rider problem.[1] The normative theory of public finance suggests efforts to provide such public goods collectively, but that traditional theory does not examine actual public sector behavior as driven by individual incentives in political markets.[2] For example, in a polity in which decisions on public spending between a pure public good and a pure private good are made with a simple majority decision rule, the majority coalition has net incentives to reduce spending on the public good and increase spending on such private goods as transfer payments to members of the majority. The static equilibrium[3] is achieved when two dollars of transfers have the same marginal value as one dollar of the public good to the members of the majority.

In short, the public good problem as it affects environmental quality in "capitalist" and "socialist" nations is the result of property rights defined and/or enforced "imperfectly."[4] To the extent that such rights, however measured, are more attenuated under socialism than capitalism, greater environmental degradation can be predicted under the former. This effect may be exacerbated if public officials in socialist systems cannot capture privately the benefits of environmental improvement to the degree available to their counterparts in capitalist economies.[5]

This traditional emphasis upon differences in property rights regimes as an explanation of environmental degradation under socialism, while important,

* Milken Institute for Job and Capital Formation; and Department of Economics, University of California, Los Angeles. The views expressed do not purport to represent those of these institutions or of any of their officers or sponsors.

143

cannot be viewed as the only explanation consistent with the evidence. For all the familiar reasons, per capita wealth under socialism is lower, *ceteris paribus*, than under capitalism; and environmental improvement seems to be a normal or superior good. Perhaps more subtle are the environmental effects of increased systemic demands under socialism for military services, and thus for the outputs of heavy industry in general and military industry in particular.[6] Such a mixture of reduced national wealth and enhanced output of heavy/military industry implies greater observed degradation of the commons, just as does the property rights model.

It is not the purpose of this chapter to disentangle these effects. Instead, the main goal here is to examine the limited and murky data on environmental degradation in Eastern Europe under socialism; the public discussion of this environmental degradation has been driven in the main by anecdotal evidence largely from the former Soviet Union. In part, this is due to the poor nature of the available data, but future efforts to explain the differing causes of East European environmental problems must be based on more systematic evidence. This chapter represents a preliminary attempt to gather such data. At the end, some brief hypotheses on socialism and military resource use are offered along with suggestions for further research effort.

ENVIRONMENTAL QUALITY IN EASTERN EUROPE

The ensuing discussion reports available data as of early and mid-1989 on environmental problems in the East European Warsaw Pact Northern Tier, that is, Czechoslovakia, the German Democratic Republic, and Poland. The available data for the other East European nations are extremely poor even by the standards of the region; and data for 1990 and later arguably do not apply to "socialism," although the lagged effects of the socialist systems obviously are important. These limitations, I believe, do not affect the central thrust of the discussion.

It is no secret that environmental pollution, particularly of air and water resources, is a serious problem in Eastern Europe. This reality is sharply at odds with socialist ideology, which maintained that environmental pollution is the result of the profit motive under capitalism.[7] Political and economic incentives for pollution control were weak, as the drive to fulfill production plans and to keep up with the West economically tended to reduce the priority of resource allocation for environmental protection. Accordingly, East European enforcement of environmental regulations was lax, and the fines imposed upon enterprises for violations typically were smaller than the cost of compliance.[8] Nonetheless, the problems became sufficiently severe in the 1980s that complaints and warnings in the official East European media became prominent,[9] and the regimes found it necessary to create official environmental groups in an attempt to preempt potential popular political opposition on this issue.[10] The success of the Greens in the former Federal

Republic of (West) Germany reinforced this political incentive in Eastern Europe. Puddington notes that the East European authorities viewed Western environmentalists with considerable wariness, a fact that indicates "the disruptive potential of ecological issues, at least as the Communist ruling elite sees things."[11]

Little consideration for environmental protection was evident in the East European central plans, as such protection, at least in the short run, was viewed as inconsistent with economic growth.[12] The low priority given environmental protection, along with the poor financial condition of the East European governments, resulted in small budgetary allocations for effluent reduction. While the cost of pollution control mandated by the US Clean Air and Clean Water Acts was about 1 percent of GNP in 1981,[13] Czech expenditure on environmental protection in 1984 was about 0.4 percent of domestic net material product (which is smaller than GNP because of the exclusion of services).[14] Polish spending was about 0.4 percent of "gross national income," while spending in the GDR was about DM 7 million for a comprehensive environmental program between 1971 and 1975. The subsequent five-year plans, however, apparently did not include separate environmental programs.[15] And, for obvious reasons, organized political pressure for environmental protection was far more difficult in Eastern Europe than in the West.

Systematic collection of data on the extent and effects of environmental pollution was not a feature of Eastern Europe under socialism, but the available evidence, while substantially qualitative, indicates that air and water pollution problems were (and are) severe in Czechoslovakia, the GDR, and Poland.[16] Czechoslovakia under socialism (and now) suffered from intense air pollution problems, resulting primarily from heavy use of high-sulfur domestic coal in industrial processes. Reliance on brown coal increased as supplies of Soviet oil were reduced. For example, of the 73.5 billion kWh of electricity generated in 1981, 64.1 billion kWh were produced by generating stations burning high-sulfur coal.[17] Accordingly, sulfur dioxide emissions in Czechoslovakia in the 1980s were roughly equal to those of the much larger FRG. The air pollution problem was (and is) particularly severe in the heavily industrialized areas of North Bohemia, and worsened steadily in the Czech lands throughout the 1980s. In the early 1960s, annual sulfur dioxide emissions were about 2.5 million tons annually, and grew to about 3 million tons by 1980. Kramer notes that emissions of all gaseous effluents grew by almost 60 percent between 1965 and 1978.[18] While not as severe as in the Czech lands, increasing sulfur dioxide emissions were a growing problem in parts of Slovakia in the 1980s.[19]

Various accounts in the Czech press indicated the magnitude of the costs imposed by the air pollution levels. Apart from increased corrosion of buildings and other structures, about 12 percent of arable land (about 1.2 million acres; 0.5 million hectares) and 1 million acres (0.4 million hectares) of timber were by the early 1980s damaged or destroyed by air pollution. Substantial human migration from North Bohemia was induced by the air pollution levels there, and approximately one-third of the population of the Czech lands are exposed permanently to air quality sufficiently poor as to constitute a serious health threat.[20]

Water pollution problems in Czechoslovakia were equally severe under the socialist regime. Official data indicated that of the 3.06 billion cubic meters of waste water produced by industrial and agricultural processes in 1981, only 0.94 billion cubic meters were subjected to waste treatment.[21] Official data show that some 70 percent of Czechoslovakia's waterways are "highly polluted," over a third of them no longer supply water fit for human consumption, and 5 percent do not support living organisms. As of 1979, about a third of the major waterways were too polluted even for industrial use. Nationally, some 4,340 miles (6,945 km) out of 15,500 miles (24,800 km) of major rivers were classified officially in the early 1980s as incapable of sustaining fish or as sustaining fish not fit for human consumption.[22] One government report noted that shortages of clean water have led to stringent limits on "the long range development of the Czech economy."[23] There is wide agreement that a major source of the problem is the inadequate level of treatment for waste water from industrial uses and sewers. Agricultural uses are important as well, although industrial water use was roughly ten times that in agriculture.[24]

Increasing official concern about environmental problems in Czechoslovakia led the central government to incorporate into the eighth five-year plan (1986–90) a series of steps designed to deal with pollution problems; apparently, there was official recognition of the limitations on economic growth caused by severe environmental problems. The steps in the five-year plan emphasized the installation of air and water purification systems, some of which were to have been imported. The cost of the program was estimated at 100 billion crowns (about $14.4 billion at the then-official exchange rate) through the year 2000, with 17 billion crowns (about $2.4 billion at the then-official exchange rate) to be spent during the eighth five-year plan. As with so many aspects of central planning, the ultimate fate of these plans, had the velvet revolution not intervened, is entirely uncertain.

The air pollution problem in the GDR may have exceeded that of Czechoslovakia. As with the Czechs (and Poland), the GDR adjusted to higher prices and reduced supplies of Soviet oil through substitution of increasing quantities of domestic brown coal for industrial use. Production of brown coal, at 258 million tons in 1980, was planned to grow to 300 million tons by 1990. As almost no desulfurization equipment had been installed in GDR factories, the GDR had the highest rate of sulfur dioxide emissions in Europe, at well over 30 tons per square kilometer in 1985, as compared with 14.5 tons for the FRG. Emissions of sulfur dioxide grew between 1980 and 1985 from 4.5 million tons annually to 5 million tons;

total sulfur dioxide emissions by the FRG in 1980 were 3 million tons. The intense air pollution resulted in significant forest deterioration along the border with the FRG and Czechoslovakia; over 432,000 acres (173,000 hectares) of forest in the Erzgebirge mountains died during the late 1970s and early through mid-1980s.[25]

The basic problem is familiar: the energy policy of the GDR was inconsistent with protection of environmental quality, and political incentives for measured economic growth were strong, as the ideological appeal of socialism no longer furthered the political support goals of the regime, if ever they did. Thus, increased production systematically had higher priority than protection of environmental quality. Although there were signs of increasing official concern about environmental degradation in the GDR before 1989, there is little evidence that plans were in development for consumption of substantial resources in efforts to alleviate the problem.[26]

Air pollution levels are severe in Poland as well. The industrial plants accounting for over two-thirds of industrial emissions are located in nineteen urban areas comprising about 18 percent of Poland's land but about half of its population. Accordingly, air pollution levels for decades have been particularly high in the leading industrial areas: Upper Silesia, the Legnitsa–Glog copper district, the Gdansk Bay region, and the Cracow region suffer from an "ecological disaster."[27] As with Czechoslovakia and the GDR, economic pressures induced substitution of coal for oil and of brown coal for low sulfur coal, which under the Jaruzelski regime was exported in increasing quantities to hard currency markets. Thus, it is not surprising that the fuels and power industries have been responsible for two-thirds of all industrial sulfur dioxide emissions, which in turn have accounted for two-thirds of all such emissions in Poland.

Environmental protection received low priority under the socialist regime. A survey in the early 1980s found that of the 1066 industrial plants that emitted about two-thirds of all atmospheric effluents, complete emission standards had been established for only 530. No standards had been set for 304 plants, and Kramer notes that treatment of industrial atmospheric emissions was "negligible."[28] Fulfillment of the production plans enjoyed far higher priority in Poland, particularly given the large hard currency debt.

By the mid-1980s about a third of Poland's main waterways were so polluted that they were unuseable. The problem was caused both by industrial effluents and by untreated or insufficiently treated sewage. The Polish Academy of Sciences study[29] noted that in 1981 4.7 billion cubic meters of sewage were produced in Poland, of which 44 percent received no treatment and another 36 percent was treated only for undissolved contaminants. More than half of the cities – including Warsaw and Lodz – do not have sewage treatment plants. Of the 3,650 major industrial plants that produced significant amounts of water effluents by the early 1980s, two-thirds disposed of their wastes without treatment.

These conditions resulted in deteriorating water quality in Poland. Between 1967 and 1977, the percentage of total river lengths classified in the highest quality category fell from 33 percent to 9.6 percent, while the lowest quality category rose from 22.8 percent to 33.1 percent. The Polish Academy of Sciences study offered a conservative (in their view) estimate of the cost of water pollution in Poland of 400 billion zloty (about $2.5 billion at the then-official exchange rate) annually. The Polish government announced a number of years ago a program to build and upgrade sewage treatment facilities in the Vistula River Basin, which was envisioned to cost 225 billion zloty (about $1.4 billion at then-official exchange rates) by 1995. The program was delayed repeatedly.

CONCLUSIONS

As noted above, differences in property rights regimes are an important source of environmental degradation under East European socialism. It is likely to be the case, however, that other factors contribute to this observed behavior as well. Reduced national wealth is likely to be one of these conditions. Foremost among them is the observed tendency of socialist (or Communist) systems toward greater militarization – that is, military resource use – than non-socialist systems, *ceteris paribus*. This systemic militarization yields an emphasis upon output by heavy/military industry, with attendant exacerbation of environmental degradation.[30]

Thus, an important task facing social scientists is the separation of these differing effects upon environmental degradation under socialism. Since the emphasis here has been on crude measurement of the environmental state of affairs under East European socialism, that research effort lies beyond the scope of this chapter.

NOTES

1 See J. Dales, *Pollution, Prices, and Property*, Toronto: University of Toronto Press, 1968, and Terry Anderson and Donald Leal, *Free Market Environmentalism*, Boulder, CO: Westview Press, 1991. See also Benjamin Zycher, "Market Allocation of the Commons," in *Protecting the Environment: A Free Market Strategy*, ed. Doug Bandow, Washington, DC: Heritage Foundation, 1986; Harold Demsetz, "Toward A Theory of Property Rights," *American Economic Review* May 1967; Harold Demsetz, "The Exchange and Enforcement of Property Rights," *Journal of Law and Economics* October 1964; and Harold Demsetz, "Some Aspects of Property Rights," *Journal of Law and Economics* October 1966.
2 See James M. Buchanan, *Demand and Supply of Public Goods*, Chicago: Rand McNally, 1968, chapters 7, 8, and 10; and James M. Buchanan, *Public Finance in Democratic Process*, Chapel Hill, NC: University of North Carolina, 1967, chapters 7 and 9. See also Geoffrey Brennan and James M. Buchanan, *The Power to Tax: Analytical Foundations of a Fiscal Constitution*, Cambridge: Cambridge University Press, 1980.

3 I ignore here the problem of non-stable majorities, or of side payments from the minority to a subset of the majority. Note that provision of such side payments in pursuit of majority status itself bears many characteristics of "publicness."

4 Let us not forget the crucial role of transaction costs. See Ronald Coase, "The Problem of Social Cost," *Journal of Law and Economics* October 1960.

5 Clearly, these benefits can be political or pecuniary. See Gordon Tullock, *Autocracy*, Boston: Kluwer, 1987, for a discussion of the similarities in incentives faced by "leaders" in democratic and undemocratic systems.

6 See Benjamin Zycher and Tad Daley, "Military Dimensions of Communist Systems," Rand Corporation R-3593-USDP, June 1988.

7 For a detailed discussion of the ideological relationship between environmental degradation and Marxism–Leninism, see Joan DeBardeleben, *The Environment and Marxism–Leninism: The Soviet and East European Experience*, Boulder, CO: Westview Press, 1985. Czech ideologists blamed ecological problems on "non-socialist individuals still surviving in the country," and argued that "the solution for ecological problems depends on the success of ideological work." See *Radio Free Europe (RFE) Situation Report* No. 8 (Czechoslovakia), May 13, 1985.

8 See Christine Zvosec, "Environmental Deterioration in Eastern Europe," *Survey* Winter 1984.

9 See Anna Zimaniova, "More Seriousness and Responsibility in Practice," *Bratislava Pravda* November 20, 1986. See also Arch Puddington, "East Bloc Ecology," *The American Spectator* March 1986.

10 An example of popular support for environmental issues was the Polish Ecology Club, which grew to over 20,000 members during the Solidarity period preceding the imposition of martial law in December 1981.

11 See Puddington, *supra*, n. 9, at 4.

12 There was a growing recognition within the East European governments in the 1980s that severe pollution problems can impose significant and explicit short run economic costs. Examples are worker absenteeism and general health problems among the population, and the cost of cleaning water used in various industrial processes. See, for example, the report of the Department of Chemistry and Environmental Engineering, Polish Academy of Sciences, *Chemical Pollution of the Environment in Poland*, translated for the US Environmental Protection Agency by SCITRAN, 1984, pp. 34–5.

13 See the US Environmental Protection Agency, *The Cost of Clean Air and Water*, Report To Congress, 1984. This estimate excludes costs due to other federal laws and regulations – in particular, the 1992 Clean Air Act Amendments – as well as costs due to state and local regulations, costs associated with voluntary actions, and economic (deadweight) losses caused by the regulatory approach.

14 See *RFE Situation Report* No. 8 (Czechoslovakia), May 13, 1985.

15 See *supra*, n. 12, at 24. See also B. V. Flow, *RFE Background Report* No. 164 (Eastern Europe), "The Environmental Crisis in the GDR," September 3, 1984.

16 The Polish government is in the process of creating a national monitoring system on the levels and effects of effluent levels. Kramer notes that the East European regimes were reluctant to publish data on environmental degradation, since such information would have proved embarrassing politically. See John M. Kramer, "The Environmental Crisis in Eastern Europe: The Price for Progress," *Slavic Review* Summer 1983.

17 See Frank Pohl, "Environmental Deterioration in Czechoslovakia," *RFE Background Report* No. 95 (Czechoslovakia), May 6, 1983.

18 See Kramer, *supra*, n. 16, at 206.

19 See "Pollution in Slovakia," *RFE Situation Report* No. 2 (Czechoslovakia), February 6, 1986.

20 See Joint Publications Research Service (JPRS), No. 79122, October 2, 1981, for a discussion of the costs caused by air pollution in Czechoslovakia.
21 See *RFE Situation Report* No. 22 (Czechoslovakia), December 10, 1982.
22 See *supra*, n. 17, at 6.
23 See JPRS, No. 73745, June 22, 1979.
24 See *supra*, n. 21, at 12.
25 See *supra*, n. 15, at 4. See also "East Germany: New Developments in Environmental Protection," *RFE Background Report* No. 81 (GDR), August 16, 1985.
26 The regime established in 1980 the Society for Nature and the Environment in an effort to defuse popular criticism of the pollution problem. The government began to participate in international conferences on environmental problems; in part because of a desire to do so, the regime no longer argued that environmental problems in a socialist state are "objectively impossible." And the GDR agreed with eighteen other nations to reduce sulfur dioxide emissions by 30 percent between 1980 and 1993. As the GDR exists no more, that objective in a certain sense has been achieved spectacularly.
27 See *supra*, n. 12, at 4.
28 See *supra*, n. 16, at 208.
29 See n. 12.
30 These pressures can be summarized as (1) a reduced social demand for military services under democracy because of the free-rider problem affecting majority choice; (2) enhanced political demands for military services under socialism as a route toward strengthened political support under conditions of reduced per capita wealth; and (3) lower opportunity costs for military services under socialism. See Zycher and Daley, n. 6 above. See also Benjamin Zycher, "Soviet Incentives in Arms Control," *Contemporary Policy Issues* October 1986.

9

FREEDOM, WEALTH, AND COERCION

Gertrud M. Fremling and John R. Lott, Jr. *

INTRODUCTION

F. A. Hayek in his classic work *The Road to Serfdom* notes that there are basically two different notions of "freedom."[1] Some, such as Hayek and Thomas Sowell, define freedom as the absence of coercion – the ability to act without the threat of physical harm – whereas others (e.g. George Stigler) define it as equivalent to wealth or welfare. Those favoring the first definition would argue that society is characterized by less freedom today than a century ago, because of the increased coercive powers of governments. For instance, Sowell (1980: 379) writes, "Past erosions of freedom are less critical than current trends which have implications for the future of freedom. Some of these trends amount to little less than the quiet piecemeal repeal of the American Revolution."

The second formulation – here labeled the "wealth definition" – on the other hand implies that people have more freedom today because their wealth, or ability to consume, has increased substantially. George Stigler, who is a proponent of this view, argues (1978: 214) "that even with the vast expansion of public controls and spending in the United States since the Civil War, there has been an enormous expansion in the average person's liberty." Not only do the two opposing definitions give different results regarding whether there is more or less freedom today, but they also give different implications for the effects of government transfer payments. To tax some to give to others would obviously increase coercion, and therefore according to the coercion definition reduce freedom. In contrast using the wealth definition, if the recipient is relatively poor, the relative increase in his or her wealth would be large and the "average" level of freedom could therefore be said to increase.

How we chose to define "freedom" fundamentally affects some important questions in economics and in law and especially affects deciding what are the proper objective functions. If one accepts Stigler's view that freedom and

* The authors would like to thank Edgar Browning, Dennis Jansen, Cass Sunstein, and Gordon Tullock for helpful comments. Any remaining errors are our own.

wealth are synonymous, there is no conflict in justifying legal rules on efficiency grounds. Those who argue that forces exist to move the common law, legal and political institutions, and the organization of firms towards efficiency should then believe that there are innate forces at work promoting freedom.[2] Yet, many economists view freedom as something unique and separate from wealth, suggesting that tradeoffs between wealth and freedom can exist. Is freedom a separate argument that we should add in our social welfare functions or is it already entered through the terms for wealth or profit maximization?

A similar dichotomy exists in public choice over whether there is an inherent tendency for political competition to tend toward adopting efficient institutions. Some, such as Becker (1976), have argued that the competition will tend to result in the most efficient methods of creating any given set of wealth transfers. Others such as Thompson (e.g. 1974 and 1979) and Wittman (1989) have advanced the view that political markets will develop institutions that maximize wealth. Again, Stigler's view of freedom obviously indicates that to varying degrees these two approaches imply that if those political institutions which exist maximize wealth, they must also be the ones best suited to maximizing freedom.[3] Those who disagree with this conclusion either must disagree that such forces are at work in forming these political institutions or they must claim that something like a desire for freedom (independent of wealth) exists in their utility functions.

This chapter critically reviews two of the existing definitions of freedom formulated by economists and suggests an alternative formulation. The next section briefly supplies an overview of two of the competing definitions. The following sections then provide critiques of definitions championed by Hayek and Stigler. The fourth section discusses a common alternative definition of freedom based upon the set of options available to an individual, and then tries to define it in terms of economics. The remaining sections of the chapter contrast the implications of this definition in terms of those offered by Hayek and Stigler.

THE "COERCION" DEFINITION AND ITS LIMITATIONS

The term "coercion" appears frequently in almost all discussions of liberty, but what is meant is often ill defined in economic terms. As a first approximation in defining freedom, F. A. Hayek simply states that freedom is "the absence of coercion" (1960: 133). Similarly, Sowell writes, "Freedom here will refer to a social relationship among people – namely, the absence of force as a prospective instrument of decision making. Freedom is reduced whenever a decision is made under threat of force" (1980: 115).[4] A difficulty arises in defining coercion or force. Coercion according to Hayek occurs "when one man's actions are made to serve another man's will, not for his own but for another man's purpose." However, what Hayek apparently overlooks is that applying this definition to economic actions would imply that market exchanges are normally associated with coercion. Just as coercion makes it costly to behave differently than the coercer desires, a higher wage likewise makes it costly to disobey my employer. Another example is the lure of profits which makes entrepreneurs produce what their customers desire. It is thus costly, in terms of opportunity costs, for the firms to "disobey" the customers' desires. As long as rents exist, it is costly for a person to change his or her actions and inframarginal rents exist in even the most competitive markets.[5]

Although Hayek later attempts to distinguish between coercion and simple market exchange as a matter of degree, the issue is not resolved. Hayek writes,

> If a hostess will invite me to her parties only if I conform to certain standards of conduct and dress, or my neighbor converse with me only if I observe conventional manners, this is certainly not coercion. . . . So long as the services of a particular person are *not crucial to my existence* or the preservation of *what I most value*, the conditions he exacts for rendering these services cannot properly be called "coercion". . . . unless a monopolist is in a position to withhold an indispensable supply, he cannot exercise coercion.
>
> (1960: 135–6, emphasis added)

The terms "crucial to my existence" or "what I most value" are all ambiguous in terms of economics. As Alchian and Allen (1977: 55) in a different context point out,

> Always, we will choose less if the price (value of the forsaken alternative) is large enough. Even the conception of some minimum necessary amount of food for sustaining life is not useful. What quality of life? How long a life? How probable a continuation of life?
>
> (see also Demsetz, 1988)

Claiming that coercion only exists if something is crucial to one's existence implies that very few government actions can be regarded as coercive. High taxes or regulation of industries seldom cause people to starve in the United States.

It is treacherous to define such concepts as coercion as a matter of degree, and counterintuitive conclusions might be reached, as shown by the following example. Costs, or more precisely *opportunity costs*, exist in many forms.[6] It seems strange to claim that it is coercion if I offer someone $1 million to jump off a bridge, but not if I only offer $10,000. In either case, I am imposing a cost on the person if he or she declines to jump. *Physical* coercion is merely one type of cost that can be imposed. There is some offer at which an individual will be indifferent between losing the offer and the threat of physical coercion. The same power would thus be exerted on altering the individual's behavior, and the amount of coercion would thus be the same. Likewise, there exists some amount of money that an individual is indifferent between losing and spending a month in jail. If I threaten not to give an individual this sum of money, this is not any different (in terms of opportunity costs) than threatening a jail term of a month. Again, according to Hayek's definition coercion would be the same.

The implications of failing to make this distinction pervade similar examples set forth both by Hayek (1960: 146–7) and by Sowell (1980: 105) relating conformity and freedom. They argue that inducing conformity can result in greater freedom by reducing the amount of force necessary by government to protect individuals from the actions of others. Social conventions and norms, unlike force, are not seen as constituting a "serious infringement of individual liberty" (Hayek, 1960: 147). Yet, their conclusion appears counterintuitive from an economic standpoint, since both methods undeniably make it *costly* for individuals to behave otherwise.[7]

Many economists have defined freedom solely in terms of relationships *between individuals* (Demsetz, 1988; Sowell, 1980: 115; Hayek, 1960: 133–47; and Von Mises, 1966: 279).[8] In this sense, Hayek (1944: 25) views liberty as the "freedom from the arbitrary power of other men." This formulation thus excludes the limiting forces exerted by nature. A problem with this version is that from the individual's perspective, restrictions made by humans and by nature cannot necessarily be distinguished but can have the exact same effects. For example, suppose that an avalanche traps somebody in a house. The individual would be regarded, according to this definition, as having more freedom if the avalanche could be attributed to Mother Nature than if humans deliberately set it in motion. However, since the individual's opportunity set is equally constrained, it seems to us that freedom should be regarded as equally limited. Further, if nobody can determine to what extent human factors were involved in triggering the avalanche, it would be impossible to use their definition to determine whether the individual's freedom was restrained or not.

To conclude, while physical coercion may be negatively correlated with freedom in that it limits one's opportunity set, it seems quite unsatisfactory to define liberty solely or even principally in terms of coercion. Limits on an individual's choices may take different forms, and when two different costs have identical effects, it is not clear what is gained by concentrating only on one particular type.

PROBLEMS WITH DEFINING FREEDOM IN TERMS OF WEALTH

Stigler (1978) suggests "freedom" to be synonymous to "wealth," "welfare," and "utility." (He switches back and forth when using the terms.) Various restrictions, including those arising from market forces, limit utility and thus

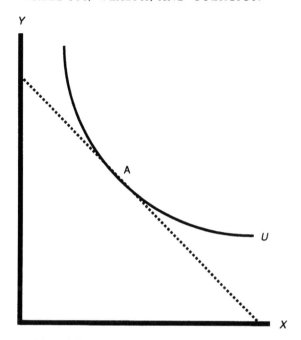

Figure 9.1 Wealth and freedom: optimal in-kind subsidies by government

freedom (p. 215): "If I cannot attend a symphony concert because there are not enough other demanders of symphony orchestra in my community, my wealth has been reduced (in utility terms) by the behavior of others."

Stigler's definition is perfectly logical and well-defined in economic terms. The problem is that defining freedom as wealth or utility begs the whole question of analyzing "freedom" as a separate concept. While utility, welfare, or wealth might generally be positively correlated with freedom, they should not be viewed as identical.

The following simple example can illustrate the usefulness of a concept of freedom separate from wealth. The dotted line in Figure 9.1 shows the original budget constraint for an individual. Given a choice, suppose this individual would consume point A along this constraint. If the government taxes away the individual's income, it can still return it in the form of X and Y so that the individual still consumes at A. According to Stigler's definition, freedom is not changed. Yet, most laypeople would probably argue that freedom is reduced, because the person no longer has the range of options he or she used to have.

Some commonly used expressions strongly suggest that freedom is frequently distinct from utility, welfare, or wealth. "Freedom to fail" (or "to be free to fail") implies that one is allowed to make choices not beneficial to one's welfare. With Stigler's definition, "freedom to fail" is a contradiction in terms, since less utility means less freedom. The expression "the golden cage" further illustrates the situation where wealth has been obtained at the *expense* of freedom, again indicating that freedom should not be regarded as synonymous with wealth.[9]

ANOTHER DEFINITION: FREEDOM AS ALTERNATIVES

Common usage, as well as dictionaries, seems to suggest that the essence of "freedom" is the ability to move between alternatives – *the ability for an individual to alter his or her consumption or behavior*. The more plentiful the alternatives, the more freedom is presumed to exist. This definition clearly refers to the size of an individual's opportunity set.

It would be easy to list examples of how additional available combinations of goods would increase the chance that choices with higher utility were found. Increased freedom would always be associated with increased utility. More options – due to technical advances, fewer government regulations, or less rigid social customs – would invariably be beneficial.

"Freedom" becomes an interesting concept separate from "utility" when we realize that tradeoffs between freedom and welfare can exist (e.g. Sowell, 1980: 114 and the authors that he cites). For example, making sunk investments might increase wealth, while raising the cost of altering behavior, as leaving the activity in which the sunk investments have been made is costly if rents are lost. Eliminating sunk investments can increase freedom and lower wealth (except if it sufficiently reduces wealth so as to preclude many consumption options). Further, as we shall demonstrate later, tradeoffs between freedom and wealth can also arise from costliness of information or from externalities. One point should also be clarified when we define freedom as the ability to move between alternatives – "the ability for an individual to alter his or her consumption or behavior." We do not mean to suggest that this is easily measured (e.g. through counting similar or trivial options).[10]

EXAMPLES OF "FREEDOM AS ALTERNATIVES": OR, WHY FREEDOM SHOULD NOT ALWAYS BE MAXIMIZED

While "freedom" typically has highly positive connotations, neither individuals nor society should always strive to maximize freedom. In the sections below some factors limiting freedom are discussed.

Social customs and property rights which limit freedom but solve externalities and increase wealth

Hayek's example of the hostess who requires "certain standards of conduct and dress" can be made to illustrate an externality point. According to the

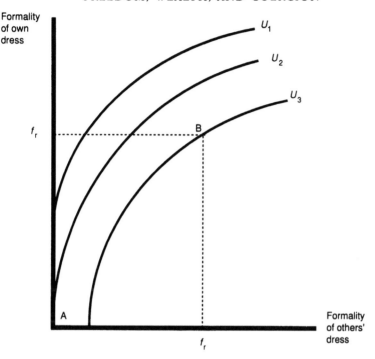

Figure 9.2 Restrictions resulting in higher utility

definition we just proposed, a guest's freedom is reduced if no such restriction had been imposed. Although an individual might be better off if he or she alone was exempt from such a requirement, the welfare of everyone invited might be higher when restrictions are imposed. This is illustrated in Figure 9.2. If we assume that all guests are alike in that they themselves prefer to dress comfortably and spend little time getting ready but enjoy looking at others who are nicely dressed, the indifference curves would have the shape shown in Figure 9.2. With no restrictions, everyone ends up being very casually dressed, as illustrated by point A at the origin on U_2. However, the hostess, who serves as a substitute to costly bargaining among potential guests, wishes to maximize the utility of the guests, and requires the formality level f_r. Every guest dresses up more than they wish, but can enjoy watching everyone else, and end up at B, at a higher indifference curve U_3. Since everyone is made better off, such a restriction can be considered beneficial.

There are a vast number of other situations where externalities are the basic reason for restrictions on an individual's freedom, for instance while property rights prevent us from using others' belongings, thus restricting our opportunity set. The restriction preventing the neighbors from using our belongings increases our freedom, since we can use our belongings whenever we wish. This is a typical restriction on somebody's freedom resulting in more freedom for someone else.

Education and freedom

Suppose that a prisoner in a POW camp could potentially escape through a well-hidden door. If, however, he does not know about this door, does he have more freedom than if there was no such door? Freedom is not only limited by the obvious constraints of government force, but equally well by information. Without the knowledge of the secret door, the prisoner does not have the freedom to escape.

Ignorance may be as fettering as "external" constraints imposed by the government, social customs, or the marketplace. Increased knowledge expands our horizons and makes us realize the additional options available. The knowledge can be in the form of "pure" information (a prison guard informing the prisoner of the secret door) or in the ability to link various facts together (by combining observations, the prisoner may discover the secret door). Education can thus contribute to freedom either through giving information or by helping the individual make inferences.[11]

Since purchasing education is costly, the individual can face a tradeoff between more freedom through more knowledge and, on the other hand, wealth. Although many types of educational investments increase both freedom and lifetime income, diminishing returns set in, and at some point the opportunity cost of further learning lowers utility.

The purchase of more consumer information may or may not increase liberty, and may or may not increase utility. A simple case where it increases both is illustrated in Figure 9.3. Point A represents the combination of X and Y that could be bought if information could be obtained costlessly. Suppose now that information about the existence of good Y is costly. With the same income, but without the knowledge of Y, the individual selects point B at the lower indifference curve U_1. If the "purchase" of gathering information about Y is indicated by the distance between the solid and dotted lines, the individual is better off making the "purchase" because he or she can now reach point C on U_2 rather than B on U_1. Depending on the required reduction in income and the shapes of the indifference curves, it is sometimes optimal to seek more information, sometimes not.[12]

The decision to purchase an education – just as much as selecting a profession, marrying, or buying a house – limits an individual's future choices.[13] Each requires investments that are not fully transferable. If for instance one chooses the education required to become a medical doctor, the time spent to acquire the degree and the license represents a sunk non-transferable investment (e.g. Lott, 1987b). Leaving the profession is costly since the quasirents associated with all the investments made in entering the profession

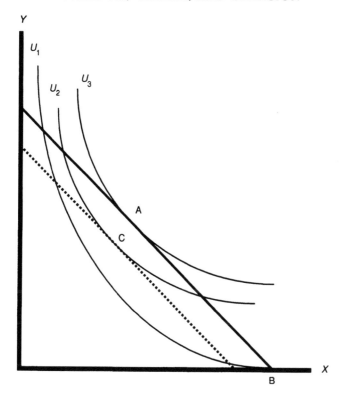

Figure 9.3 The purchase of consumer information

cannot easily be transferred to others. The decision to enter a particular profession produces opportunity costs making it costly to later alter one's chosen career paths. The doctor will remain in the profession as long as he or she obtains some quasi-rents even though it may not pay the doctor to enter the profession now if he or she had the decision to do it all over again. Likewise, individuals could put off making a decision on choosing a profession and thus maintain a higher degree of freedom. As time passes, however, the payoff to education would gradually get lower as the number of years for which one could remain in the profession falls. The additional years of increased freedom are obtained at the cost of a lower lifetime income.

Thus, although each individual may have a great deal of freedom early in life to make decisions about the way that individual will live the rest of his or her life, once choices have been made, freedom is reduced. The extent to which commitments have already been made is thus another factor that is specific to the individual and that determines the degree of freedom to be faced.

"Freedom" usually has positive connotations, and it is ironic that those who in their own life try to maximize freedom at every stage, would accomplish little. In a complex world, with heavy competition, one cannot switch in and out of medicine, engineering, poetry, economics, etc., as getting ahead in an area requires a great deal of sunk investment at an early age.

Protecting others from their own mistakes and the "freedom to fail"

Economists presume that an individual chooses the alternative he or she perceives as the best one. Given costly information, this does not always turn out to be the best choice. The definition of freedom we propose does not imply that the *ex post* choice is correct, and thus it is assumed that individuals are "free to fail." According to our framework, it is possible that increased freedom, with more "bad" alternatives (those not chosen by anybody if the consequences had been known *ex ante*), would make individuals worse off, because some people happen to choose them. These individuals who made mistakes were "free" to reduce their wealth and thus reduce their future options.

Often, restrictions on freedom are imposed, not in order to prevent damage to others, but to prevent damage to the individual. An illustration is the monitoring of children's activities by parents in order to protect children from injury. Many government restrictions are based on similar "parental" intentions. Examples include regulations on the selling and usage of drugs and food products as well as mandatory seat belt laws.

Even if parents or governments had vastly greater wisdom, there are, however, two objections that would have to be met before someone willingly would entrust an authority to make such decisions. First, the authority should know the person's utility function, and, second, the authority's utility function should be sufficiently positively dependent on the subject's utility. With a population that is very homogenous (racially, religiously, culturally) these two conditions seem more likely to be obtained, and less freedom should be expected.

Since those who are better informed can make relatively better use of increased freedom, it may appear that higher levels of education should be associated with a greater quest for freedom and thus lower reliance on authority. This is only partly true: only if people become *more equal* in their knowledge should this happen. If more advanced technology results in experts in narrow areas, many people would still have to rely on others' judgments most of the time. For instance, with more medicines and food additives available, individuals increasingly have to rely on expert opinions. The greater the divergence of knowledge, the greater the potential opportunity costs for not deferring to the judgment of others.

FREEDOM AS AN "OPTION VALUE"

Freedom is often viewed as having a value in and of itself. This would suggest that it can be viewed as simply another good that enters into the utility function, and that different people can have different tastes for it. However, as indicated by the preceding discussions, we believe that a different analysis is warranted.

We argue that what is commonly referred to as "the value of freedom" can be viewed as an "option value" just like options in the stock market derive their value. When dealing with keeping possible future choices open, it is, however, difficult to define exactly under what circumstances certain options would be valuable and how valuable they would be. Stating that somebody "values freedom" may be a convenient way of expressing that leaving choices open has a substantial option value, without going into the details of the nature of the options. In the case of the medical student, mentioned in the previous section, an evaluation of the option value of keeping choices open (rather than making the sunk investment) would have to consider under what circumstances the student would prefer to switch to some other profession; the probability that such circumstances would occur; and the value of the switch under each circumstance. Factors entering into such a calculation would be the probability distribution of the different professions' wage rates, as well as the likelihood that the student's own tastes for different professions will change in the future. Thus, the apparent "taste" for freedom may well be a reflection of the individual's perception of the degree to which the environment or tastes will change.

Casual observations suggest that it is those who have the most to gain from the additional choices that have the highest "tastes" for freedom: it seems that the young, rather than the old, desire freedom the most. This is consistent with the value of freedom being a complex option, because the longer the remaining life-span, the higher is the payoff for any given option. Perhaps surprisingly, increased freedom can often be similar to insurance. If, for instance, the wage rate in one's profession falls, freedom to alter this profession can mitigate the impact on one's income. In other cases, greater freedom instead allows a person to take advantage of the new opportunities opening up.

Notice that under the option value approach, the individual attempts to maximize lifetime *expected utility* by choosing the appropriate level of freedom (i.e. options purchased). Thus freedom is not maximized.[14]

CONCLUSIONS

This chapter has not sought to develop a "new" definition of freedom, but has defined freedom in a way that we think is consistent with common usage, in terms of options. We have emphasized how this definition can fit in with traditional economic analysis.

Perfect freedom is impossible since we live in a world of scarcity, and constraints limit our ability to alter our consumption or behavior. The marketplace, the government, as well as costly information, all limit our freedom. While wealth and freedom can indeed be correlated with each other, there are many tradeoffs that we face between the two. More freedom frequently comes at the expense of decreased wealth. If individuals do value freedom independently from wealth, measuring the efficiency of institutions will be even more difficult than it was previously since it will require a method of attaching a value to differing degrees of freedom.

NOTES

1 See Hayek (1944: 25–6; 1960: 17).
2 See for example Alchian (1950), Easterbrook (1983), Lott (1987d), and Rubin (1977) as proponents of the views that there are innate forces for efficiency.
3 One can believe that wealth and freedom are separate objectives and still believe that there is an innate tendency for institutions to advance both. For instance, the earlier discussions concerning political markets could be rephrased to say that those politicians who can create transfers at the lowest total costs in terms of deadweight losses and reductions in freedom will create the most support and win. Individuals will weight their votes in terms of how much they value each.
4 Von Mises (1966: 281) writes, "Thus we may define freedom as that state of affairs in which the individual's discretion to choose is not constrained by government violence."
5 See Klein and Leffler (1981) for a discussion of how rents make certain types of behavior very costly for firms.
6 Lott (1987a, 1987b) discusses how important opportunity costs can be in altering individual behavior.
7 Alfred Marshall (1920: 622) implies a relationship between freedom and social convention when he writes of the "individual slavery to custom." James Buchanan (1985) and Lott (1987c) write of morals as constraints on peoples' opportunity sets. (See also Nozick, 1974: 28.)
8 For a similar position see also John Locke (Second Treatise of Government, 1689–90: chapter II).
9 Adam Smith, at least according to Buchanan (1976: 7–8), also recognized this tradeoff between freedom and wealth. As Buchanan (p. 8) writes, "Smith sanctioned interferences (by government) only when efficiency criteria overweighed those of justice, conceived here not in distributional terms at all, but in terms of the value of natural liberty." Stigler (1978), however, does not acknowledge such a tradeoff since he defines freedom as wealth or utility (p. 217).
10 As Cass Sunstein has pointed out to us, if one were to merely count options, regardless of the nature of such options, a prisoner could be viewed as having a lot of freedom: prisoners, as opposed to most working people, can choose when to eat, sleep, watch television, etc. Raz (1986: 373–5) has a similar discussion. For instance, Raz (p. 375) writes:

> Another consideration concerning adequacy relates to the variety of options available. Clearly not number but variety matters. A choice between hundreds of identical and identically situated houses is no choice, compared with a choice between a town flat and a suburban house.

11 Increased education, however, should not be taken to invariably increase freedom. It might be used as a tool for the government to indoctrinate people. As J. S. Mill (1859: 108) notes, "A general State education is a mere contrivance for molding people to be exactly like one another and the mold in which it casts

them is that which pleases the predominant power in the government." As we shall discuss later, the sunk investment in a specialized training can also limit future freedom.

When people believe that a particular set of social convictions or norms is "fair" or "legitimate" it is more costly to behave differently. Instilling certain views in a person may actually serve as a substitute for coercion (Lott, 1990). A possible example involves the caste system in India. Before the British arrived, the caste system was universally accepted – even by those in the lowest caste, the "untouchables." The bonds of these social traditions were so strong they were often compared to physical coercion. J. H. Hutton (1946: 105) approvingly quotes S. C. Hill as calling the caste system:

> the only Social System ever proposed upon a basis stronger than force . . . entirely independent of any form of political government. . . . The system is permanently stable because of the complete absence of any motive on the part of the ruled for seeking alterations . . .

These groups had supposedly not even perceived of alternative arrangements as possible. The introduction of competing ideas with the arrival of the British at least brought up the possibility that caste members had choices where previously none had existed (Ghurye, 1969: 270–305).

12 Of course, the information-gathering problem is a difficult one confronting the individual. Without knowing what one might learn – such as the existence of another good – one cannot easily evaluate how valuable the additional knowledge is.

13 Raz (1986: 374, n. 1) touches very briefly on this: "Given that every decision at least once implemented, closes options previously open to one . . . the question of whether, and when, one's own decisions may limit one's autonomy raises tricky issues."

14 To value freedom because additional options allow us to maximize expected utility is not the same as freedom being identical to utility.

REFERENCES

Alchian, Armen A. (1950) "Uncertainty, Evolution, and Economic Theory," *Journal of Political Economy* 58: 211–21.

Alchian, Armen A. and William R. Allen (1977) *Exchange and Production: Competition, Coordination and Control*, 2nd edn. Belmont, CA: Wadsworth.

Becker, Gary S. (1976) "Comment on Peltzman," *Journal of Law and Economics* 19: 245–8.

Buchanan, James M. (1976) "The Justice of Natural Liberty," *Journal of Legal Studies* 5: 1–16.

—— (1985) "The Moral Dimension of Debt Financing," *Economic Inquiry* 23: 1–6.

Demsetz, Harold (1982) *Economic, Legal, and Political Dimensions of Competition*. New York: North-Holland.

—— (1988) "The Meaning of Freedom," in *Ownership, Control, and the Firm: The Organization of Economic Activity*, Vol. 1. New York: Basil Blackwell.

Easterbrook, F. H. (1983) "Criminal Procedure and a Market System," *Journal of Legal Studies* 12,2: 333–44.

Ghurye, Govind S. (1969) *Caste and Race in India*. Bombay: Popular Prakashan.

Hayek, Friedrich A. (1944) *The Road to Serfdom*. Chicago: University of Chicago Press.

—— (1960) *The Constitution of Liberty*. Chicago: University of Chicago Press.

Hutton, J.H. (1946) *The India Caste System*. London: Cambridge University Press.

Klein, Benjamin and Keith B. Leffler (1981) "The Role of Market Forces in Assuring Contractual Performance," *Journal of Political Economy* 89: 615–41.

Locke, John *First and Second Treatises Concerning Civil Government*. Many editions and reprints, the first one in 1689–90.

Lott, John R., Jr. (1987a) "The Effect of Nontransferable Property Rights on the Efficiency of Political Markets: Some Evidence," *Journal of Public Economics* 32: 231–46.

— (1987b) "Licensing and Nontransferable Rents," *American Economic Review* 77: 453–5.

— (1987c) "Political Cheating," *Public Choice* 52: 169–87.

— (1987d) "Should the Wealthy be Able to 'Buy Justice'?," *Journal of Political Economy* 95: 1307–16.

— (1990) "An Explanation of Public Provision of Schooling: The Importance of Indoctrination," *Journal of Law and Economics* 33: 199–231.

Marshall, Alfred (1920) *Principles of Economics*, 8th edn, reprinted. New York: Macmillian.

Mill, John Stuart (1859) *On Liberty*, reprinted 1947. New York: Appleton-Century-Crofts.

Nozick, Robert (1974) *Anarchy, State, and Utopia*. New York: Basic Books.

Raz, Joseph (1986) *The Morality of Freedom*. Oxford: Clarendon Press.

Rubin, Paul H. (1977) "Is the Common Law Efficient?," *Journal of Legal Studies* 6: 51–64.

Sowell, Thomas (1980) *Knowledge and Decisions*. New York: Basic Books.

Stigler, George J. (1975) *The Citizen and the State*. Chicago: University of Chicago Press.

— (1978) "Wealth and Possibly Liberty," *Journal of Legal Studies* 7: 213–17.

Thompson, Earl (1974) "Taxation and National Defense," *Journal of Political Economy* 82: 755–82.

— (1979) "An Economic Basis for the 'National Defense Argument' for Aiding Certain Industries," *Journal of Political Economy* 87: 1–36.

Von Mises, Ludwig (1966) *Human Action*, 3rd edn. Chicago: Henry Regnery.

Wittman, Donald (1989) "Are Democracies Efficient?," *Journal of Political Economy* 97: 1395–424.

10

DISCOVERY FACTORS OF ECONOMIC FREEDOM

Respondence, epiphany, and serendipity

Daniel B. Klein*

If decisions were a choice between alternatives, decisions would come easy. Decision is the selection and formulation of alternatives.

(Kenneth Burke, 1932: 215)

Abstract: Economists place a heavy emphasis on equilibrium model building, and this emphasis leads them to think of economic freedom as the freedom to choose in a neatly characterized setting. Three other facets of economic freedom, facets that tend to be eclipsed by model building, are the freedom to respond flexibly to opportunities (which I associate with Coase), the freedom to discover opportunities by epiphany (associated with Kirzner), and the freedom to discover opportunities by serendipity (associated with Alchian). Neglect of these discovery factors tends toward an under-appreciation of freedom.

INTRODUCTION

The economics profession as a whole puts a heavy emphasis on formal equilibrium model building. The norms of formal model building do much to give the profession a set of standards for how economic research is to proceed and what constitutes good work. A scientific community can't run without norms and standards. This fact is sometimes neglected by those who complain about formal model building; sometimes they seem to view formal model building as an unnecessary hinderance on discourse. It is as though they see the "true" way of good work, and but for the emphasis on model building that truth would become apparent to all.

If the critics neglect the need for standards, they do, however, have a point about predominant norms possibly restricting discourse. Any mode of

* Associate Professor of Economics, Santa Clara University. The author has benefitted from comments by Tyler Cowen, Andrew Dick, Arthur De Vany, Walter Grinder, and Adrian Moore.

discourse, although clarifying, enriching, and expanding knowledge in some respects, is also bound to confine and limit knowledge in other respects. There is no reason to suppose that all important facets of a subject will be amenable to a single well-delineated mode of discourse, or "paradigm" (Kuhn, 1970). Some facets of the subject, especially in the social sciences, are not aptly rendered in the dominant mode of discourse. When rigidly demanding that all discourse conform to that mode, the scientific community throws some facets of its subject into the shadows (Sen, 1977; Hirschman, 1986). This is the "essential tension" of scientific advance, as described by Thomas Kuhn (1959), the tension between one's commitment to a dominant mode of discourse and one's understanding of facets of the subject which that mode of discourse cannot capture.[1]

This chapter discusses three facets of the market process. More pointedly, I take up the three facets as a way of exploring the economist's understanding of the free market. I argue that the heavy emphasis on model building has led economists to a somewhat narrow understanding of freedom. Dynamic and particularistic facets of freedom, though of great practical importance, cannot very well be made to shine in formal models, and consequently are underappreciated in economic research and underemphasized in economic education.

FREEDOM TO CHOOSE AS BUT ONE FACET OF THE FREEDOM TO ACT

The economics profession as a whole is accustomed to model-based stories in which it is presumed that the analysts, if not the players in the stories themselves, know the opportunities and objectives that describe the market context. Economists must posit such setting and background material to frame the tale. Such exercises sharpen our eye for strategy, investment, and economizing, but overexposure can impair our vision for other features of economic processes.

In particular, model building sometimes limits our notion of economic freedom. Beginning with introductory courses, the talk of economists is so centered on equilibrium models, as opposed to public issues, that freedom is understood only for what it achieves (or fails to achieve) in blackboard models. Equilibrium stories of price ceilings, price floors, and entry barriers lead us to think of markets as *neatly characterized procedures*, and of freedom as little more than the *freedom to choose* within these characterizations. (Note Kenneth Burke's use of the word "choice" in the opening quotation.) It may be the freedom of tenants to choose high-rent apartments, of workers to choose low wage employment, or of consumers to choose the services of unlicensed electricians. Because our equilibrium stories posit the industry, the preferences, and the opportunities, all that freedom accomplishes is a more efficient utilization of *given* resources.

In their professional discourse economists rarely talk of factors of economic change like discovery, imagination, or serendipity, and consequently they tend to neglect these as vital components of economic progress. Trained well in their professional thinking, economists often carry over their habits of analysis to thinking about public policy.[2] They are left insensible to the fact that government restrictions on freedom tend to choke off the vital components.

For example, the economist might think that in making policy for urban transit, government experts can, after much careful study, adequately determine the transit technologies and systems that would suit the city's needs, and then implement the system. I submit that that approach reveals poor appreciation of how economic freedom functions.

The notion of economic freedom used here is a legalistic notion of the *freedom to act*. I mean Isaiah Berlin's (1969) "negative" and more empirical conception of freedom, with the legal details filled in, so far as is practicable, by the Friedmans (Milton, Rose, and David) (1962, 1989). Specifically, I mean freedom (and reasonable safeguarding) of property, consent, and contract. This is freedom in the flesh, with hair and sweat and pigment. I prefer to call it the "freedom to act," rather than the "freedom to compete," as Hayek (1978) has called it, because, as Frank Knight (1935: 292) notes, this freedom includes "freedom to organize to eliminate competition."

Freedom to choose is but one facet of the freedom to act, and it is heavily emphasized in academic research. I will discuss three underemphasized facets of the freedom to act. These other facets are important in making a full case for freedom, but are difficult, if not impossible, to render in the dominant mode of discourse, namely equilibrium model building.

FREEDOM TO RESPOND AND TO FORM CONTRACTS

Short-lived opportunities or imminent troubles often visit the entrepreneur. Fortune emerges – perhaps at an unexpected time or in an unexpected form – and the entrepreneur needs to respond. The entrepreneur's situation calls for a flexibility – that is, freedom – to respond to the special bits of fortune that come knocking. When confronting the continual gale of change, our economic agent comes to resemble a busy switchboard operator.

Research in the tradition of George Stigler's papers on information (1961, 1962) shows that model building can incorporate search by comparison shoppers and the like who are uncertain about price or quality at a given store. In other models, events come stochastically to the agent, who then carries out planned contingent response. In this sense uncertainty can be incorporated into the model building paradigm of solving for individually optimal behaviors. But stochastic events and appropriate respondence certainly complicate the model, and typically such complications are not worth the trouble. In practice, the economist does not incorporate such features into equilibrium storytelling, unless stochasticity and respondence are the very focus of the paper.

An economist can best come to understand the element of change and the importance of flexible respondence by studying the individuated circumstances of the firm, the industry, or the particular market. Such study grants the economist a view of the variety of possible realizations, and how entrepreneurs in fact cope with not knowing which will come to pass. Exploration of actual economic practices, and appreciation of the freedom to respond, has been greatly advanced by the law and economics community, led by Ronald Coase, Aaron Director, Harold Demsetz, and Armen Alchian (see especially 1977: chapters 1 and 2).[3] In "The Problem of Social Cost," Coase (1960: 19) pressed the point that to understand an institutional or regulatory issue we would need "detailed investigation of the actual results of handling the problem in different ways" (see also Coase, 1972).

Coase and his colleagues have encouraged economists to plumb the dark depths of actual institutions and to describe cases where market participants recognize probabilistic events and plan responses for each contingency. Good recent examples are the works of Arthur De Vany and Gail Frey (1981), Dennis Carlton (1991), and Andrew Dick (1992), on the role of stochastic processes in a variety of industries, including steel production, plastics, and semiconductors. These authors explore how basic uncertainty gives rise to economic practices that economists might otherwise have difficulty explaining – practices like queuing, order backlogging, second sourcing, and vertical integration. These papers often show an appreciation for individuation and uncertainty in local conditions, and how infringements on freedom prevent proper response to those conditions.

The freedom to act carries not only a flexibility in making one's choices in isolation, but also the freedom to form elaborate contracts that grant one flexibility in relations with others. Though hoping to follow plan A, one might contract in advance for the *option* of pursuing plan B, or plan C, or whatever plan meets the contingency. Accordingly, Coase has beckoned economists to explore how economic agents form contracts to cope with the stormy seas of commerce and industry. For example, De Vany and Eckert (1991) tell how, in the golden age, motion-picture companies worked on a contract system with film stars and others talents, and vertically integrated into exhibition, because of severe and pervasive uncertainties on both the supply side and the demand side of the industry. They argue that the Supreme Court's *Paramount* decision (1948), which broke up the production house system, was based on an oversimplified notion of "restraint of trade," and resulted in losses for film makers and viewers alike. The Coasian community has generated numerous studies of how restrictions on freedom of contract have hobbled the ability of business to cope with uncertainty.

In the case of free-enterprise urban transit, for example, severe uncertainty and individuation might be fundamental, and adaptation crucial. Carriers might not expect current conditions to persist. New competitors might invade their routes, or current competitors drop out. The carrier companies may wish to abandon certain routes or add others. For such reasons carriers may wish to lease their buses and vans, and form contracts that permit them to alter vehicle utilization on short notice. Carriers may form flexible contracts with their drivers, allowing the company to alter hours and remuneration. In unregulated private enterprise, flexible respondence, as common practice, is an important source of both cost containment and effective service delivery. But equilibrium storytelling seldom includes the complicated apparatus of stochastic processes and so on which would be necessary to capture the role of flexible respondence.

FREEDOM TO HAVE EPIPHANY

It is one thing for the entrepreneur to greet fortune when it comes knocking. It is something else to apprehend fortune in its hidden forms, and seize it. Here we have the distinction between responding to the realization of events within a framework of recognized variables and relationships, and the discovery of a fresh opportunity to embrace a new and better framework. Here is the distinction between information and insight. This element of epiphany, of finding fortune by interpreting the world differently, is the subtle and vital element in human decision making. Yet this element of decision making is absent from equilibrium model building.

An example of epiphany is found in W. Somerset Maugham's short story "The Verger." A new vicar came to St Peter's, Neville Square, and called in the church verger to discuss a troubling matter. "I discovered to my astonishment that you could neither read nor write," he told Albert Edward Foreman, the verger of sixteen years. When directed to learn to read and write, Albert Edward replied "I'm too old a dog," and bid the vicar a friendly farewell. He hung up his verger's gown and went into the street. He was a non-smoker, but with a certain latitude, and it occurred to him that a cigarette would comfort him. He looked up and down the long street without finding a shop that sold cigarettes.

"I can't be the only man as walks along this street and wants a fag," he said. "I shouldn't wonder but what a fellow might do very well with a little shop here. Tobacco and sweets, you know."

He gave a sudden start.

"That's an idea," he said. "Strange 'ow things come to you when you least expect it."

He turned, walked home, and had his tea.

"You're very silent this afternoon, Albert," his wife remarked.

"I'm thinking," he said.

The former verger set up in business as a tobacconist and newsagent. Soon he set up more shops, and in time accumulated a small fortune. The distinguished gentleman went to the bank to put his wealth into securities and startled the bank manager by announcing that he could not read or write. "Good God, man, what would you be now if you had been able to?" – "I can tell you that, sir," replied Mr Foreman. "I'd be verger of St Peter's, Neville Square."

Maugham's story tells of a man who not only discovered something he wasn't looking for, but discovered something *he quite possibly might not have discovered at all*. In Israel Kirzner's terms, the verger was *alert* to a profit opportunity. The verger's apprehension of the street as a-bad-place-to-find-a-cigarette was a realization in his working framework. Apprehending it as a-good-place-to-set-up-a-tobacco-shop was not. The opportunity could have been missed entirely, or noticed only fleetingly.

Economists give some attention to innovation in the sense of significant and identifiable technological advance, but they give very little attention to alertness or epiphany in all its buzzing, blooming – yet very often mundane – manifestations. The verger's story is material neither for a news headline nor an elegant model, nor is it captured in a variable called "education" or "R and D," but it is nonetheless the kind of small breakthrough everyone makes now and then, and which, in aggregate, accounts for significant economic improvement. It is creativity and imagination, achieved countless times over, in the individuated worlds of individuals. Whereas Coasian respondence explores the individual's adaptation within his or her individuated world, Kirzner's alertness is the individual's reformulation of his or her individuated world.[4] This human experience of reformulating, or *reinterpreting*, one's world, this element of epiphany, is, by its very nature, *impossible* to capture in an equilibrium model.[5]

Too often economists neglect the effects of public policy on alertness and the discovery process. Kirzner, however, queries: what economic and political institutions can be expected most successfully to evoke entrepreneurial alertness?

In the Somerset Maugham story, the verger noticed something that was now *in his interest to notice*. Here is the heart of Kirzner's distinctive argument for economic freedom (1985: 28):

> Two individuals walk through the same city block teeming with hundreds of people in a variety of garbs, with shops of different kinds, advertising signs of many goods, buildings of different architectural styles. Each of these individuals will notice a different set of items out of these countless impressions impinging on his senses. What is noticed by the one is not what is noticed by the other. The difference will not merely be one of chance. It is a difference that can be ascribed, in part, to the *interests* of the two individuals. Each tends to notice that which is of interest *to him*.

Kirzner claims that "human beings tend to notice that which it is in their interest to notice."[6] The claim is natural enough and beyond doubt. It implies that profit opportunities will be best discovered and seized in a legal framework that gives individuals an interest in discovering them.

Every Ph.D. economist understands that under a regime of economic freedom (and a host of other assumptions), the market generates efficient outcomes; model builders have refined the logic in the "fundamental welfare theorems" of general equilibrium. But Kirzner's argument for freedom is totally missed by such logic, and arises only because the ancillary assumptions of the model do *not* hold. In real life, many opportunities lie hidden from view; there is no set of "common knowledge." Not only are preferences, constraints, and opportunities individuated in minute detail, but each actor's interpretations of them are individuated.

The market process generates a system of human activities each of which is performed in partial ignorance. There are always discrepancies between available opportunities and market recognition of those opportunities. We therefore value, Kirzner argues (1985: 30), a legal system "which offers entrepreneurs the required incentives for the discrepancies to be noticed and corrected." The legal system that best does so is economic freedom, which keeps individuals alert to profit opportunities because it grants them an interest in seizing them. To Kirzner, the most impressive aspect of the free market system is not its ability to generate efficient allocations within a framework of fully recognized ends and means. Rather, "the most impressive aspect of the market system is the tendency for [previously unrecognized ends and means] to be discovered." Yet this most impressive aspect, which cannot be captured in the dominant mode of discourse, is poorly recognized in academic economic research and poorly imparted in economic education.

Consider the case of making policy for urban transit. It is typical for local governments to fix the price of taxi services, and to require official meters in taxicabs. An economist might argue that this policy remedies problems of bad consumer information, infrequent dealings, and cabby opportunism. With a model of supply and demand in his or her head, the economist might reason that so long as regulators don't set the price too far from "the equilibrium price," the downside of price fixing may not be so bad.

Kirzner would argue that this reasoning is glaringly inadequate. Price competition, Kirzner would argue, is crucial to the vibrancy of the market and should not be seen in isolation from other activities in the market process.

Perhaps an upstart company seeks to enter a sleepy local taxi market. It plans to utilize a new maintenance system to keep the cabs in repair, or a new contracting policy to assure itself loyal drivers, or a new dispatching system to provide prompter service to customers. It might offer new stylish cabs, and bring this new service to the consumer's attention by a clever advertising campaign. Finally, it plans on cracking the traditional market by offering – at least temporarily – a well-publicized low price – the lowest in town.

Kirzner's point is that when the government fixes taxi rates, besides running the risk of getting a shortage or surplus, we run the risk of regimenting the industry and choking off the vital process of discovery. If the upstart company cannot offer a new low price, then it is likely to forgo the campaign altogether. In fact, there would not even be an upstart company to devise such a campaign. Society loses not merely some "quantity supplied," but an entire foray into a local economic terrain, a vital entrepreneurial investigation into new services and new ways of producing services. In carrying out the would-be campaign, the upstart company would have undergone a series of fresh decisions, each of which would have involved entrepreneurial discoveries. (Listen again to Kenneth Burke's words: "Decision is the selection and formulation of alternatives.") The overschooled economic perspective, which sees the freedom to act as little more than the freedom to choose, fails to appreciate this larger social loss from government assaults on freedom (cf. Kirzner, 1992: 53–4).

FREEDOM TO FIND SERENDIPITY

The freedom to choose points up how freedom allows individuals to adapt their strategy to a neatly characterized competitive environment. In our discussion of Coasian respondence we saw how freedom allows individuals to adapt to individuated conditions, by responding in step with changes in those conditions and forming contracts to cope with those conditions. In our discussion of Kirznerian alertness we saw how freedom sparks individuals to adapt their interpretations of local conditions, to incorporate available-but-undiscovered profit opportunities into their interpretive framework. Thus we have seen three ways in which freedom promotes appropriate adaptation of behavior to underlying opportunity.

There is yet another facet of freedom which helps to achieve a meeting of appropriate behavior and opportunity. In an article entitled "Uncertainty, Evolution, and Economic Theory" (in the *Journal of Political Economy*, 1950), Armen Alchian pointed out that in a market system not only does behavior tend to adapt appropriately to opportunity, but opportunity tends to adopt appropriate behavior. The survivors in a market system, he explains, "may appear to be those having *adapted* themselves to the environment, whereas the truth may well be that the environment has *adopted* them" (1977: 22).

Alchian gives an unreal but useful example:

Assume that thousands of travelers set out from Chicago, selecting their roads completely at random and without foresight. Only our "economist" knows that on but one road are there any gasoline stations. He can state categorically that travelers will *continue* to travel only on that road; those on other roads will soon run out of gas. . . . If gasoline supplies were now moved to a new road, some formerly luckless travelers again would be able to move; and a new pattern of travel would be observed, although none of the travelers had changed his particular

172

path. . . . All that is needed is a set of varied, risk-taking (adoptable) travelers. The correct direction of travel will be established.

Alchian's point was principally methodological: Economists are so caught up in stories of optimization, stories of appropriate adaptation, that they neglect stories of adoption of the appropriate by the evolutionary process of experimentation and selection. Alchian asks for an economic understanding that does not limit behavior to the tidy forms of optimization that make equilibrium models cohere. He asks for a more evolutionary understanding that allows "imitative, venturesome, innovative, trial-and-error adaptive behavior" (p. 32). Alchian's perspective gives the economist a loose framework for explaining the survival of the fittest that includes, and goes beyond, the idea of fit adaptation to survival requirements. Indeed, some researchers are now using tournaments (Axelrod, 1984), evolutionary games (Maynard Smith, 1982), and models of experimentation and learning in games (Kreps, 1990: 164f.; De Vany, this volume) to illustrate how trial and error behavior may evolve through time and generate emergent conventions.

Alchian's idea of opportunity adopting appropriate behavior points us toward another facet of economic freedom, again a facet eclipsed by equilibrium model building. Whereas the virtues of the freedom to choose, to respond, and to discover were, in each case, predicated on the display of purposive behavior, Alchian's point tells us to value freedom even for human behavior that is foolhardy, romantic, or arbitrary. Economic freedom carries the freedom to act regardless of one's permits, licenses, certification, or other forms of government permission to use one's own property or to enter consensually into affairs with others.

To use Alchian's biological metaphor, economic freedom is the system that generates the widest possible spawning of different phenotypes – that is, different particular expressions of the genotype (pp. 22–3). In conjunction with the freedom to experiment comes the responsibility of failure: only if the "phenotype" carries the responsibility of failure will the selection mechanism of the competitive market operate to adopt appropriate behavior. In Alchian's lesson, "[s]uccess is discovered . . . not by the individual through a converging search . . . [but] by the economic system through a blanketing shotgun process" (p. 31). I think of Jed Clampett, the television character of *The Beverly Hill Billies*, who inadvertently discovered crude oil while out shooting for some food.[7] Once a particular phenotype – be it a type of restaurant entrepreneur, wholesale distributer, or textile manufacturer – hits upon success, this type is imitated and the social benefits increase. Phenotypes that do not hit upon success perish.

Sometimes beneficial "phenotypic" variation comes about not by random spawning but by positive error. Many of us have had the experience of making a mistake in using our word-processing program, and, in figuring out how to fix the mistake, discovering some wonderful feature we hadn't known about. Error turns out to be a blessing. The element of serendipity is also present in Maugham's story of the verger, in that the verger in fact had made a wrong turn when he headed down the street where he discovered commercial opportunity.

Serendipity might be said to be an inadvertant discovery which is on net socially beneficial. It need not be beneficial from the point of view of the discoverer, however, or even of his or her long term self. The historian Samuel Eliot Morison tells of such a case in the early pages of *The Oxford History of the American People* (1965: 23): "America was discovered accidentally by a great seaman who was looking for something else; when discovered it was not wanted; and most of the exploration for the next fifty years was done in the hope of getting through or around it." Alchian (1977: 30) points out that a great deal of "pioneering and leadership" in the economic realm occurs by failed attempts at imitation. Economic freedom presses entrepreneurs into contact and experimentation with their environment.

Compare Alchian's idea of spawning with Kirzner's theory of discovery based on interest. In his example of two individuals who walk down the same city block, Kirzner argues that each tends to notice things that the individual would best be able to make use of. But even if discovery is not led by interest but is merely random, there is a definite benefit to having two, rather than one, encounters with the environment, since with two it is more likely that at least one will serendipitously discover an as-yet undiscovered opportunity.[8] And Alchian's spawning idea is especially important if discovery depends not only on individual interest, as Kirzner maintains, but also on distinctive talents in perceiving the environment; thus it has been argued that immigrant entrepreneurs sometimes succeed by virtue of their peculiar outlook on things.[9] Each type of mind may have its own special propensity to have beneficial accidents.

In our example of urban transit, market experimentation might mean new modes, new vehicles, new pricing schemes, new routes, new schedules, new aspects of service, new techniques in providing service, etc. These changes might come from within the industry, from newcomers, or from entrepreneurs initially based in other industries, perhaps in hotel services, delivery services, or even used-car dealing. A free-enterprise transit policy would invite all comers to make their bid in the market, and let travelers select the worthy. Depending on their discoveries, niche finders would survive, or prosper, or induce imitation.

CONCLUDING DISCUSSION

Discovery as positive externality

In placing heavy emphasis on equilibrium model building, economists eclipse the discovery factors of economic activity: respondence, epiphany, and serendipity. Unlike other important elements of economic activity, like price

Table 10.1 Facets of decision making, representing economists, and character examples

Static choice	Respondence	Epiphany	Serendipity
Samuelson	Coasians	Kirzner	Alchian
Max utility	Switchboard operator	The verger	Jed Clampett
No discovery	Small discovery within one's interpretive framework	Discovery that alters one's interpretive framework	
More deliberate			Less deliberate

competition, strategic commitment, and economizing, which are beautifully rendered by model-building tales of optimizing agents, these more dynamic factors are thrown into the shadows.[10] Coasian respondence to the gale of change can be very rigidly and narrowly worked into equilibrium storytelling, with much cumbersome apparatus. Alchianian serendipity can be mimicked by computer simulation studies, which themselves are outside the optimization mode of discourse, but again the rendering is rigid and mechanical. Kirznerian discovery, the epiphany of the individual to see a new interpretation of what is before him or her, is, virtually by definition, impossible to capture in equilibrium storytelling.

Within the neatly characterized settings of economic models, the opportunities are posited at the outset and often assumed to be common knowledge among homogeneous agents. In such a context, when a producer enters a market or expands output, there is no consumer benefit associated specifically with that producer's activity, since the opportunity would have been filled by some other producer anyway. Consumers get their surplus regardless of the activities of any particular producer. The consumer surplus is virtually an *endowment*, embodied in the intial conditions posited by the analyst.

Once the scholar breaks free from formal model building and admits of discovery in his or her storytelling, we can see that discovery is a lot like a positive externality. Discovery creates differentiated products, new markets, better consumer information, new cost conditions, and so forth. These are not gains that must happen in any event. Discovery generates whole regions of consumer and producer surplus that had not been previously imagined. These fresh blocks of consumer and producer surplus are like "public goods" (Cowen, 1985).

If the economics profession were to allow more attention to the discovery factors, it might find itself in stronger support of economic freedom. The ideas I have associated with Coase, Kirzner, and Alchian are all linked in their illumination of the following two points: (1) knowledge and opportunity are extremely local and individuated, (2) knowledge and opportunity are constantly changing. These points humble us by telling us, the academicians and intellectuals, that the economy will always be unknowable (Hayek, 1948, 1955, 1988; O'Driscoll and Rizzo, 1985). We really know less about economic processes, transforming inputs into outputs, than we sometimes pretend. Too often we mistake a thorough knowledge of the representations that other intellectuals make of a subject for a thorough knowledge of the subject itself (Schopenhauer, 1851: 199). To the extent that the economy is unknown and opportunity is hidden, the discovery fount of positive externalities gains in importance.

If, despite the best intellectual efforts, economic processes will remain largely unknown, it makes little sense for the regulator, aided by the academic economist, to try to alter the outputs by regulating the inputs. The regulator is apt to specify inappropriate inputs, or presently obsolete inputs, or uniform inputs in a situation that calls for individuated inputs. The regulator is apt to choke off the discovery fount of positive externalities. The wiser course very often is simply to treat outputs directly – notably, by safeguarding the relatively simple tort rules of property, consent, and contract – and leave the inputs free to discover themselves and to dance their own steps within that legal framework.

On giving evidence for discovery

If the Hayekians are correct both about economics and about economists, we should observe the following pattern: economists who neglect the discovery factors underpredicting the harms of regulation and the benefits of deregulation. Needless to say, good data for such a test are elusive. Clifford Winston (1993) reviews the deregulation experience for a number of industries, comparing the benefits as predicted beforehand by economists with the benefits as assessed afterward. The results, not surprisingly, are ambiguous, but perhaps mildly supportive of the Hayekians. For the benefits arising from changes in service quality, which especially eludes quantification, Winston remarks (1993: 1277):

> Most of these changes made deregulation more valuable to society. Economists effectively predicted lower bounds by not recognizing further adjustments by firms. These developments were not anticipated because economists' predictions generally rely on models that assume no technological change.

Until we have good data on the ability of economists who neglect discovery to predict the effects of policy changes, data that in effect isolate the significance of the discovery factors, our exploration of this most crucial matter shall have to rely on other scientific methods – introspection, thought experiment, metaphor, parable, case study – like those employed by Coase, Kirzner, and Alchian.

What should economists do?

If a better understanding of discovery is to be had, it would seem that it will not be by virtue of fancier and more advanced model building. Although advanced storytelling of that sort can be instructive, it is likely to generate a somewhat narrow and esoteric understanding of such dynamic features of economic activity. Economics is already suffering from an autarkic specialization, in which researchers are developing highly specialized intellectual products that are not profitably traded to others (McCloskey, 1994: 74f.). Indeed the one form of intellectual specialization that the profession seems to neglect, sometimes with a vengeance, is the middleman.

There are other ways to tell stories, and they may be better suited to the task. Economists might do well to focus more of their energy on learning to tell stories of business and economic history, case studies, or economic biography. An even more radical, but I hope effective, departure from respectability was occasioned in the present chapter by the use of a piece of fiction. Yet another form of discourse that might broaden understanding is open policy dialogue, where serious scholars engage in open advocacy, if they have something to advocate, and submit to public debate. That would certainly be welcome by students, our customers. These suggested other ways of telling stories are probably better suited to the study of discovery.

But, of course, all of these suggestions do exacerbate the problem of deciding standards of good and bad work. That problem recedes when we all insist on model building as the one legitimate way of telling stories.

NOTES

1 Stated differently, and perhaps more directly in line with Kuhn's discussion, the essential tension is that scientists must have enough of a commitment to traditional paradigms that something becomes important because it is anomalous to those paradigms, yet enough flexibility, or lack of commitment to the paradigms, that they are willing to break from them, so that they may capture the anomaly with some innovative mode of speaking. As Kuhn (1959: 227) puts it: "Very often the successful scientist must simultaneously display the characteristics of the traditionalist and the iconoclast." For a valuable discussion of this tension in modern economics, arguing that mainstream economics is logically sound but too paradigmatic, see Boettke (1995).

2 Hayek (1979: 67):

> To use as a standard by which we measure the actual achievement of competition the hypothetical arrangements made by an omniscient dictator comes naturally to the economist whose analysis must proceed on the fictitious assumption that *he* knows all the facts which determine the order of the market.

3 On the development of law and economics, see Coase (1993).

4 Kirzner (1985: 7): "The crucial element in behavior expressing entrepreneurial alertness is that it expresses the decision maker's ability spontaneously to transcend an existing framework of perceived opportunities."

5 Kirzner (1979: 155) says that the distinctive aspect of entrepreneurial activity is "its inability to be compressed within the equilibrium conception of the market."

6 For example, it is not in the interest of economic graduate students to notice discovery.

7 The genuine counterpart to Jed Clampett is James Marshall, a frontiersman who undertook to build a sawmill in the Sierra Nevadas in 1848. Instead he struck gold and triggered the California gold rush.

8 Compare Kirzner's "Alertness, Luck, and Entrepreneurial Profit," esp. p. 178, in Kirzner (1979).

9 Hoselitz (1964: 157). Alchian himself might serve as an example of this point. In his Introduction to Alchian's selected works (1977: 8), Ronald Coase writes:

> Armen Alchian was born on April 12, 1914, in Fresno, California. He was brought up in a tightly-knit Armenian community, a community which was subject to intense discrimination. This discrimination, which does not now exist, was not the result, Armen Alchian believes, of any natural unfriendliness or unreasonableness on the part of the other inhabitants of Fresno but was due to the strangeness of the Armenians' manners and customs, which, because they were unusual and not quickly altered, were not understood or tolerated initially.

> This led Alchian to think about discrimination as a problem of information costs, and to produce great papers treating information cost issues. Thus, one might argue, it was the peculiar cultural experience of an Armenian American that spawned, within the economics profession, the Alchian phenotype that appreciates information costs, and this type was adopted by the economics profession because of the gains it yielded.

10 For a valuable study of the disappearance of the entrepreneur in economics, see Frank Machovec (1995).

REFERENCES

Alchian, Armen (1977) *Economic Forces at Work*. Indianapolis: Liberty Press.

Axelrod, Robert (1984) *The Evolution of Cooperation*. New York: Basic Books.

Berlin, Isaiah (1969) "Two Concepts of Liberty," in *Four Essays on Liberty*. New York: Oxford University Press. From his lecture in 1958, pp. 118–72.

Boettke, Peter J. (1995) "What Is Wrong with Neoclassical Economics?," Ms., New York University.

Burke, Kenneth (1966 (1932)) *Towards a Better Life*. Berkeley, CA: University of California Press.

Carlton, Dennis W. (1991) "The Theory of Allocation and Its Implications for Marketing and Industrial Structure: Why Rationing is Efficient," *Journal of Law and Economics* 34: 231–62.

Coase, Ronald H. (1960) "The Problem of Social Cost," *Journal of Law and Economics* 3: 1–44.

—— (1972) "Industrial Organization: A Proposal for Research," in *Policy Issues and Research Opportunities in Industrial Organization*, ed. Victor R. Fuchs. New York: National Bureau of Economic Research, pp. 59–73.

—— (1993) "Law and Economics at Chicago," *Journal of Law and Economics* 36: 239–54.

Cowen, Tyler (1985) "Public Goods Definitions and their Institutional Context: A Critique of Public Goods Theory," *Review of Social Economy* 43: 53–63.

De Vany, Arthur and Ross D. Eckert (1991) "Motion Picture Antitrust: The Paramount Case Revisited," *Research in Law and Economics* 14: 51–112.

De Vany, Arthur and N. G. Frey (1981) "Stochastic Equilibrium and Capacity Utilization in the Steel Industry," *American Economic Review* 71: 53–7.

Dick, Andrew R. (1992) "An Efficiency Explanation for Why Firms Second Source," *Economic Inquiry*, 30: 332–54.

Friedman, David (1989) *The Machinery of Freedom: Guide to Radical Capitalism*, 2nd edn. La Salle, IL: Open Court.

Friedman, Milton (1962, with Rose D. Friedman) *Capitalism and Freedom*. Chicago: University of Chicago Press.

Hayek, Friedrich A. (1948) *Individualism and Economic Order*. Chicago: University of Chicago Press.

—— (1955) *The Counter-Revolution of Science: Studies on the Abuse of Reason*. New York: Free Press.

—— (1978) "Competition as a Discovery Procedure," in *New Studies in Philosophy, Politics, Economics and the History of Ideas*. Chicago: University of Chicago Press, pp. 179–90.

—— (1979) "Law, Legislation and Liberty," in *The Political Order of a Free People*. Chicago: University of Chicago Press, p. 3.

—— (1988) *The Fatal Conceit: The Errors of Socialism*. Chicago: University of Chicago Press.

Hirschman, Albert O. (1986) "Against Parsimony: Three Easy Ways of Complicating Some Categories of Economic Discourse," in *Rival Views of Market Society*, ed. Albert O. Hirschman. New York: Viking, pp. 142–60.

Hoselitz, Bert F. (1964) "A Sociological Approach to Economic Development," in *Development and Society: The Dynamics of Economic Change*, ed. David E. Novack and Robert Lekachman. New York: St Martins Press, pp. 150–63.

Kirzner, Israel M. (1979) *Perception, Opportunity, and Profit: Studies in the Theory of Entrepreneurship*. Chicago: University of Chicago Press.

—— (1985) *Discovery and the Capitalist Process*. Chicago: University of Chicago Press.

—— (1992) *The Meaning of the Market Process: Essays in the Development of Modern Austrian Economics*. London: Routledge.

Knight, Frank H. (1935) "Economic Theory and Nationalism," in *The Ethics of Competition and Other Essays*. London: Allen and Unwin, pp. 277–359.

Kreps, David M. (1990) *Game Theory and Economic Modelling*. Oxford: Clarendon Press.

Kuhn, Thomas S. (1977, essay appeared in 1959) "The Essential Tension: Tradition and Innovation in Scientific Research," in *The Essential Tension: Selected Studies in Scientific Tradition and Change*. Chicago: University of Chicago Press, pp. 225–39.

—— (1970) *The Structure of Scientific Revolutions*, 2nd edn. Chicago: University of Chicago Press.

McCloskey, Donald N. (1994) *Knowledge and Persuasion in Economics*. New York: Cambridge University Press.

Machovec, Frank M. (1995) *Perfect Competition and the Transformation of Economics*. London: Routledge.

Maugham, W. Somerset (1952) "The Verger," in *The Complete Short Stories of W. Somerset Maugham*, Vol. III. Garden City, NY: Doubleday, pp. 572–8.

Maynard Smith, John (1982) *Evolution and the Theory of Games*. Cambridge: Cambridge University Press.

Morison, Samuel Eliot (1965) *The Oxford History of the American People*. New York: Oxford University Press.

O'Driscoll, Gerald P. and Mario J. Rizzo (1985) *The Economics of Time and Ignorance*. New York: Basil Blackwell.

179

Schopenhauer, Arthur (1970, 1851) *Essays and Aphorisms*. New York: Penguin.

Sen, Amartya K. (1977) "Rational Fools: A Critique of the Behavioral Foundations of Economic Theory," *Philosophy and Public Affairs* 6: 317–44.

Stigler, George J. (1961) "Economics of Information," *Journal of Political Economy* 69: 213–25.

—— (1962) "Information in the Labor Market," *Journal of Political Economy* 70: 94–105.

Winston, Clifford (1993) "Economic Deregulation: Days of Reckoning for Microeconomists," *Journal of Economic Literature* 31: 1263–89.

11

IN CELEBRATION OF ARMEN ALCHIAN'S EIGHTIETH BIRTHDAY

John R. Lott, Jr.

John Lott: When we first attempted to put this program together, I was a little bit worried that with a general session, a luncheon, and five paper sessions it might be a little difficult to find enough participants. Well, I can assure you, those concerns were pretty short lived. In fact I have a little more appreciation for what it might be like to be a journal editor, because I think I have probably ended up offending about three or four times more people for not including them in sessions such as this than I have possibly made friends by having them included. So far, we have had one session of original papers in Armen's honor, and immediately after this, Ben Klein will address the luncheon, and tomorrow we have four more sessions.

Right now, we are going to hear the thoughts of five extremely prominent individuals as they speak about Armen's influence as a teacher, researcher, coauthor, and colleague. Two of the people here are Nobel Prize winners: Bill Sharpe had Armen as his dissertation advisor, and incidentally he also had Harold Demsetz on his committee, so this is kind of old home week for him; Jim Buchanan, another Nobel Prize winner, had Armen as a colleague; Axel Leijonhufvud has been in the same economics department as Armen for thirty years. Others have had him as a teacher, like Bob Topel, and as both a colleague and as a coauthor, like Harold Demsetz.

I thought I would take advantage of my position as moderator and organizer to personally reflect on what Armen has meant to me. He may not want to own up to the responsibility for the blame or credit that I attribute to him. When I was in high school, the summer after my sophomore year, an economics professor moved in next door to me – M. Bruce Johnson who teaches now at the University of California at Santa Barbara. I went over and asked Bruce what types of economics textbooks I should look at, and he gave me seven of them. I think the first three that I looked through seemed OK, but they were nothing particularly exciting. Then I got to Armen's textbook with Bill Allen, *University Economics*, and I think that book was responsible for me not only becoming an academic but also deciding to go to UCLA. It is hard to explain now, though I guess some of you can relate to how exciting reading the questions in the back of the chapters were. Whether it be things like "Why are Rose Bowl ticket prices set low so that they have more people demanding them than the supply of tickets available?" Or the shipping of good apples out; or why rent control results in students not obtaining apartments, but elderly old ladies who are less likely to damage the apartment buildings. The exciting thing was that such clear and simple insights could provide such powerful implications and it seemed amazing to me that people could actually go and make an income thinking about such fun and interesting problems. I suppose that was responsible for me wanting to become an academic. To give you an idea of the youthful enthusiasm that I had, I decided at that point I was going to go to UCLA. My Mom, who was living in Miami, felt that California was a dangerous place all the way across the continent, and she was unwilling to let me apply there. So I went to school in the south for a year and then for my sophomore year I said, "Well, it's still a plane trip away, it's still going to be a plane trip away in California, it can't be that much worse." So, I ended up at UCLA. Less than a week after I had moved there, I went over and knocked on Armen's door because I wanted to go in and offer my services and see if he would be willing to hire me for a research assistant. He was not in his office and so I went over to Bill Allen's office and I knocked on the door, and he was in. So I told him how anxious I was for him to hire me as an RA, and he said, "Well, how about $4.50 an hour?" And I said, "Oh, that's great!" I didn't notice at that time that Clay LaForce had walked in behind me, and his response was, "Bill, I think you're paying too much."

The other thing I wanted to briefly relate was one lecture that Armen gave in his class as the third lecture in his graduate Price Theory class. I'm not sure how many of you can relate back to one lecture in one class that so completely transformed your views about economics and kind of served as the guiding light for your research in the rest of your career, but I think I can relate back to one lecture in my own case. That was when Armen defined the notion of efficiency. He defined efficiency as "Whatever is, is efficient." If it wasn't efficient it would have been something different. Of course, if you try to change anything that is there, that is efficient, too.

I suppose the best way to relate this to you is to point out something like the notion of optimal taxes. Armen would ask the question, "If something is so optimal, why don't we see it then?" The notion being essentially that there must be other costs that you left out of your model: costs involved either in the political system, in organizing support, or in changes for this other solution which might seem to be such a low cost option. And the basic point of his argument was: why are we only weighting some costs and not others? Why are these costs (involved in minimizing the particular dead-weight losses that would be involved in setting a particular tax) less important than other types of costs (those involved in informing people of what the options are or of organizing them to go and try to adopt the alternative option)?

I think it's important to understand that type of lecture in order to realize the effect it had on so many graduate students there and the divergent effect it had on so many people. You have people who'd come in, like Walter Williams, who in my understanding was kind of a leftist or even a Marxist when he first went to UCLA, and anybody who listens to the Rush Limbaugh show from time to time and hears Walter filling in for Rush can notice that there has been some change that has occurred over time. You can also have testimonials from many other UCLA Ph.D.s. Ted Frech, who I was talking to a few months ago, told me he was a rabid libertarian when he went to UCLA and now he is kind of confused, or at least much less certain of his libertarian ways than he used to be, and that is basically because of the type of lecture I was just talking about. You can say, "Well, this is the way the world should be." But then the question comes up, "If that is so obvious, then why isn't the world like that?"

These individuals that we have here I am sure want to talk, and I don't want to tread too much on their time. However, I couldn't help but take a few minutes myself and motivate where I am coming from on this. Bill Sharpe is the next person we have here, and Bill, would you like to come up here?

Bill Sharpe: John asked me if I would be willing to come up and mainly reminisce. He did actually give me another assignment, I can't remember what it was, but I didn't undertake that. I am going to undertake the first assignment which is by far the more pleasant and more personal, so I would like to very much reminisce about my days, and in particular, my days as a masters student when I took Armen's course in 1956, when he was a relatively young associate professor. First let me first say that Armen, along with Fred Weston and Harry Markowitz, I count as my three mentors, and Armen in very, very large part, so I owe a great deal to him. That being said, there is a tendency, as I'm sure you know, on occasions such as this for speakers to gush and become overly saccharin, and I want to avoid that as much as I can. On the other hand I don't want to do a Friars Club roast.

One of the things you do when you get to this stage in your career is to recycle your earlier material and engage in what could be called self-plagiarism. On two occasions, people were foolish enough to ask me to write a piece on how I got "this way" (whatever "this way" may be). And on those two occasions, I of course said something about Armen. So I am going to read you what I wrote on other occasions about Armen, presumably away from this particularly emotional and hot-house situation.

First, something I wrote in 1990 which you will see is the more formal of the two:

Armen Alchian, a professor of economics, was my role model at UCLA. He taught his students to question everything, to always begin an analysis with first principles, to concentrate on essential elements and abstract form secondary ones, and to play devil's advocate with one's own ideas." [Let me say, parenthetically, I think that's probably the most important of the lessons that Armen taught.] In his classes we were able to watch a first-rate mind and work on a host of fascinating problems. I have attempted to emulate his approach to research ever since.

All of this was true in 1990, it was true in 1956, and it is certainly true today. Let me quote from another of these pieces, one that I wrote in 1992:

> It was during this year [1956] that I irrevocably crossed the line to become an economist. Much of the credit or blame for which goes to Armen Alchian, who taught the graduate microeconomics sequence at UCLA. While personally gentle and traditional, Armen was and is clearly an eccentric economic theorist. He started the course by asserting that 95 percent of the material in economics journals was wrong or irrelevant. He then proceeded to discuss the economics of the illegal market for buying babies. At one point, he spent five or six lectures wrestling somewhat unsuccessfully with the meaning of profit. Indeed, most of his classes had the characteristics of a wrestling match. We witnessed a brilliant mind grappling, usually very successfully, with the most difficult concepts in economics in creative and innovative ways. There could be no better training for a fledgling theorist and no higher standard. After two semesters with Armen Alchian, I was hooked, I wanted to be a microeconomist.

In my time at UCLA (which I suppose was a simpler time), all the teaching assistants had one room with a bunch of desks and a blackboard. We would all go to Armen's class, then rush to the room, race to the blackboard, and typically spend several hours trying to figure out just what had gone on – trying to unscramble all of this very difficult material. I think those sessions were, next only to Armen's class itself, the most important part of my education at UCLA. It was this process – Armen provoking and the rest of us trying to understand, expand, and consolidate – which made economists out of some pretty raw material at that time.

I also want to say a little bit about the textbooks, because the textbooks are a reflection of the material to which we were exposed. As you know, there is *University Economics*, which includes both microeconomics and macroeconomics, and then the micro-only portion published under the title *Exchange and Production Theory in Use*. In just flipping through the latter in the last day or two, I was rather appalled to find a number of ideas which I thought I had invented. I guess that is the mark of a good teacher: that you are taught so well it becomes subliminal and you think in later years that you came up with the ideas yourself. I have a quote for you, from a book called *Economics and Charity*. (Computer searches are wonderful things;

I turned up this book when I said "Alchian" to my computer.) In it is a small excerpt, slightly Anglicized, from *University Economics*. The editor of *Economics and Charity* called *University Economics* "Perhaps the most penetrating introductory economics textbook in the English language." It appears that he was hedging his bets; I wondered if he thought that another had a better book. In any event, there is no doubt that it really is a remarkable book. I taught from *University Economics* at the University of Washington and experienced, as many of you have, how difficult it is to use a textbook with undergraduates that sings the praises of unfettered market solutions to allocating resources. If you look at the book, you will see that both Armen and Bill Allen were very, very careful to say over and over, "Now look, there are many ways of looking at these problems." Sensible people may well disagree as to the efficacy of market solutions as opposed to command economies, as we would say today. But somehow or other, the students were able to discern just a *tiny* bit of a preference on the part of the authors for market solutions. That approach, in today's terminology, was kind of "in your face" economics. And I commend that term to you as you think about the kind of things Armen does. I might also say that some of it borders on what would be politically incorrect, at least in the kinds of institutions you read about in "Doonesbury."

It won't surprise at least some of you that I was particularly enamored with Armen's work on allocating goods over time and allocating risk among members of the society. You will find all of that discussed in particular in the text *circa* 1964, but he was dealing with those issues much earlier. At the time, microeconomics textbooks resolutely preceded as if the world was one of certainty. The notion of uncertainty was just not something you found in a microeconomics text, or indeed, in many economics departments. This now seems ludicrous because uncertainty has now permeated not only economics but also the field that we now call financial economics. But it was not standard at that time, and Armen's work, in the literature, in the course, and in the textbooks, was really instrumental in beginning that movement. Here is a quote from the 1969 edition of *Exchange and Production* that shows how current the material is:

> The news spreads that the next coffee crop, now blossoming in Brazil, has been nipped by unseasonable cold weather. Immediately the flow of coffee out of current stocks of consumption is reduced, therefore the current price of coffee to consumers will rise as coffee is released for current consumption.

As you probably all know that is precisely what happened in recent months. And what we now await is the prediction that Armen made that there will very soon be calls from political and other quarters for the heads of the speculators who have caused everyday working people to have to pay more for their coffee when in fact "nothing" has changed.

Let me give you one more personal anecdote that brings home what an unusual man we honor today. When I took my Ph.D. oral exam, Armen and two of his colleagues proceeded to ask me question after question, not a single one of which I could definitively answer. The only person who asked any questions to which I knew the answer with any assurance was Fred Weston, who came late to the dissertation. After two or three hours of living hell, I was dismissed, and went out to await the verdict. And the minutes passed, and passed, and passed, I was going down the list of other careers I might pursue. Eventually Armen appeared and I braced myself for the response. Armen said,

> Well of course you passed, but I suppose I should tell you that the three of us, before you came in, decided that we would ask you questions to which we didn't know the answers because it would just be a lot more interesting. And we got so excited that the discussion went on and we forgot to come out and tell you the verdict.

Armen Alchian – truly unusual economist, an innovator, a major contributor, a superb teacher, and one to whom I owe a great, great personal debt. Armen, Happy Birthday.

John Lott: Thank you very much Bill. Our next speaker is someone I am sure you all know, Jim Buchanan, who was a colleague of Armen's briefly in the late 1960s when he was at UCLA and has known him in many other contexts.

Jim Buchanan: I appreciate the opportunity to come here and join this tribute to Armen. As many of you know, I am on record as classifying Armen as the best blackboard economist I have ever known. And I refer here to Armen's unbounded curiosity in the face of any problem posed to him and to his willingness to help anyone who stands confused, and, finally, to his ultimate confidence in the economists' tool kit. The challenge to Armen is always in the chase. Give him a problem and he will, with a bit of blackboard exercise, come up with some solution. I thought the analogy with the wrestling match that Bill mentioned was very good. I look back with fondness on my brief time at UCLA when Armen shared the office next door. I would go next door and Armen would immediately go to the blackboard and really work out whatever problem happened to be bothering me. And of course those sessions were exciting and interesting, but they got much more exciting and interesting when Earl Thompson happened by. Then they went on and on and on.

At the end of these brief remarks, I am going to give Armen a problem, one for which the several explanations I have heard do not seem convincing. But John Lott instructed me to do more than that. I was told to try to develop a constructive argument within the few minutes here assigned to me. An argument that might be related to Armen's contributions. And, perhaps predictably, my starting point is Armen's seminal 1950 paper on profit maximization as a survival strategy, behavior that exhibits evolutionary stability in a competitive economic environment. Now let me digress to say, for most of you, this will not seem as seminal as it does to those of us who were around in 1950. As I was noting to Jack Hirshleifer last night, evolutionary thinking permeates economics and it is now becoming a very natural way of thinking, but nobody thought about evolutionary processes in the 1950s. It's part of the intellectual environment in social sciences, and this makes it difficult to appreciate the genuinely innovative quality of Armen's 1950 enterprise.

I think we need to recall the analytical setting out of which the Alchian paper emerged. In the late 1940s economists had witnessed a fierce controversy within their own ranks between those who used behaviorally descriptive evidence to suggest that firms do not maximize profits, at least in accordance with the textbook calculus, people like Lester, Hall, and Hitch, on that side of the debate, and they were opposed by those who extended the precepts of ordinary rationality to deduce profit maximization as a part of rational choice. Here you think of Fritz Machlup on that side of the debate. Armen Alchian's point in his 1950 article, which now seems simple enough, was that the controversy was essentially irrelevant. In order to survive, firms must behave so as to cover costs, which as Ronald Coase had told us much earlier, although none of us were then familiar with the argument. Ronald Coase had told us that to cover costs is the same thing as maximizing profits anyway. Now behaviorally, the Alchian survivalist definition for profit maximization may not seem to get us very far, but I think that Armen really intended to suggest the enormousness of the implications for allocative efficiency that followed from that. Now this interpretation of Armen's purpose does provide, it seems to me, a link with his work in the late 1950s and 1960s, work that introduced the incentive incompatibility resulting from the attenuation of property rights of the decision makers. Some of this work was done jointly with Reuben Kessel. Those of us who are old enough to remember, will remember Armen's excitement and discussion about his examples that he drew from the non-proprietary sector where property rights were attenuated, with his hypothesis about the Ford Foundation having prettier secretaries and thicker carpets than profit maximization would suggest.

But I want to come back to the initial model and try to unravel the survivalist criterion in terms of its implied behavioral limits. I want to suggest that the normative status of this criterion may be quite different in differing institutional settings. Patterns of behavior that ensure survival in the technological complexity of today's extended, but highly politicized, markets may not, independently of some ethical reinforcement, carry with them the normative implications that emerged so clearly in the stylized textbook constructions. Think first then about a setting in which all the participating units, whether individuals or firms, are engaged in a continuing sequence of trades or exchanges. Here, Adam Smith's discipline of continuous dealings will surely ensure that firms which survive will be those that maximize profit without exploitative practice. Deliver value for money, in other words. Consider by comparison a setting where there are few if any repeated interactions between buyers and sellers. And here you think immediately of the service station along the interstate highway. Like many of you, I suspect I have been taken by one or two scams in my life on that, either on shocks or alternators or whatever. Once or twice, I learned and was not taken anymore, but I was taken. Here the disciplinary feedbacks are quite different. Now of course marketwide trademarks and brand names emerge to substitute for more disciplinary feedback, but the scope for opportunistic behavior is at hand.

More generally, I think there is cause for concern, or at least for further inquiry, as technology develops so as to create further erosion in the continuity of buyer–seller relationships and to replace personal by impersonal dealings. And this concern is exacerbated by the accelerated potential politicization of any and all transactions. Some of us are not nearly so sanguine as Gary Becker about the efficiency-enhancing properties of political competition. And I must say I was a little bit worried by John Lott slipping over into that today in some of his remarks. The rent seekers who survive and prosper may not be behaving so as to ensure that resources are moved to their most productive use.

At this point, I think it might be useful to refer to Hayek's introduction of cultural evolution. Specifically, think about the possibility that many of the behavior traits that we now observe may well have evolved in commercial settings in which survival depended on the maintenance of mutual trust among traders. My concern is whether such standards of trust and respect are dictated by the technological and political superstructure in the modern economy. Is it not possible that there has already been some erosion in the effective strengths of the disciplinary feedbacks so as to make survival alone carry less normative implication than it did in earlier periods? Despite the dramatic reductions in transactions costs that the extended market facilitates, along with the enhanced availability of the exit option, just how dependent are we on those codes of conduct, to use a Hayek term? How dependent are we on those codes of conduct that few of us understand, without which our economy might not function nearly so well as it does? Social critics of the market and of market evaluation, that is the socialists who will always be with us (we might have thought their zeal would be a bit tarnished by the mid-1990s, but it does not seem to be tarnished nearly so much as might have been predicted), they will always continue to equate profit maximization with opportunistic exploitation of each and every buyer and seller relationship in each and every exchange. And I think it should be incumbent on us as economists to identify the flaws in such a vision. The profit-maximizing behavior that survives in the appropriately defined institutional setting does carry normative implications as implied in the original 1950 Alchian paper. But the proviso there is all important. As political economists, we should pay more attention to what the appropriately defined institutional setting is and must be.

Finally, and as I promised you, let me pose a problem to Armen Alchian, the problem of the familiar and much discussed CEO stipends. To me the theories of marginal productivity, the theories of non-competing groups, and the theories of tournaments, which I have heard as explanations here, do not measure up. And I would like to pose to Armen: just how do we explain what we now observe? Thank you very much.

John Lott: Our next speaker is someone who has probably known Armen for the most continuous length of time or at least has been in the same department as him, and that is Axel Leijonhufvud.

Axel Leijonhufvud: Continuity yes, but complexity no. I should explain that Harold Demsetz substituted for me in the morning session, and so I am here in my capacity as substitute for Harold Demsetz. In what capacity he is here, I can't say.

I came to UCLA in 1964 so I have been Armen's pupil and colleague for thirty years. Through the 1960s and 1970s, the UCLA economics department was Armen's department. You associated UCLA with Armen the same way you did MIT with Paul Samuelson or Chicago with Milton Friedman. These decades, when Alchian was the intellectually dominant figure, were also the years when UCLA economics had an independent intellectual profile in the profession. UCLA then was like no other school. Its distinctiveness, and the significance of it in the larger scheme of things, was for some reason better appreciated in Europe and generally abroad than in the United States. But, UCLA in Armen's great days was not just a school where we tried to do economics the way it was done in Cambridge, Massachusetts, and in Chicago, and did it almost as well, it was a different place. We had our own segment of the frontier of the subject.

Like others who have had the privilege of being Armen's students and colleagues, I have learned a great deal from his ideas. Indeed, I probably have learned more than I can honestly account for, because much of what Armen taught has become second nature to me. Looking back, I find that the *manner* in which Armen exerted his influence just as interesting to reflect on as *what* his influence was. When we categorize Armen's work, we stress first property rights and contracts theory as his main subject areas, perhaps, and incomplete information and transactions costs as the characteristic conceptual tools.

But to understand Alchian's importance, it will not suffice to enumerate original insights and ideas that were specifically his. You have to realize that he, more than anyone else (and I would include Ronald Coase), made property rights, contracts, and business practices in general into the field of study that they have now become. And he did so by multiplying the questions that price theory could and should address – and by making us understand how interesting these questions were.

Most of the people present today, I think, will have a hard time realizing what microeconomics was like thirty years ago because you were not there, and the rest of you will have a hard time remembering because it was a long time ago. Jim Buchanan has a good memory actually; he remembered what it was like in the 1940s, when he said no one thought of economics in evolutionary terms in the 1950s. What I learned in graduate school ten years later than that time was arid stuff, trivial optimization exercises combined with equilibrium conditions that had no foundation in any examination of how actual markets work. This was not the fault of my teachers – this was the state of the art in the profession in general.

But at UCLA, there was Alchian, full of curiosity about actual, everyday business practices. Why do people do what they do? Why is the practice this or that? Always observing. My theory courses were deductive. You started from convexity and continuity assumptions and the like and built elaborate structures in that way. Armen came at it from the inductive end, from observation always.

Let me mention his work on production functions and cost curves as an example. It often seems to me that hardly anyone has really studied production the last sixty years or more. Marshall used to visit factories to understand production, and so did Karl Marx before him. But once the Cobb–Douglas was invented, economists have been doing production theory by sitting in their offices and taking derivatives on the damn thing and never looking outside. Armen is one of the few exceptions. His work in this area stems from the work on airframe manufacturing that he did at RAND during the war. What he found, of course, was that the production sets that he was dealing with were not convex in all dimensions. And if that work of his had the influence that it should have had or might have had, production theory would today be very different. We might be studying production in an empirical way. I would say, by the way, that the "learning-by-doing" interpretation popularized by Ken Arrow is one that makes Armen's work look fairly harmless from the standpoint of standard theory, and that Armen's work is more subversive than it appears in Arrow's version. So Armen taught us at UCLA that there were whole classes, rich classes of questions, that price theory could and should address. That was his great importance to us.

Now for those of you who had the privilege of associating with him there was something else that was equally important, at least speaking for myself. There was not only the influence of his questions, and the influence about how he went about finding answers, but the manner in which his influence was exerted over students and over colleagues. What always comes first to my mind in thinking about him is his personal lack of pretentiousness, lack of self importance and pomposity. I learned from Armen to (I hope) take economics seriously, but not to take economists too seriously. Armen always had this tolerant amusement at the overweening ambition, and what the British call puffery, of economists, academics in general, and public figures talking about economics. If Armen's own attitude was more prevalent, economics would not have turned from a scholarly endeavor into the competitive sport that it often resembles today, where what counts is what league you're playing in and the most papers into the most prestigious journals.

You are asking, why would I stress unpretentiousness? Can unpretentiousness be an important quality? In Armen Alchian's case I think it has been important in at least three respects.

First, I feel that it is at the bottom of Armen's so-called conservatism. This amused skepticism extends into a skepticism in general of people who claim they will improve the world by using the powers of government. This was an unpopular attitude back then, far more unpopular than it was in the 1980s. But it was a personal attitude that I perceived as very, very different from the hard-edged ideological conservatism of the 1990s of the libertarian conservatives. Because Armen's amused skepticism extended also to those people who would say, "I have a method for improving the world – abolish government."

Now it is important in another way, because his lack of self-promotion and his abstentiousness from it I think is what more than anything else has kept him from the Nobel Prize so far. I can find no other explanation of the behavior of my countrymen. He will, of course, be amused at my saying so, thinking me pretentious on his behalf.

The openness of the place to new ideas was often not appreciated by outsiders. Let me simply recount my own experience. When I was in the market for graduate school, my choices eventually came down to Yale or UCLA, and back at that time the difference in the perceived professional prestige between the schools was much larger than subsequently. When the rumor went around Brookings, where I was for that year, that I was going to go to UCLA, a very well-known economist came to me and put his hand on my shoulder and said, "Axel, I hear you are leaning towards UCLA. I have something you must think about. With your Keynesian interests, you will never be happy at UCLA." The very opposite was the case. I came to UCLA with no particular intention of staying for a long time; I thought I was going back to Europe for one thing. But I became a UCLA loyalist and have stayed one until today. Alchian's UCLA was the right place for someone with my interests. I'm not at all sure that my kind of Keynesian interests would have flourished in the citadels of that era's Keynesianism.

If in the microeconomics of the 1960s few people thought about contracts, property rights, and business practices, in the macroeconomics of the 1960s no one, but no one, talked about information. You cannot imagine how completely lacking from the literature this was unless you take the time to go back and read a broad sample of the stuff and what it was like then.

When I came to UCLA I was a bit shyer than I am today, so I was sitting in my office trying to make sense of Keynesian economics and its relationship to micro theory by thinking of the economy as an information network where things could go wrong under certain conditions. But I didn't have very much confidence that my way of thinking about it was right or a fruitful way to go, and without Armen's support and encouragement, I doubt very much that anything would have come of it.

This came about in a funny way because back then students used to tape your lectures. You would often find yourself talking to a line of tape recorders in the front row with the students sleeping peacefully behind. Armen had this habit of spying on us assistant professor types by borrowing the tapes and playing them when he was driving in his car. So he heard some tape of mine where I was worrying about price adjustments in competitive markets in this macro setting, and arguing that price adjustment velocities couldn't be infinite generally speaking, and that the notions about flexibilities and inflexibilities in micro were not well defined. And so he came to me – I had not dared come to him – and borrowed some of the pieces of manuscripts that I had. Then he gave me out of his desk drawer his classical paper on "Information Costs, Pricing and Resource Unemployment." that eventually appeared in the famous Phelps volume that played such an important role in changing how microeconomics was done. And I learned a lot from that and from the long discussions we had.

The final point I now want to make is this. Why was this paper in his desk drawer? I have no idea how long it had been there, but the version I got was pretty yellow. I think of this every week because papers come across my desk today and you know what they look like. The author says,

Now here is a somewhat puzzling phenomenon.

And then says,

I will make a few *ad hoc* assumptions and I will take the license of as-if methodology, which allows me to do anything, and then I will show that there is at least one possible optimizing model that exists that really implies this phenomenon or my characterization of this phenomenon, and now I am ready to go into print.

Armen started from a set of phenomena that he had observed, and figured out a plausible explanation – model, if you want, of these phenomenon – and then put it into a drawer. Over time he would think of more behavioral phenomena that would fit this explanation, but he would wait for such confirmation by empirical evidence, confirmation by phenomena that were not part of the original question. And if we had the same discipline today in the profession as the self-discipline that Armen put into his work, the volume of publication in economics today would be cut to a small fraction of what it actually is and our lives would all be easier.

John Lott: Well, on that wistful last hope, I would like to turn to Bob Topel. Bob was a graduate student at UCLA, and he has become one of its few most successful Ph.D.s, and that alone would be sufficient to include him in the prestigious company that we have here. But I had the opportunity to sit in some classes that Bob taught at the University of Chicago in 1980, and I have to say that out of most of the people whose classes I have had the opportunity to sit in on, Bob's style reminded me very closely of Armen's. It was Socratic, probing, demanding of the students when they say something that they justify what they meant by the terms they used, and relentlessly giving them a tough time whenever they would be willing to open their mouths. And if they didn't open their mouths, he would cold call on them. But anyway it's primarily because of that, despite the other reasons, that I also include Bob in this.

Bob Topel: My wife recently described to me the first time she met Armen. It was in Hawaii over twenty years ago. Making small talk, she asked if Armen had been to Molokai, which she said was very beautiful and interesting because of the former leper colony there. Armen asked, "Does it have a golf course?" "No," she replied. Said Armen, "I'm not interested."

It's a special honor for me to be asked to present some comments in honor of Armen Alchian's eightieth birthday. But the episode I just described makes me suspect that the speakers get greater "personal value in use" as he would put it from this gathering than Armen does, who I'm sure would rather spend his time doing something else. So, I am going to lead with what might be the only thing any of us will say that will capture his imagination.

Armen, on Monday I will play Royal Lytham St Anne's, a British Open course in the Lake District of England. I plan to shoot your age. [Postscript: I failed.] Years ago, when I was a graduate student, our late friend and golf partner, George Stigler, spoke at another birthday celebration for Armen. He recalled how he had started Milton Friedman's career by holding up a copy of Pigou's *Economics of Welfare* and saying, "Milton, there is a mistake in this book." With this in mind, I picked up my copy of Armen's collected works to look for a mistake – there is one – and to renew my perspective on what kind of an economist Armen is.

To me, the unique thing about Armen is his unquenchable desire to understand the things he observes in the world. Armen is not a theorist or a model builder in the usual sense. In fact he does not suffer theory lightly, though he has a powerful paragon that he applies to real world problems. He is not an empirical economist in the modern sense either. Beyond the number of Jews working for public utilities, there isn't much hard data or formal testing in Armen's papers. Armen simply seeks to understand without trying to show how clever he is. All of Armen's papers – from his classic on evolution to his explanation for why we professors have tenure (because we like it) – have this approach. Why do people do one thing and not another? Why are businesses organized as they are? Why have certain institutions arisen, and what role do they play? These are not the questions of a crusading economist who wants to change the world, like Friedman: they are the questions raised by a scholar who would simply like to understand the world, like Stigler. Armen taught us to approach economics the same way, with a physical scientist's intense desire to understand the way things work. Armen is an extremely clever man, but I count as one of the great virtues of his work that it contains no cleverness for the sake of being clever.

For many, Armen's classic papers are "Evolution" and his methodological piece on utility measurement. These are nice, but my favorite is his paper on information costs and resource unemployment. It challenged the profession to apply tools of optimizing behavior to understand a whole range of problems related to unemployment and the apparent failure of markets to clear. Many of the arguments in this paper were compelling, some less so. But the major contribution came in his approach to the problem. This was extremely refreshing, bridging the gap between the firm foundations of microeconomics and the dull "ad hocery" that then passed for macroeconomics. It affected the way I think about everything, and its theme runs through the work that I have done on unemployment. This paper had a lasting and enormously positive impact on our profession.

Looking over the list of speakers, it appears that my role is to say something about being a student in Armen's department. I have a few stories.

I'm a bit of an odd choice to speak about Armen. Unlike generations of UCLA graduate students, I was never enrolled in a single class that Armen taught. Yet, like all of the other students at UCLA from the 1950s through the 1980s, Armen had a tremendous impact on my education and on the way I think about markets and institutions.

I started my graduate studies at another school. Axel and Harold attended the same one, but only I had the good sense to leave it so I could be educated by them. Also, it didn't have palm trees. In pondering this move, my advisor (who is a famous theorist) told me that UCLA was OK and that Alchian in particular was probably good enough to have a job at Chicago's Business School. This was high enough praise for me, and given the way my career turned out I like that opinion even more today.

So I went to UCLA and tried to pass myself off as a second-year student. Now such was my naiveté that I thought graduate courses would be pretty much the same no matter where you took them. So I decided to take the Ph.D. qualifying exam in economics theory. Armen was the chairman. Just to be on the safe side, I went to Armen's office and showed him my well-pondered and well-marked up copy of Malinvaud's *Lectures on Microeconomic Theory*. I told him of my thorough understanding of all the results in Arrow and Hahn's *General Competitive Analysis*. With a completely straight face, Armen told me this was excellent preparation, and that if I also understood everything in his principles book I would have no trouble at all. And he shut the door.

194

I was reassured.

When the important day came, the exam was Armen at his best. It began by saying, "There are 28 questions on this exam. Answer them all. There is no time for thinking; you should have done that during the previous year." I sensed right off I was at a disadvantage. The questions were all of Armen's favorites, which I subsequently came to know and love, but about which I hadn't a clue at the time. (Of course, some macroeconomics was appended to the exam, but everyone knew it didn't count.) Things did not look good.

My confidence rose enormously, however, when a particular question caught my eye. It was about a theorem, and I was sure there were no important theorems in economics that I couldn't prove – Kakutani, Brouwer Minkowski, or Hestenes, I was ready for anything. The question read: "State the Coase theorem and explain why it is important." Who was this obscure mathematician Coase and what important theorem could he have proved? It wasn't a good day.

I ultimately recovered from that educational setback by hanging around Armen's class and by teaching from his book. His original advice was right: you can be a pretty good economist by knowing what is in his principles book. In fact, my publisher calls Alchian and Allen a terrific principles book for people who already have a Ph.D.

Any graduate student will tell you that Armen's class was something. He came straight from the golf course on a mission to make you realize how little you understood. He was a man who announced on the first day: "If you people were any good, you would have gotten into MIT. So you aren't any good. We will make economists out of you anyway." He would single a student out and ask him a question. Then two things could happen. First, you could answer incorrectly, in which case Armen would drag you through his inexorable logic until you did it right. Or, if you got it right, he would change the assumptions and put you through the same thing. You were wrong and he was right. It was really quite simple once you caught on.

Armen even used class to demonstrate important principles. Ben Zycher, who was around when I was, created externalities by asking too many questions. There being a lack of property rights in the room, we needed either a social planner or some prices. Of course the former wouldn't do, so Armen charged Ben a quarter for every question he asked. From this I learned a very important principle of economics: rectangles are much bigger than triangles. Ben asked just as many questions as before, and Armen got a big stack of quarters.

Armen's influence at UCLA went well beyond the classroom and beyond the articles he wrote. Armen was a presence. The UCLA department in those days was Armen's department. Alchian defined the intellectual environment at UCLA, even for those students that never interacted with him directly. Students learned economics by hanging around and tackling problems together. More often than not the problems we tackled, and our approach to them, were Armen's.

My comments may have left the impression that Armen cut an intimidating figure among the students, and he did. But that is Alchian's educational style, and we all knew it. We knew him to be the charming and kindhearted gentleman that we honor here today. My fondest memories of Armen come from my one year as his colleague at UCLA in 1985–6. If I circulated a paper, Armen's copy would come back the next day covered with comment. Then he would stop by the office to argue about it. I loved it.

I have said enough. Happy Birthday, Armen; may there be many more. You should view this milestone I look forward to as an opportunity to shoot your age. I look forward to hearing that you have done it.

John Lott: Thank you very much, Bob. The last person that we have here – we wanted to include a coauthor of Armen's to get a slightly different perspective on things – is Harold Demsetz.

Harold Demsetz: Thank you. I am here today as a utility infielder. John called me a night or two ago, saying he thought he had more time in the session than the words you four were going to say. I thought to myself that John hasn't been around the profession long enough to have a good appraisal of the speaking prowess of academics. But nonetheless, I agreed to put together a few notes about Armen just in case – only thirty pages.

First, Armen, let me congratulate you on surviving for eighty years. Some of you may not know that this is a very remarkable achievement given the terrible stock tips he has given his colleagues over the last several years. I have always considered myself lucky and privileged to have the office next to Armen's except for these stock tips.

My introduction to Armen's work took place forty years ago when I was working on my Ph.D. at Northwestern University. The theory course was taught by Bob Strotz who then was much involved in utility theory. Armen's article explaining cardinal utility was on the reading list. The paper was well crafted and intelligible, and it really did help me pass the course, but neither it nor cardinal utility nor the course was much help after that. Armen showed good judgment in dropping this line of inquiry. He also gave a seminar at Northwestern in which he dealt with an old topic, production cost, that has been referred to by other speakers, and especially by Axel. Theorists had left this topic untouched after Jacob Viner's assistant had convinced him that only at the bottom of a long run average cost curve would minimum short run average costs equal long run average costs. Whereas Armen's article on cardinal utility was purely expository, his seminar on production costs was very innovative. It appeared in 1959 in his notable article on costs and outputs, and is part of Armen's work on the economics of the firm. Since we both worked on the firm, I will focus on this part of his work.

Neoclassical theory treated costs only as a function of output rate and exogenously given technology. But Armen, through work done by himself and others at RAND, realized that output rate alone could not explain several facts about the airframe industry and he proposed that total output should be included in the firm's cost function. This made facts relating to firm size, use of machinery, and learning over time much more understandable. He may not know it, but his presentation at the Northwestern Seminar helped guide me some two and a half years later to the decision to leave my first job at the University of Michigan for UCLA. Armen, you may regret having given that lecture.

It is clear that Armen's mode of thinking begins by asking questions. One of the three jobs I held when I first came to UCLA was to consult at RAND one day a week. During a lunch hour, I remember Bill Meckling, Armen, and me shopping for a camera. We went from shop to shop. Armen would ask the shopkeeper questions, questions, questions, questions, and he kept shopping, shopping, shopping. He never bought the camera. Similarly, he seldom buys the latest wrinkle on economic theory.

The innovative capability that showed itself in his work on production costs was no fluke. It reveals itself again and again in a variety of topics such as unemployment, inflation, property rights, and the firm. Confining myself to his writings on the firm, I note first *Competition, Monopoly and the Pursuit of Profits*, published in 1962 with Reuben Kessel as a coauthor. It examined the novel consequence of price regulation (or discrimination). Reuben and Armen argued that price regulation exacerbates discrimination by personal characteristics and they provided statistical evidence in support of their theory. The paper was eye opening in the conclusions it derived about discrimination, and it motivated me to write a paper subsequently, published in the *North Carolina Law Review*, on minorities in the marketplace.

Production Information Costs and Economic Organization (that's Armen's title) came out in 1972, coauthored by myself and Armen. Armen and I began this work in 1968 when Armen came to visit Chicago for a year as a Ford Foundation Distinguished Visiting Professor. In this role, his commitments were trivial, and it was quite natural for him to become aware of shirking behavior. In fact, we saw little of him on campus for many weeks. He claims he was down with a serious case of flu, and he even had his lovely wife Pauline join in this claim. Once we teamed up to write this article, since it was a team, we both faced even stronger incentives to shirk. But there must be something to the productivity of team effort, even though neither Armen nor I practiced team writing very much, for this paper, as most of you know, has become a mainstay of the economics of the firm. The only aspect of this coauthorship that I regret is that Alchian begins with an "A."

Without going into detail, certain contentions of the paper should be noted here. These are that team effort is productive, that it gives rise to shirking problems, and that the organization of the firm is at least partly explained by the attempt to mitigate these problems. Exacerbation of the shirking problem occurs precisely because it is a team that is at work. This makes it difficult to apportion product across individual workers. In the very next paper he wrote on the theory of the firm, Armen altered his position on this topic. In "Vertical Integration, Appropriable Rents, and Competitive Contracting Processes," coauthored with Klein and Crawford, the argument is that enlarging the size of the team through vertical integration ameliorates the problem of shirking across markets. Now when Armen and I wrote our paper on the theory of the firm, I was under the impression that we agreed that team production exacerbates shirking problems as compared with transactions across the market. In what might be described as postcontractual opportunistic behavior, Armen reneged on this agreement in the vertical integration paper. In this vertical integration paper, market transactions are the source of shirking and team production is the cure. This paper is rapidly catching up in citations to our paper, so I am especially aggrieved.

I have not discussed one of Armen's more important papers relating to the theory of the firm, his classic "Uncertainty, Evolution, and Economic Behavior" that Jim referred to. This well-known paper, deserving of the attention it has received, delivers a perspective of competition that still makes waves in the profession. In an earlier session today, I delivered a paper devoted entirely to discussing this classic. I shall not repeat myself here.

As we all know, Armen's impact is not restricted to scholarly articles. His principles text, coauthored with Bill Allen, continues to serve an elite audience, and UCLA graduate students have produced a literature much influenced by Armen's teaching. He can be quite proud of what he has accomplished. His insights into the way the world works merit admiration and appreciation. Thank you Armen, and as token of my appreciation, I have a stock tip for you . . .

John Lott: I would like to thank you Harold. Harold, as he said, has served double duty today. He just got off giving an earlier session dealing with Armen. I would like to invite Armen to give him a chance to respond a little bit to the various comments that have been made, to try to clear his name so to speak.

Armen Alchian: I suppose I should thank my mother and father like everybody else does, and God. But I do thank the people who are here for coming. I presume a lot of you are former graduate students otherwise I don't know why you would come. And you know I have abused you a lot. I used to enjoy class, because I could abuse you a lot. You were very tolerant. I thank you for having tolerated that. I should express thanks to the speakers here. But I am not going to because I have a lot of stories about each one of them that I could tell you. I won't tell any, except one. It is my general premise that the university has two functions; I'm not sure which is the most important one. One is education, the other is a marriage market. And I am convinced that UCLA is a superb marriage market. My daughter married a man she met at UCLA. And I went to Hawaii once for a quarter and met a young lady named Lynn Shishido whom I seduced into coming to UCLA as a graduate student. She's now Bob's wife. And it stuck, which is also unusual. So my test of a first-class university is to ask the student alumni, "Did you marry a woman or man that you met at the university?" And I would rate colleges on that basis. A lot of parents ask me about UCLA or Santa Barbara or Berkeley, and I talk about the departments. When I say, "You know, the people he or she is going to meet there are important," their eyes light up. When you mention the cohort of students with whom their child is going to associate, they understand that. When I talk about the departments and what they are like, their eyes glaze over, and I think that is a sensible response.

I would like to tell a story about Bill Sharpe. When he got his Nobel award, I ran to the library and got his dissertation. There was my name as thesis advisor, and I thought that's great. The odd part is, I didn't have much to do with that thesis. I had met Harry Markowitz at RAND and told Harry about this student working on financial aspects and said, "Harry you get in touch with Bill Sharpe." And he made it go. But it's my name as the thesis advisor on the dissertation. That's very nice.

Now I express my gratitude to the students I had; they're the ones that count. I could have done as well as with any other colleagues than with these fellows. It's the students you have that make the big difference. So I had planned, but I didn't have the guts to do it, which may surprise some of you who have been in some of my classes, to come here and start disrobing. Taking off this jacket, taking off my tie, then taking off my shirt, and ending up with a T-shirt that the UCLA graduate students have made this year, which indicates something about UCLA in the background. But what I *have* done is put on this shirt, in my hand, the signatures of my colleagues and all the graduate students I could get to sign, and some I have added myself. I have got some very distinguished names on it.

There is one tradition I have in giving public talks. It is to always mention my wife, and she is here. Thank you and good luck.

NAME INDEX

SUBJECT INDEX

For Product Safety Concerns and Information please contact our EU
representative GPSR@taylorandfrancis.com
Taylor & Francis Verlag GmbH, Kaufingerstraße 24, 80331 München, Germany

www.ingramcontent.com/pod-product-compliance
Ingram Content Group UK Ltd.
Pitfield, Milton Keynes, MK11 3LW, UK
UKHW020955180425
457613UK00019B/700